THE GALLANT
PIONEERS
150TH ANNIVERSARY EDITION

The Gallant Pioneers

150th Anniversary Edition

Gary Halston

DEDICATIONS

Gary: To Lewis and Jennifer and my wee mum, Marion.

Gordon: To Pam and Alfie – Pam, for her help and time with the tours, presentations and grave hunting.

Iain: For my late parents Emma and Archie and my two grandsons, George and Lewis.

In memory of Walter Smith, 1948-2021.

I've had my share of pastime, and I've done my share of toil,
And life is short – the longest life a span;
I care not now to tarry for the corn or for the oil,
Or for wine that maketh glad the heart of man.
For good undone, and gifts misspent, and resolutions vain,
'Tis somewhat late to trouble. This I know –
I should live the same life over, if I had to live again;
And the chances are I go where most men go.

The Sick Stockrider
by Adam Lindsay Gordon, 1833–1870

The above verse by the Australian poet was read by Tom Vallance on the evening of Wednesday April 13 1898 at his restaurant, The Metropolitan, in Hutchison Street, Glasgow.

The occasion was the 21st anniversary of the 1877 Scottish Cup final between Rangers and Vale of Leven and 30 former players and friends of both clubs accepted the invite from the first great captain of the Light Blues to attend.

He told his guests: "The same spirit that characterised football in the old days has gone. It has been reduced to a purely mercenary matter."

* * *

"Our very success, gained you will agree by skill, will draw more people than ever to see it. And that will benefit many more clubs than Rangers. Let the others come after us. We welcome the chase. It is healthy for us. We will never hide from it. Never fear, inevitably we shall have our years of failure, and when they arrive, we must reveal tolerance and sanity. No matter the days of anxiety that come our way, we shall emerge stronger because of the trials to be overcome. That has been the philosophy of the Rangers since the days of the gallant pioneers."

Bill Struth, Glasgow, May 1953

Four lads had a dream
To start a football team
They had no money, no kit, not even a ball
But they carried on
And the Rangers were born
55 titles
We're still going strong

CONTENTS

FOREWORDS

John Brown
Rangers FC 1988-1997

Four teenage boys took a walk around Kelvingrove Park in 1872 and laid the foundations for the greatest football club in the world.

How could they have known, 140 years later, their beloved club would be struggling for its very survival?

I have loved Glasgow Rangers for as long as I can remember. It's part of me. It's in my blood.

It is a big enough honour to be a fan of the club, but to have actually played for the team? That really was the stuff of dreams.

I was part of a squad that won nine-in-a-row, as well as cups and silverware galore, including the Treble, and we even came within a whisker of reaching the first Champions League final in 1993.

But the biggest challenge I ever faced at Ibrox was on a warm summer's night in the summer of 2012 when I stood on the steps of the stadium and voiced my concerns to worried fans about the direction I feared the club was heading.

I believed our club had been infiltrated by people who did not have its best interests at heart. The danger signs were there, but too many had chosen to ignore them.

I could not turn away. I owed it to Moses McNeil, Peter McNeil, Peter Campbell and William McBeath to stay and fight and tell the truth as I saw it.

My speech on the steps that night was not scripted or rehearsed. It came from the heart and was delivered in the moment.

As I stood there, memories of my childhood came flooding back – sitting glued to that little black and white telly in our house in Blackburn, West Lothian in 1972 with my parents, Andy and Irene, and my brother, David, watching Bud Johnston and Colin Stein score against Dynamo Moscow to win the Cup Winners' Cup.

It was difficult to suppress my emotions when I thought of my dad taking me to the Centenary Scottish Cup final in 1973, the euphoria of Tam Forsyth's winning goal at Hampden sealing one of the club's finest ever victories over Celtic.

I thought of our great European nights at Ibrox too, special occasions such as the 2-0 win over Juventus in 1978 under John Greig. It still ranks as one of our greatest European performances of all time.

Watching those games as a kid was life changing, but to represent my club on so many big occasions was off the scale incredible. Walking out at Elland Road for the Battle of Britain against Leeds, or playing Marseille at Ibrox and the Stade Velodrome? Those moments will live with me forever.

Those who don't have Rangers in their hearts would struggle to understand what it means to players, fans and custodians. It's much more than a football club. It's a way of life. It runs through our veins. It's family. Those gallant pioneers created something matched by no other club or institution the world over – a sense of pride, honour and integrity.

I shudder when I think back less than a decade. We were so close to losing our club and I genuinely feared seeing it dismantled, red brick by red brick. The thought makes me sick even now. It was a very frightening time. The threat of our club going down and not coming back was real. I still maintain that opinion today – and no-one will ever convince me otherwise.

My phone didn't stop ringing during that period with people asking: 'Bomber, what are you going to do?' I knew I had to do something, but what? There was an increasing feeling of helplessness among the fans, but I had been given information about what was going to happen to my club.

The Rangers fans had always supported me throughout my career and this was my opportunity to pay them back. It was time to speak out.

People I had previously respected advised me not to stand on the steps in front of those big, oak doors on Edmiston Drive. They told me to keep my head down, keep quiet. Thankfully, I listened to others.

They implored me to tell the fans what was going on. As absurd as some of the information I was given seemed, I was assured it was correct – and that I would be proved right in the end.

I had the full support of my wife, Sandra, and my daughters, Lauren and Megan, but I had embarked on a journey that was not without its difficulties for me, my reputation, my family – and my club.

It was particularly tough on my parents, who were in their mid-70s, as I had to put up with abuse on the streets and on social media. The girls were told their old man was a rocket and it's probably best not to dwell on some of the personal threats I received. It's a time I'd never wish to re-live.

However, no matter what was thrown at me, giving up was never an option. I had to focus on one thing only – the future of Rangers. I spoke out at every opportunity and to anyone who would listen, from fan groups to journalists, on the dangers I believed the club were facing.

Others you would have expected to want to save the club were elsewhere, cosying up to the very people I believed were in danger of destroying Rangers. I'll leave that to them and their conscience.

It cost me, professionally and personally. Managerial jobs that followed at Clyde and Dundee were compromised because, to supporters there, I was the permanently angry man who only had Rangers at heart. I became persona non grata in some circles.

But they say time is a healer – and what a healing period Rangers have enjoyed under the guidance of our manager, Steven Gerrard.

We've celebrated our 55th title and it was momentous in many ways, not least because winning the championship prevented our fiercest rivals across the city from reaching their dream of 10-in-a-row.

What a great job Steven has done, transforming a group of players into a winning squad, all within a couple of years and only a handful of transfer windows.

People ask my proudest moment at Rangers and I have no hesitation in telling them. It was the day I stood shoulder to shoulder with the fans and shouted at the top of my voice until I was eventually heard.

I'd be thrilled to think Moses, the two Peters and William were up there cheering me on, all the way.

After all they have given us, battling to return to the club into the hands of people who truly have Rangers at heart was the very least their legacy deserved.

Rangers till I die.

John Brown
October 2021

Gary Ralston

We have cherished the scale of their ambitions for 150 years and for the first time in history we can finally picture them all together.

Four lads had a dream – mine, as a writer on the early years of Rangers, was to gather the images of the founding fathers and tell of the formation of a great football club.

As we celebrate a momentous milestone for the club, they have been brought together again for the first time since the 1870s, re-born here in the pages of The Gallant Pioneers. We finally have a picture of William McBeath to go with Moses McNeil, brother Peter and Peter Campbell.

The story behind that new-found image is in chapter nine, one small but very significant tale from a century and a half of amazing adventures.

Well Moses, here's hoping you are looking down on Edmiston Drive with justified pride at all you have created.

As for our two Peters, McNeil and Campbell? Your achievements and names remain cherished still, 150 years after that quiet walk around West End Park, where an idea for a football team began to take root.

Poor William, you may have died penniless and alone in a corner of an English field, but you have been the richest benefactor and brought priceless joys to millions around the world.

As for Tom Vallance, dear Tom? Let the scale of your efforts to establish Rangers Football Club as the finest in the land never be forgotten or diminished.

You may have arrived on the scene a few months after your four friends, three of them boyhood chums from the Gare Loch, but you contributed immensely on and off the park. Thankfully, like boyhood pal Moses, you lived long enough to see the scale of what your beloved Light Blues would become.

The spirit of the founding fathers shines through today as much as it did in 1872 as Rangers celebrate a birthday only few clubs in the world game can claim – and of those, surely, none have been as successful.

In May 1953, a dinner was hosted by Glasgow Council to honour the achievements of Bill Struth. He was presented with a portrait that now hangs in the Ibrox Trophy Room and the legendary Rangers manager delivered a powerful oratory that many among the Light Blues legions have clung to in recent years.

There must be tolerance and sanity, urged Struth, for the years of failure that would inevitably occur. He insisted, however, that Rangers would emerge stronger for it all. After all, he maintained, that had been the philosophy of the club since the days of the gallant pioneers.

His words rang more true for the decade up to the invincible league title victory under Steven Gerrard in 2021 than at any point in the history of the club.

Those greedy, rapacious carpetbaggers who seized control of Rangers from 2011 brought the club to its knees. How cruel and haunting was the thought of Struth, buried high above Ibrox at Craigton Cemetery, so close to the financial carnage a mile away.

Their bloated salaries and bonus packages were as unedifying as the continuing zeal to deny Rangers their history, even if the decision to begin the process of liquidating the old holding company in June 2012 caused widespread confusion initially.

Thankfully, Rangers men of stature emerged, just as president George Goudie had done in 1883 when his loan of £30 saved the club from going under little more than a decade after it had been formed.

Dave King, Douglas and Graeme Park, John Bennett, George Letham and George Taylor invested significantly, followed by others who had come to see that Rangers had been returned to safe hands, bolstered by record season ticket sales of more than 47,500.

Front and centre at the worst of times were also Paul Murray, John Gilligan, Chris Graham, Craig Houston and John Brown. They played crucial roles in uniting fans and shareholders against those who had come to be despised.

'Bomber' has always been my favourite Rangers player, for many reasons. How typical of the man that he stood up to be counted, speaking out when others sat quietly and said nothing. It was a genuine honour when he agreed to write the foreword for this new edition.

In truth, the support never wavered, even as doubts about the integrity of those in the boardroom grew. Rangers played consistently to sell out crowds from the Third Division onwards, with season ticket sales never dropping below 38,500.

The authenticity of the men in the boardroom, slowly but surely, was matched by the players on the pitch as Gerrard gave the fans a team with whom they could once again identify and trust as he further underlined his own reputation as a football man of substance.

Three times they have emerged in recent years from the earliest Europa League preliminary rounds to reach the group stages and beyond before that stunning 55th title win in 2021, forever destined to be the pinnacle of Gerrard's reign in the eyes of supporters.

In qualifying for the group stages of the Europa League again in August 2021, Gerrard took Rangers into the top 50 of co-efficient ranked clubs in Europe. In 2017, Rangers were a lowly 265 in UEFA's ratings. Gerrard took them to 40th after their aggregate victory over Armenian champions FC Alashkert.

Remarkably, that was 10 places higher than Celtic, who had banked a shot at the Champions League for five years without a challenge from Rangers after their collapse into the financial wilderness in 2012. Little wonder billboards declared 'Legend in Liverpool, God in Glasgow' after winning 55.

Rangers, of course, went 38 league games unbeaten under Gerrard, arguably the most impressive championship – certainly the most important – in the long and fabled history of the club. That surely includes even the campaign of 1898/99 when a world record of 18 wins from 18 games was set – how that must have pleased Moses, his brother Peter and Tom as they looked on, their playing days long behind them.

Rangers have organised a festival of events to mark the 150th anniversary of the club and are constructing a museum where the story of its humble foundations will surely be recognised for future generations to celebrate and give thanks.

Nothing of the history of Rangers – absolutely nothing – would have been written without the determination and pride of four boys who had no money, no kit and even had to borrow a ball to play their first matches on Glasgow Green.

It's hoped the publication of The Gallant Pioneers – this is now its fourth edition – has also helped inform supporters of the passion and principles behind the formation of the club. Those teenagers took a walk in West End Park and gave voice to an ambition that amounted to little more than the creation of a team to play the new craze of association football.

The early years' research, particularly the fastidious efforts of Gordon Bell and Iain McColl, is ongoing still. In this edition we reach back through the mists of time and, we hope, offer further clarity on the beginnings of Rangers, not to mention that picture of William.

Some may find our conclusions controversial, including our belief the club played as a side known as Western before adopting the name of Rangers, most likely in September 1873. We'll let our opinion, backed by our evidence, speak for itself.

There is a pride in the legacy left by the book. I received a phone call from a club executive, shortly after The Gallant Pioneers was first published in 2009, and they revealed Sandy Jardine had read it and proposed plans to change the date of the club's formation from 1873 to 1872 atop the stand that now carries his name.

It was a towering gesture from Sandy, who was such a passionate advocate of the story of the club's early years before his sad passing in 2014.

More than most, Sandy appreciated that planning for future meant honouring the past. Moses, the two Peters, William and Tom deserve every bit of recognition that comes their way in the 150th year for the fabulous club they helped build.

Gary Ralston
October 2021

1

THE BIRTH OF THE BLUES

There are days, months and years that will remain woven like silk ribbons into the red, white and blue reflections of Rangers fans forevermore.

The memories of success are sewn from Barcelona in May 1972 with Willie Waddell at the helm, to Walter Smith's Wednesday night in April 1997 when nine-in-a-row was won, all the way to the clinching of title number 55 under Steven Gerrard in March 2021.

Life is a constant casting off and there are still thousands of those among the Light Blues legions whose recollections are rooted deeper in the past, perhaps to Scot Symon's Treble winners of 1964 with Slim Jim in his glorious pomp.

Maybe they can even go back to old man Struth himself, the legendary manager who led the club to a record 18 championships and the first grand slam in Scottish football history in 1949.

Understandably, for the tales of derring dos before the Second World War – and there were many – we have to increasingly rely on dusty memoirs and faded newspaper clippings to tell us of the wonders of David Meiklejohn, Bob McPhail, Sandy Archibald, Alan Morton et al, who arguably made Rangers the best team in the world for several seasons between the wars.

Reaching even further into the past, John 'Kitey' McPherson was the colossus who helped the Light Blues to their first Scottish Cup triumph in 1894 and then, with team-mates such as Nicol Smith, played a pivotal role in the unique title win of 1898/99.

Back then, 18 wins out of 18 were secured, an unprecedented achievement rightly and repeatedly referenced when Gerrard's class of 2021 went unbeaten in the Premiership from first to last.

Journalist John Allan was around to witness and recount many of those earliest feats and the former Daily Record editor produced the three most authoritative works on the history of Rangers before his death in 1953.

Even today, 'The Story of the Rangers', 'Eleven Great Years' and '18 Eventful Years', which recorded the story of the club to 1951, retain much credibility and authenticity.

Allan is owed an apology from these pages. It was noted in previous editions that he had the clasp of a loyal Ranger, as Bill Struth once remarked, but that the strength of his grip on historical reality had become a bone of contention.

Undoubtedly Allan, born in Kinning Park in 1879, romanticised the formation of the club he quickly grew to support and did not do enough to clarify the old chestnut – thankfully now settled and resolved – around the formation of the club in 1872 rather than, as he insisted, 12 months later.

Allan's influence stretched beyond the written page to the very corridors of power at Ibrox itself, where he was recognised as a confidant of Struth in particular. The greatest ever Rangers boss was effusive in his praise in an obituary for Allan that appeared under his byline in the Rangers Supporters' Association annual of 1954, his last of 34 years as Ibrox manager.

Struth recalled of Allan: "I still see him walk into my room with the smile of the kindly heart and the clasp of a loyal Ranger. He knew many of my secrets. They were sacred to him. No confidence was ever in danger when given to John. Our success was his success, yet in his role of critic he was a forthright, honest chronicler who sought no favours and gave none in the line of duty."

He added: "I have known him to leave his office after many hours of exacting work, slip quietly into his home and pen the deeds of our great teams of the past until roused from his labours by the dawn breaking in on his thoughts.

"A few hours sleep and he was back at his desk. So brilliant a pen as his could have told an absorbing story without the necessity of detail. But as he said to me: 'Without the facts to prove the greatness of the club, my task would be incomplete.' It meant days of research – yes, months if measured in the hours he spent among his unique record books and in the old files that took him back to the beginning of the game."

Allan insisted the birth of the club came in 1873, a year still celebrated on the intricate mosaics on either side of the Ibrox Main Stand, opened in 1929. It was a date the club happily accepted for decades after the publication of 'The Story of the Rangers' in 1923, the first great book on its history, before rightly re-committing to 1872 shortly after publication of The Gallant Pioneers in 2009.

The correct date is now celebrated on top of the Sandy Jardine Stand, in all Rangers media, literature and marketing material and, of course, forms the basis for the club's 150th anniversary celebrations in 2022.

Allan's book was published to celebrate its jubilee and opened with: "In the summer evenings of 1873 a number of lusty, laughing lads, mere boys some of them, flushed and happy from the exhilaration of a finishing dash with the oars, could be seen hauling their craft ashore on the upper reaches of the River Clyde at Glasgow Green."

Allan went further and categorically stated the club was born from a match played on a Tuesday night at Glasgow Green on July 15 1873 between two teams, Argyle and Clyde. He added: "These names did not represent organised clubs. The two sides were selected for the purpose of providing a game and names were chosen to give the event some individuality."

He went on to list the names of the players from the two competing sides including, for Argyle, Moses and Peter McNeil, William McBeath, Tom Vallance and Peter Campbell. He continued: "It is recorded in a news print of the period that the game was very exciting and ended in a draw."

Fresh research has, indeed, unearthed the article in question, which appeared in the Glasgow Herald three days after the match was played on Glasgow Green, noting it was between *Argill* and Clyde. In total, five players – including David Hill of Clyde – would go on to represent Rangers in their pivotal Scottish Cup final against Vale of Leven four years later.

There was another match involving the teams on Saturday September 20 1873, also on the Green, which is of huge historical significance.

It stands as the earliest match report – we argue THE earliest match report – in which the name of the Rangers countless supporters know and love today was used for the first time.

In actual fact, the club was listed as 'Rangers (late Western)' and therein lies a new story on the origins of the club which we will examine later in the chapter.

The Glasgow News of September 22 reported the game against Clyde as being the "return match between these two clubs" which, in truth, is unlikely to be a reference to the first match two months previously.

In his book, Allan mentioned a subsequent meeting between Rangers and Clyde, which finished 11-0 in favour of the Light Blues. Sadly, reports of the encounter do not appear to have been published in newspapers of the time.

The match in September was likely to have been a follow on from that rout and, again, Rangers emerged emphatic winners, with William McBeath scoring five goals in a 7-1 victory. The report mentioned three Clyde players favourably, all of whom had played in the July fixture.

Two of them, John Baird and John Rankin, also went on to play for the fledgling Rangers as their Clyde team, short lived like so many others of the period, disappeared soon after (the Clyde team we know today was not formed until 1877).

Evidence to support the formation of Rangers in 1873, not 12 months earlier, was provided by Moses McNeil himself, in the only ever newspaper interview with the co-founder intensive research has uncovered.

Significantly, however, his first-person piece was printed in Allan's own Daily Record in April 1935, 48 hours after Rangers had won the Scottish Cup against Hamilton Accies.

The influence of Allan loomed large over the copy, which appeared under McNeil's byline and a headline stating: 'When Rangers First Reached the Final'.

McNeil, reminiscing on his career three years before his death at the age of 82, wrote: "In the summer of 1873 my brothers Peter and Willie and myself, along with some Gareloch lads, banded together on Glasgow Green with the object of forming a football club."

It would be mean-spirited to pin the inaccuracy of 1873 solely on Moses McNeil or John Allan, and the club's date of formation was a source of debate around Ibrox in the early 1920s as its jubilee loomed.

A celebratory dinner hosted by chairman Sir John Ure Primrose and attended by the greats of the Scottish game took place at the 'Ferguson and Forrester's' restaurant on Buchanan Street on April 9 1923 and received widespread coverage in all newspapers the following day.

The Evening Times recorded: "There has been some difference of opinion as to the year in which the Rangers Football Club originated, but it has been settled to the satisfaction of the gentlemen who at present control the club that the foundation was laid in 1873."

Nevertheless, a stronger body of evidence exists to prove 1872 was the real date of Rangers' formation. Firstly, the Scottish Football Association annuals, published as early as season 1875–76, carried details of every club operating in the game at that time, with information provided by each club secretary.

Rangers, with their background most likely recorded by Peter McNeil, were acknowledged from the very first edition as being instituted in 1872.

Their entry in one of the earliest editions of the respected handbook even gives a brief, potted history of that period and states: "This club has been one of the most successful of our Scottish football clubs, having played on Glasgow Green as a junior club from 1872 to 1874."

One of the earliest and most respected histories of the British game, published in 1905, also declared 1872 to be the year. Furthermore, the article on 'The Game in Scotland', part of a four-volume series 'Association Football And The Men Who Made It' was penned by Robert Livingstone, the former president of the SFA.

He wrote: "The seed sown by Queen's Park did not all fall on stony ground, however, for in 1872 there sprang into life two clubs which today stand at the very forefront. These were Rangers and

5

Third Lanark and they were accompanied before the footlights of the world by Vale of Leven, destined for a chequered existence, but a still plucky survival."

The official Rangers handbook – known affectionately to generations of Ibrox followers as the 'Wee Blue Book' – was published every year from the turn of the 20th century until the 1980s.

From its first edition, Rangers were acknowledged as having been formed in 1872. As late as the edition for season 1920–21, under a section listing historical data, the club's birth was given as 1872.

Significantly, the section of historical data did not appear in the following year's edition, or in the handbook published for 1922–23. However, it returned for season 1923–24 when, lo and behold, the club's birth was listed as 1873. Perhaps surprisingly, no explanation was ever offered by the handbook's editor – John Allan.

A theory has surfaced over the years that Allan was under such pressure to publish a jubilee history that he altered the year of formation to suit his own punishing deadline – and historical ends. Allan certainly appears in a literary rush as he gallops through the very early years of Rangers in his book.

Further weight to the claim it was expedient for Allan to overlook 1872 as the year of formation comes from the fact that the earlier date does not even merit a mention at all. Surely Allan, with a reputation for such painstaking research, would have at least attempted to explain, in the first great history of the club, why the formation of 1872 that had been universally recognised up to that point was actually wrong?

That first written review of Rangers, by William 'Daddy' Dunlop in 1881, is also adamant the club was formed in 1872 – late March to be precise – by the three lads from the Gare Loch and William McBeath as they strolled in Glasgow's West End Park.

Naturally, Dunlop was writing closer to the club's birth date than anyone, so his evidence carries more authority. Certainly, few would disagree with his overall assertion in his essay that Rangers, formed from such humble roots, were "a self made club".

If Moses McNeil, writing in the 1920s and 1930s under the influence of Allan, was convinced the club was formed in 1873 then Tom Vallance, speaking much earlier in 1887, believed otherwise.

At the grand opening of the first Ibrox Park in August of that year, at the Copland Road end of today's stadium, that most gallant of pioneers toasted the future of the club.

In his speech, printed in the press at the time, he stated: "Well, about 15 years ago, a few lads who came from Gare Loch to Glasgow met and endeavoured to scrape together as much as would buy a football and we went to the Glasgow Green, where we played for a year or two. That, gentlemen, was the foundation of the Rangers Football Club."

Former player Archibald Steel, who played for the club in the 1870s before moving to Bolton, wrote one of the first authoritative histories of Scottish football in 1896 under the pen name of Old International. His book '25 Years Football' mines a rich seam of anecdote and first-hand experiences of playing against almost all the major clubs in the early years of the game in Scotland.

Steel emphasised 1872 as the year of Rangers' foundation as he recalled: "In the west, particularly, the game quickly took root and any spare ground where football could be followed was seized upon with avidity by the eager aspirants to dribbling proficiency.

"Two of the earliest I may mention were the Queen's Park juniors and the Parkgrove, besides which a year later – in 1871 – the Dumbreck and in the 12 months afterwards the Clydesdale, Rangers, Rovers and Third Lanark."

There has been less ambiguity about the origins of the Rangers name but fresh research has offered new insights into the early years of the club and may, in part, explain the confusion that arose around the time of the 50th anniversary on the debates of 1872 versus 1873.

Let there be no doubt Rangers were formed in 1872 but new evidence, not least the match report against Clyde, indicates they did not take their famous name until the following year.

If, as Allan states, they played a game in July 1873 under the name Argyll – surely derived from the Gare Loch roots of most of the founders – then a compelling theory emerges they soon changed to play under the name Western before settling on the moniker with which they would soon achieve renown.

The architect of the theory is none other than Daddy Dunlop himself, a behemoth of the early years and whose term as president in 1879-80 coincided with a stellar career as a player between 1876-1880, before he left for Queen's Park.

He wrote under the nom de plume 'True Blue' and his essay on 'The Rangers FC' was carried in the 1880-81 edition of The Scottish Football Annual before being re-printed in full in the Scottish Athletic Journal in August 1887 to mark the club's move to the first Ibrox Park.

He claimed the three monumental Scottish Cup final matches against Vale of Leven in 1877 were only slightly more talked about by the first generation of Rangers fans than the three games against early pace setters of the Scottish scene, known as the Rovers and "a stiff club to beat," according to Dunlop.

Rangers earned their early breakthrough, Dunlop maintained, on the back of the series of matches, known as the 'Wee Internationals' and which all ended in draws.

He recalled: "The Rangers had then but little experience from which they might gain knowledge. Common sense and the wisdom of the times pointed to practice as the high road to victory – and to practice they accordingly betook themselves.

"Three matches played on either the Green or Queen's Park did not decide their respective merits. But what themes for appreciative conversation did they furnish to the most ardent and enthusiastic spectators."

A club called Western did exist in the early 1870s but, crucially, they were a cricket team who had been formed in 1862 and played out of Regent's Park, a ground today occupied by the car park of the Kelvin Hall.

On September 15 1873 the North British Daily Mail reported on a cricket match from two days' previously involving all members of the Western club as the first XI took on the rest in the closing match of their season.

Meanwhile, across the river Clyde at South Side Park – also known as Queen's Park – a football team named Western were playing out a goalless draw against the Rovers on the same Saturday, also reported in the North British Daily Mail.

How could members of a cricket team called Western find players for a football match on the same day, across the other side of the city, on what was their annual, end of season gala occasion?

The cricketers and their friends retired to the Regent's Park pavilion after their match "where a most agreeable evening was spent". Frustratingly, no teams were listed from the football game played that day, but it's unlikely to have involved any cricketers.

The following Monday, September 22, the Glasgow News reported on that 7-1 thumping of Clyde by 'Rangers (late Western)', including the five goal haul by McBeath. We assert that this is the first match report ever to publicly mention the club by its now famous name – along with that nod to how it had been previously, even if briefly, known.

The North British Daily Mail also reported on a match between Rovers and Rangers on November 10 that year. It was played at Glasgow Green and finished goalless, with the game cut short because of fading light – and the Light Blues' side was packed with its famous pioneers.

It has not been possible to find the third game of the series from an era when football reporting, like the sport itself, was only beginning to evolve.

But why call themselves Western – and why change the name towards the end of September? Firstly, it's possible the McNeils, Cambells and Vallances took the title in homage to the Eastern club, which they had come to admire when watching that powerhouse play on Glasgow Green in the earliest days of the round ball game.

Of course, the heritage of the teenagers in the seaside villages to the west of Glasgow would also have made the name particularly apt.

The change of name is more easily explained – it was forced on Moses and Co after the Western cricket club decided to enter a team in the first season of the Scottish Cup in 1873-74.

Football league seasons run today, for the most part, from August to May because many of the fledgling teams in the Victorian era grew from cricket clubs who needed sporting challenges for their members outside their traditional summer term.

Two Western cricket club committee members, an RM Liddle and JH Kelly, became honorary treasurer and committee member respectively of the first SFA executive in late summer 1873, with clubs given until 30 September to enter that season's Scottish Cup competition as the first round draw took place the following day.

In short, as soon as the well established Western Cricket Club decided to turn to football, the hopes of the Gare Loch lads in keeping their new-found name were doomed.

Still an infant outfit in their own right, the club that soon became known as Rangers lacked the acumen at that stage to enter a competition to play with the big boys, but they would earn their place within 12 months.

For what it's worth, Western were humbled in the first round of the cup, losing 1-0 to Blythswood at their Regent's Park ground on October 18.

Match reports from that time onwards involving Western feature players who were inextricably linked to the cricket club. Not one player with a Rangers connection can be identified, further underlining the belief that the two Western football teams from the period were distinct and different.

But what's in a name? A flattering profile of Harry McNeil, the great Queen's Park winger and occasional Ranger, in the Scottish Athletic Journal of October 27 1885 reads like a Victorian version of Hello! magazine and credits him with naming the club Rangers.

Likewise, Daddy Dunlop claimed the club was named Rangers as rudimentary rhyming slang after the fact so many of its earliest players were strangers to Glasgow.

Neither tale rings as true as Allan's account in his book that "Moses McNeil proposed that it should be called the Rangers Association Football Club and to the young minds the name had an alluring appeal. It was adopted unanimously. Mr McNeil has related that he had been reading C.W. Alcock's 'English Football Annual' and had been attracted by the name he had seen belonging to an English rugby club."

McNeil's claims, made through Allan and again in the pages of the Daily Record in 1935, hold water. Alcock's annuals were elementary guides to the newly formed clubs across Britain and their preference for the various codes of football, including association and rugby.

They were first published in 1868 and are so rare that even the British Library does not boast any copies dating from before 1873. The RFU Museum at Twickenham does, however, and their issues make for fascinating reading.

Before 1870 no rugby team in England featured the Rangers name, although other wonderful handles included the Mohicans, Owls, Pirates and Red Rovers.

However, in the 1870 edition of Alcock's annuals a team called Rangers does appear, based in Swindon, with a kit that included white trousers, white jersey with a blue star on the breast.

The Rangers football team that lost the Scottish Cup to Vale of Leven after three games in 1877 were pictured in the photographer's studio shortly afterwards in a very similar kit, including a star on the breast of their shirts.

However, it can be no more than a coincidence as the Rangers star arguably owed more to their connection with Clyde Rowing Club, who used it then – and still do now – as their club emblem. (As an aside, there is no evidence to suggest Rangers ever wore the shirts with the star outside the photographer's studio. In all three games against Vale, for example, they wore blue).

In Alcock's 1871 edition Rangers are again mentioned, still at Gorse Hill in Swindon, but with the additional information that they had been formed in 1868 and played a form of rugby known as Marlborough. It's entirely possible the Swindon rugby team are the club from whom the Glasgow side took its name.

Still, as always, there is scope for debate, because by the publication of Alcock's next edition, in the autumn of 1872, the Swindon club had disappeared and another club named Rangers (formed in 1870, but making its first appearance in the annual) had taken its place. This second club played rugby union and were based on Clapham Common in London.

We believe Rangers were formed in 1872 and named in September 1873 and it is most likely they took their title from either the club in Swindon or Clapham Common, depending on the Alcock annual McNeil had studied.

Further evidence to suggest the club was named the year after its formation is provided by the arrival of Tom Vallance to join his friends in the spring of 1873, as Dunlop wrote. In the Nottingham Evening Post, of all papers, Rangers and Vallance were mentioned on December 31 1928, on the eve of a 3-0 Ne'erday victory over Celtic at Ibrox.

The Post mentioned: "Mr Tom Vallance, one of the founders of the Rangers, is to be present tomorrow. He gave his vote to the adoption of Rangers as a name for the club, the proposal having been made by one who had seen the name in one of CW Alcock's old English rugby annuals. A choice little piece of history!"

The beginnings of Rangers may have been humble, but they were also able to boast a royal connection in its infancy as a membership card from season 1874–75 announced the patron of the club as the Most Noble, the Marquis of Lorne, who would go on to become the 9th Duke of Argyll.

It is clear that the new association football clubs saw patronage by the aristocracy as lending authority to their new ventures – not to forget, of course, the financial support that often came with the acceptance of an honorary position at the fledgling clubs.

Queen's Park, for example, charged captain William Ker with finding a patron in 1873 and he immediately set his sights on the Prince of Wales, who politely declined. The Earl of Glasgow, however, agreed and quickly forwarded a donation of £5 to his new-found favourites.

In all likelihood the Marquis of Lorne, John Douglas Sutherland Campbell, would have donated a similar sum to his fellow lads from Argyll to boost their new enterprise.

The Marquis was 27 years old when Rangers were formed and clearly had a level of interest in the association game as he was also an honorary president of the SFA at the time and was still listed as a patron of the association in the 1890s.

It was something of a coup for the Rangers committee to persuade him to patronise their infant venture, not least because only a year earlier he had married Princess Louise, daughter of Queen Victoria, at Windsor, and had become one of the most high profile figures in British public life even if, as a Liberal member of parliament, he was regarded as something of a political plodder on the back benches at Westminster.

As future Clan Campbell chief, the Marquis of Lorne is likely to have been acquainted with John Campbell, his namesake and father of Peter, who would have enjoyed a position of standing in the Argyll community as a result of his successful steamboat enterprises.

The McNeils would also surely have had access to high society, even if indirectly, through their father's position as head gardener at Belmore House on the shores of the Gare Loch.

The Marquis, or Lorne as he was best known, was also a keen supporter of sporting pastimes, particularly those with an Argyll connection. The landed gentry viewed patronage of such healthy pastimes as an extension of their traditional responsibilities as clan chiefs, even in the latter half of the 19th century.

It is unlikely Lorne ever watched Rangers play in the early years – there is no record of it – as his life in London and Argyll was demanding, not to mention the fact that in 1878 he left British shores to become Governor General of Canada.

He and Louise made a massive contribution to Canadian life at the time – Lake Louise was named after Victoria's daughter. Their patronage of the arts and letters was underlined with the establishment of institutions such as the Royal Canadian Academy of Arts and the National Gallery of Canada.

Lorne and Louise returned to Britain in 1883 and he became ninth Duke of Argyll following the death of his father in April 1900. Lorne died of pneumonia on the Isle of Wight in May 1914, aged 68 and was buried at Kilmun – not the first with a Rangers connection to be buried at that peaceful graveyard by the shores of the Holy Loch.

Louise, his wife of 43 years, lived out the rest of her long life at Rosneath Castle, although she died at Kensington Palace in 1939, aged 91. In her latter years she thought nothing of using her royal status to walk into any house in Rosneath unannounced to ensure all within were well.

She even shared the village for many years with Moses McNeil, who lived out his latter years in the close-knit community where he had been raised for part of his younger life.

History has not recorded if they were ever on speaking terms. They may have led two very different existences, but they could claim without fear of contradiction membership of special institutions that still mean so much to so many.

2
THE GALLANT PIONEERS

The story of the formation of Rangers is a simple tale too often told wrong. Over the years, sadly, ignorance and malevolence have become cosy bedfellows in shaping an uncomfortable narrative for those who reflect on the humble and innocent origins of the club with pride.

The publication of The Gallant Pioneers in 2009, coupled with the wonderful work of The Founders' Trail, orchestrated by Gordon Bell and Iain McColl, has helped connect thousands of Rangers supporters with the early years of the Light Blues over the last decade.

The success of both projects – as well as the imminent opening of the new Rangers museum at Ibrox – also serves as a timely reminder of the appetite among fans for the history of the club, something publishers openly doubted when the idea of The Gallant Pioneers was first mooted all those years ago.

The book was motivated, in part, by the openly erroneous interpretation of the early years of Rangers by media commentators and even public bodies.

The Kelvingrove Art Gallery and Museum, for example, opened its doors in the summer of 2006 after a three-year refurbishment at a cost of £28 million. The beautifully restored Victorian landmark boasts 8,000 works of art and – as many Rangers fans were quick to point out – one work of fiction.

In a section of the ground floor devoted to Glasgow Stories, space was given over to an exhibition of 'Symbols That Divide', which included flags, banners and colours, many of them associated with the city's two great clubs, Rangers and Celtic.

To the annoyance of many fans of the Light Blues, the script associated with their favourites (which was changed following a string of complaints) started: "Rangers began as a Protestant club…"

In an article in The Times to mark the 130th anniversary of the very first Scottish Cup tie played by Rangers in 1874, a 2–0 victory over Oxford at Queen's Park Recreation Ground on the south side of Glasgow, it was noted: "It was only thanks to large lashings of luck that Rangers were able to evolve from the primeval soup of Scottish football's prehistoric era."

In March 2007, as the debate on sectarianism raged back and forth in the pages of the Scottish press, Sun columnist Bill Leckie – one of the sharpest tabloid writers in the business – took Rangers to task and declared it: "a club which has had its entire history to drive bigotry from the terraces."

As an institution that has been part of the social fabric of Scotland for 150 years it is inevitable that Rangers – in particular its early years – have attracted myth, mischief-making and mis-perception on a scale to match their triumphs over the decades.

This success includes a trophy haul unsurpassed in world football: 55 top flight championships, 33 Scottish Cups and 27 League Cups, not to mention the European Cup-Winners' Cup in 1972, appearances in the final in 1961 and 1967 and a run to the UEFA Cup final in Manchester in 2008.

Lest we forget, Rangers also won lower league championships from 2013 as it began to claw its way back following the carnage of financial vandalism and underhand corporate chicanery.

At a time when Rangers and its supporters are being more closely scrutinised than ever before, including some potent self-analysis, history has a vital role to play in reminding every fan (not just of Rangers) of the club's humble origins and how the Light Blues were moulded by its earliest personalities.

Their fates, failures and fledgling successes may even, in turn, help re-define the future of a club they could never have dared dream would grow to become one of the biggest in the world.

However, much of what has been recorded on the early years has been fictionalised and regurgitated as truth to create a fog of fable as thick as any haar that rolls across the floodlit pitch at Ibrox from the Clyde during a midweek game.

So, no, Rangers were not established as a sporting front for the teachings of Knox, Calvin and Luther, even if the upbringing of the club's gallant pioneers was undeniably Protestant and the ethos of the club remains indelibly so, while still embracing players and fans from across the religious and social spectrum of 21st-century Scotland and beyond.

If there was any criticism aimed at the club's membership list in the 1870s it was in relation to the clannish nature of its Gare Loch influence, with many of the club's early members associated with a shared upbringing on the Clyde peninsula.

Questions on the importance of religion as a defining factor of the club in its formative years are as relevant as asking a survivor from the Titanic how they had otherwise enjoyed their voyage.

To pin the Protestant yin to the Catholic yang of Celtic – the Parkhead club were formed in 1887 to help provide succour to the members of that religious community in the east end of Glasgow – is lazy historical shorthand.

It seeks to place the debate on the Old Firm and both clubs' formations, rivalries, politics and problems into snug, pre-assembled pigeonholes, including a shared ideological birth based on religious motivation, albeit from different tenets of the Christian faith.

However, the formation of Rangers does not fit. The inspiration of Peter and Moses McNeil, Peter Campbell and William McBeath as they walked through the Glasgow park in early 1872 near the spot that would later house the museum that stood and misrepresented their motives, was pure and simple.

They sought nothing more than to add prowess in association football to a range of sporting interests that already included 'manly' pastimes such as shinty, rowing and athletics.

Likewise, the formation of their club and its progress throughout that decade and beyond owed absolutely nothing to good fortune and everything to solid friendships (or Gare Loch clannishness), sound organisation and a firm structure.

How else, within 18 months of their humble beginnings at Flesher's Haugh on Glasgow Green, could they have persuaded the Marquis of Lorne, future 9th Duke of Argyll, Governor of Canada and son-in-law to Queen Victoria, to become their first patron?

Finally, Rangers has not had its whole history to address and resolve affairs nowadays associated with sectarianism. Such emotive issues did not arise until at least 40 years after the earliest players, most of them still dressed in their street clothes, kicked the club's first, battered piece of leather around a patch of open ground.

They were driven on by the altruistic ideal of sport for sport's sake and the dream of scoring a game-winning goal against their debut opponents, Callander (it never came, the match finished goalless).

Wider debates on sectarianism are tangled in a labyrinth of landmine topics ranging from Irish nationalism, militant republicanism and the nature of Scottish, Irish and British identity at the turn of the 20th century.

In short and in truth, the story of Rangers is one of the most romantic of the greatest sporting clubs formed. It was born uniquely and totally out of a love for the new craze of association football that spread throughout Scotland and England in the 1860s and 1870s.

The founding fathers of the club were, in fact, no more than young boys who had come to Glasgow seeking their fortune in business and industry and who, instead, went on to develop an unintentional relationship with fame that keeps their names alive and cherishes the scale of their achievements to this very day.

Campbell and McBeath were only 15 years old, Moses McNeil was 16 and his older brother, Peter, was the senior statesman at just 17. Tom Vallance was not there at the conception but he certainly helped in the delivery of the club and was also a mere pup, barely 16 years old.

The images and memories of that time are passed down through the yellowed pages of 19th-century newspapers such as the Scottish Athletic Journal, Scottish Umpire, Scottish Sport and Scottish Referee, recalling on-field successes and off-field intrigues.

Other, more personal and often harrowing stories come from the vaults and archives of museums and libraries across Britain, including long-hidden horrors of death at sea, insanity and loss of life as a result of business worries, the tag of certified imbecility, a trial for fraud and life in the poorhouse, not to mention a second marriage for one of the founding fathers that was most likely bigamous.

Thankfully, there are happier tales to recollect, stories of fascinating relationships, directly and indirectly, with the growth of the steam trade on the Clyde, Charles Rennie Mackintosh and even the gift of the club's first ball from the owner of the company that would go on to become House of Fraser (Mike Ashley, take note).

The pattern of Rangers' development is woven inextricably into the rich tapestry that chronicles the growth of Glasgow, where the dominant sporting threads have been coloured blue and green for well over a century.

The second city of the empire is as central to the story of the club as the River Clyde was to its earliest trade in tobacco and cotton. In 1765, a little more than 100 years before Rangers staked their first claim to a pitch at Flesher's Haugh, James Watt was walking deep in thought on Glasgow Green when a vision of an innovative use for steam power came to him and triggered one of the most important developments of the Industrial Revolution.

In 1820 there were 21 steam engines operating in the city, yet within a quarter of a century that number had increased to over 300, powering operations in a range of industries including cotton and textiles, chemicals, glass, paper and soap.

Later, heavier industries came to dominate, including ironworks, locomotive construction and the aforementioned shipbuilding. In 1831 the first railway arrived in Glasgow, complementing the existing Forth and Clyde and Monklands canals, which had been completed in the early 1790s and were vital to transport raw materials such as coal and ironstone from the bountiful fields of nearby Lanarkshire.

On the Clyde, technological developments saw shipbuilding advance at such a pace from the 1820s that within 50 years more than half the British shipbuilding workforce was based on the river, including teenager Peter Campbell, producing half of Britain's tonnage of shipping – up to 500,000 a year by 1900.

It was a chaotic recipe for growth that over the course of the century absorbed hundreds of thousands of new inhabitants, the population increasing from 66,000 in 1791 to 658,000 in 1891.

By the 1820s, thousands of Scots had been forcibly driven into the clutches of the new industrial age through rural depopulation and Clearances in the Highlands on the back of social reconstruction following the failed Jacobite uprisings.

By 1821 the population of Glasgow had risen almost fivefold from 32,000 in 1750, much of it a result of immigration, particularly from Ireland. Many of those who settled in the city in the late 18th century were Irish Presbyterians, drawn by the common ancestry and shared sense of cultural heritage with lowland Scots.

They were particularly skilled in weaving and settled in the communities in the east end of the city that traditionally nurtured the trade, such as Bridgeton and Calton. By 1820, it was estimated that up to a third of the area's weavers were of Irish origin – many of their descendants are Rangers supporters today.

In the late 1840s, further Irish immigration as a result of the potato famine also increased the city's population. The majority of those who arrived in Glasgow as a result of the famine were Catholic, although up to 25 per cent of all those who arrived in Scotland from across the water in the 19th century were Protestant.

These were the best and worst of times. In the 1820s and 1830s the average life expectancy for men in Glasgow was just 37, and women fared little better at 40. By the 1880s it had increased, but only slightly, to 42 and 45.

There were typhoid epidemics in 1837 and 1847 and Scotland's first cholera epidemic also hit the city, killing 10,000 people. There were further outbreaks of the deadly disease in 1849 and 1854 when over 7,500 citizens lost their lives.

Between the 1830s and the late 1850s, death rates rose to peaks not seen since the 17th century. Even 20 years later there was still a very high infant mortality rate, with up to half of all children born never seeing their fifth birthday.

As late as 1906 a school board survey revealed a 14-year-old boy living in a poor area of Glasgow was, on average, four inches shorter than a child of a similar age from the city's west end. It came as only a perverse crumb of comfort that the extra inches in the city's poorer quarters would not have been welcomed, given Glasgow's status at the time as the most overcrowded population centre in Britain.

However, the west end symbolised the self-confidence of Glasgow's burgconing mercantile classes and the two Great Exhibitions of 1881 and 1901 in Kelvingrove Park showcased its pride in its reputation as the second city of the Empire.

By 1820, the development of the city westwards had reached Blythswood Square, with gridded Georgian terraces extending along Bath Street, St Vincent Street and West George Street. By the 1850s many of these buildings had been commandeered by the city's business community, which were constructed around George Square and extended up Blythswood Hill as banks, insurance houses and shipping companies expanded in size and influence.

As the city's wealth increased, so was the isolated countryside further west swallowed up from the mid-1800s, particularly with the completion of the Great Western Road and the establishment of the Botanic Gardens on the Kelvinside Estate.

The relocation of Glasgow University from the High Street to Gilmorehill in 1870 added an academic aura still prevalent today and, all the time, the construction of handsome mansions and elegant townhouses in yellow, pink and red sandstone gathered pace, overseen by architects such as Rennie Mackintosh and Alexander 'Greek' Thomson around spacious crescents and a plethora of public parks.

Glasgow has long claimed more public recreation areas per head of population than any other major European city, giving rise to its proud nickname of the 'Dear Green Place'.

Fittingly, the story of the birth of Rangers straddles both sides of the city. Peter Campbell apart, the founding fathers and their earliest teammates could not be easily tagged as representative of either of the polar opposite communities that confidently sprang up or rose falteringly and with raspish breath in their adopted city.

They represented the everyman; neither rich nor poor, privileged nor disadvantaged. They did not come from nor live in the disease-ridden wynds of the Gallowgate, Saltmarket, Calton or High Street, but neither did their addresses declare them as young men of particular wealth or substance.

Their homes, like themselves, stood on the fringes of prosperity: close to, but not part of, the affluent west end. To a man, they lived exclusively in the Sandyford area in addresses such as Berkeley

Street, Kent Road, Cleveland Street, Elderslie Street and Bentinck Street. They worked, for the most part, in the service industry or white-collar occupations such as drapers, hosiers, clerks and commercial travellers.

As Moses and Peter McNeil, William McBeath and Peter Campbell walked through West End Park in March 1872, discussing their desire to form a football club, they may have looked up the hill and been similarly driven to aspire to the lifestyle of those who had just constructed their handsome and spacious homes in the Park district, with panoramic views offering a dramatic sweep across an everchanging Glasgow cityscape.

In time, their fledgling club would climb to lofty peaks in European football, but for many different reasons, personal tragedies among them, none of them would clamber from the foothills towards wealth and prosperity and all would die with their contribution to the history of Rangers virtually unheralded.

Until now, their life stories have remained largely unknown and unacknowledged by all but a sympathetic few.

In those heady days their sights were set not on the west, but to the east and the public park of Glasgow Green that had been laid out over 36 acres between 1815 and 1826 by the city fathers, offering a rare opportunity for residents from the claustrophobic lanes and alleyways to sample open spaces.

The park provided a vital escape to the people of the east end who existed in appalling conditions, even after the City Improvement Trust had been established in 1866 to clear the slum dwellings and improve squalid living conditions.

The park served the recreational needs of the city at the time despite, bizarrely, a bye-law introduced in 1819 prohibiting sporting and leisure pursuits. Cricket and shinty were popular pastimes, as was bowling, and there was even a huge wooden framed gymnasium on site.

Rowers could be found on the Clyde and the Clydesdale Amateur Rowing Club, formed in 1857, and the Clyde Rowing Club, formed in 1865, catered for eager enthusiasts, including the McNeils, Campbells and Vallances, who had grown up participating in the pastime from a young age on the waters of the Gare Loch.

It came as no surprise that the young friends should decide to form a club of their own, inspired by the likes of Queen's Park, who were founded on July 9 1867 when a group of young men met at No. 3 Eglinton Terrace to establish a new club, settling on their club's name only after rejecting a string of alternatives including Morayshire, The Celts and The Northern, which undoubtedly reflected the Highland roots of their founding sons.

Rivals were in such short supply in the early months of Queen's Park that members were forced to find new and innovative ways to split their numbers into teams on the local recreation ground – at one point smokers played non-smokers. It must have come as some relief when, in August 1868, they finally found opponents named Thistle and rules were quickly agreed between club secretaries.

The game was a 20-a-side affair, played over two hours and Queen's Park won 2–0, setting a pattern for success that would become all too familiar over the subsequent two decades. The Spiders have lifted the Scottish Cup 10 times, which still stands as the most victories in the famous old competition by any club outwith the Old Firm.

Association football had grown increasingly popular in the public schools of England in the first half of the 19th century, although as a sport it had been around for hundreds of years and had been present in China since before the birth of Christ.

Rapid advancements were made in football during the Victorian era, not least as a result of the Saturday half-day holiday. It allowed workers who toiled in industry a rare few hours of recreation time beyond the usual Sabbath observance to take part in, or look in on, various leisure activities.

On the field, crucial rule changes were adopted soon after the formation of the English FA in October 1863, following a meeting of a dozen clubs from London and the surrounding areas at the Freemasons' Tavern in Great Queen Street. Until then, there had been little to distinguish the games of football and rugby.

By the mid-1860s, however, it had become forbidden for players of the association game to dart forward with the ball in hand as the focus switched to a dribbling game played on the ground.

The Scots quickly adapted to new tactics and techniques, developing an early team framework far superior to anything being played south of the border. Queen's Park were among the first clubs to grasp the benefits of a more structured formation, playing a 2–2–6 formation: two full-backs, two half-backs and six forwards, with two players on the left wing, two on the right and two through the middle.

The English clubs persisted with their 1–1–8, but its folly was exposed when the Spiders, playing a short, sharp passing game, saw off top English side Notts County 6–0 at Hampden. Ultimately, it prompted a demand for Scottish players by English clubs that continues to this day.

The FA Cup was instituted in 1871, two years before its Scottish equivalent, and international football also began to develop from the club game, thanks in the first instance to Charles W. Alcock, the administrator, journalist and publisher who would provide the eponymously titled football annual from which Moses McNeil took the Rangers name.

It was in November 1870 when, as secretary of the FA, he wrote to the Glasgow Herald suggesting a game between players from both countries. He cajoled: "In Scotland, once essentially the land of football, there should still be a spark left of the old fire, and I confidently appeal to Scotsmen to aid to their utmost the efforts of the committee to confer success on what London hopes to be found, an annual trial of skill between the champions of England and Scotland."

In total, Alcock arranged four games in London, but the Scots team was plucked from the ranks of anglos working in the capital, as well as a couple of moonlighters, most notably W.H. Gladstone, the son of the Prime Minister. It came as no great shock when Scotland lost all the games played and the 'Alcock Internationals' have no official standing to this day.

Still, sporting history has correctly lauded Alcock as a football visionary and it came as no surprise when the first official international between Scotland and England was played in Glasgow, fittingly on St Andrew's Day 1872.

Queen's Park represented the nation that November afternoon after handing over £10 to the West of Scotland Cricket Club for the use of their ground in Hamilton Crescent, Partick, with the promise of a further £10 if takings for the game exceeded £50.

In the end, 4,000 people paid £103 to watch the scoreless draw, but there was one notable absentee – the official photographer, who left the ground when players refused to promise they would purchase prints from the game.

The overwhelming popularity of the game ensured the fixture's place in the fledgling football calendar and Scotland soon underlined its supremacy, winning eight and losing only two of the first 12 international matches played against the Auld Enemy.

It was against such a backdrop that Rangers had been formed in 1872, most likely towards the end of March if the earliest account of the club's history is to be taken as read. And while one or two of the facts are open to question, it carries the strong whiff of authenticity, particularly written so close to the birth itself.

One of the leading lights of the earliest Rangers team, William Dunlop, penned that history of the early years for the 1881–82 edition of the Scottish Football Annual under the pseudonym True Blue.

Dunlop had joined the club in 1876 (his sister, Mary, would go on to marry Tom Vallance) and was a Scottish Cup finalist against Vale of Leven in 1877 and again in 1879; that same year he began a 12-month term as president of the club. In looking back at the game against Callander he recalled of Rangers: "Thus ended their first match, played about the latter end of May 1872, some two months after the inauguration of the club."

The idea for a football club had been discussed by the teenage pioneers during walks in West End Park, nowadays known as Kelvingrove Park, close to the residences and lodging houses of the youngsters.

In the 1871 census Peter McNeil, a 16-year-old clerk, lived at No. 17 Cleveland Street with his oldest sister, Elizabeth, 30, and brothers James, 27, Henry, 21, and William, 19. Moses, a trainee clerk, made his way to join his siblings on his arrival in Glasgow, most likely towards the end of 1871, by which time Elizabeth was head of the household that had subsequently moved around the corner to No. 169 Berkeley Street.

Peter Campbell, born and raised in Garelochhead, knew the Shandon brothers from childhood and he was also employed near his friends on moving to Glasgow, at the Barclay Curle shipyard at Stobcross Quay.

The quartet was completed by William McBeath, an assistant sales-man, who had been born in Callander but arrived in Glasgow from Perthshire with his mother, Jane, soon after the death of his father Peter in 1864.

The birth of Rangers symbolised a new beginning for William, who lived in the same tenement close in Cleveland Street as the McNeils. His mother died in March 1872 of chronic bronchitis, aged just 53, with her son's youthful scrawl officially certifying her death.

Dunlop wrote: "A friend of ours, and member of the Rangers, certainly not noted for his accurate knowledge of history, used to remark that there were only two incidents in the history of Scotland specially worth remembering. Jeffrey, Brougham and Sydney Smith met in an old garret in Edinburgh and as a result of their 'crack' determined to found the Edinburgh Review.

"P McNeil, W McBeith [sic], M McNeil and P Campbell, as the result of a quiet chat carried on without any attempt at brilliancy in the West End Park, determined to found the Rangers FC. These old Rangers had been exercised: in fact, their feelings had been wrought upon, on seeing matches between the Queen's Park, the Vale (of Leven), and 3rd L.R.V. (Third Lanark).

"Viewing the interesting and exciting points of the game, even then brilliantly elucidated by the Queen's Park, had given rise to the itching toe, which could only be relieved by procuring a ball and bestowing upon it an unlimited amount of abuse."

Friends, particularly those with a Gare Loch connection, were rounded up, Harry McNeil and three chums from Queen's Park agreed to second and soon Rangers were off and running (most of them in their civvies) at Flesher's Haugh.

To be fair, Dunlop freely admitted that the game against Callander was considered a "terrible" spectacle and poor McBeath was so exhausted by his efforts "he was laid up for a week," although he was named man of the match. Nevertheless, inspired and motivated by that first encounter, office bearers were quickly elected and further games arranged.

Soon, the youthful Rangers team were the most popular draw on Glasgow Green, courtesy of their exuberant, energetic and winning brand of football.

Their earliest fans would undoubtedly have included the residents of the east end of the city, many of them Irish Catholic immigrants, who would subsequently flock to watch Celtic when they were formed 15 years later.

Indeed, former Celt Tom Maley, brother of legendary Parkhead manager Willie, fondly recalled going along to watch Rangers play their first Scottish Cup tie at Queen's Park Recreation Ground in 1874 in an article for the Sunday Post in February 1927.

He said: "It is a far cry, and when one, looking at the great spacious and splendidly equipped enclosure that the Rangers now possess, trace their career from Glasgow Green to Ibrox, and dwell on their vicissitudes and triumphs, one is constrained, be he even churlish, to say of them that they have a just claim to be included among those 'who have achieved greatness.'"

The ghostly whispers of the founding fathers of yesteryear are now but breezes blowing on the wind, from Flesher's Haugh up and over the city centre to Great Western Road and Burnbank, swirling across the Clyde to Kinning Park before moving on towards Copland Road, the site of the first Ibrox Park.

This early year history, now in its fourth edition, was always an attempt to present the formation of a great football club against the backdrop of almighty social change in industrialised Glasgow.

Rangers survived and prospered, but not all those teenagers who took it upon themselves in the spring of 1872 to form their very own club would, unfortunately, be able to say the same.

3

MOSES MCNEIL

Moses McNeil beguiled Scottish defences at his peak and then went on to run rings around Rangers historians for decades afterwards. Finally, however, we can paint a picture of this giant of Scottish football.

There were those of a certain vintage still around at the turn of the 21st century who could remember Moses living out his latter years in the village of Rosneath on his beloved Clyde peninsula, where he was born on October 29 1855.

He existed fairly modestly for the final years of his life before his death from heart disease at the age of 82 on April 9 1938 at Townend Hospital in Dumbarton.

The house he shared latterly with his sister Isabella, Craig Cottage, is still standing, tucked up off the main road leading into Rosneath, away from prying eyes. It is somehow fitting because this giant of Scottish football appeared to withdraw gradually in his latter years from all he had helped create, including Rangers.

Moses is buried in the local graveyard at St Modan's Parish Church, interred with Isabella and her husband, former sea captain Duncan Gray, and the McNeils' eldest sister, Elizabeth. As the last of his family line, it was unsurprising the name of Moses was missing from the gravestone under which he lies.

The Restoration of Rangers Graves Project, under the respectful leadership of Iain and Gordon, made the acknowledgement of Moses' final resting place one of their first missions when it was formed in 2014.

In June 2015 they were joined by Reverend Christine Murdoch from St Modan's and former Rangers skipper Ally Dawson, who sadly passed away at the age of 63 in July 2021. They unveiled a stone in memory of Moses which stated, simply and fittingly: 'A local man and founder of Rangers Football Club.'

In the village of Kilcreggan, boatyard owner Ronnie MacGrowther, born in 1932, could still picture Moses, a small man with a navy blue suit and walking stick and very rarely without his bowler hat. "He always looked respectable, but I don't think there was a lot of money around," he recalled. "A lot of people in the community didn't know about his connection with Rangers, but my father did. Moses was a nice old man, but he could also be a wee bit prickly on occasions."

Another former neighbour recalls Moses leaving for Glasgow once a month, they believed to pick up a pension from Rangers. More often than not, there was a spring in his step, a glint in his eye and a slight slur in his speech by the time he returned home much later in the day.

Time, thankfully, was not playing tricks with Ronnie's memory as the rich mosaic of Rangers history was coloured still further with the delightful discovery of a new picture of Moses. The family snap was taken at Rosneath in the early 1930s, shortly before his death, and only came to light in the aftermath of the first edition of The Gallant Pioneers in 2009.

It showed a dapper Moses with nieces Mary Margaret Stewart and Isabel Scott and Mary Margaret's husband, Archie. Mary Margaret and Isabel were grand-daughters of Harry McNeil, Moses' brother – the great Queen's Park and Scotland winger who guested for Rangers in their first game, that 0-0 draw against Callander at Flesher's Haugh in May 1872.

The snap is significant as it is the only picture of Moses from the 20th century our research has unearthed. It came from the family scrapbook of Anne Law, great granddaughter of Harry. Anne, from Glasgow, sadly passed away early in 2021 but was happy she played a role in helping inform fans of the club founder.

Interviewed at the time, she said: "Mary Margaret was my mother and Moses was very fond of her. My mother and father used to visit

Moses and his sister Bella in Rosneath quite often in the 1930s and my own middle name is McNeil. I didn't realise the significance of the photograph until recently, but I was delighted to share it with Rangers fans because I'm also a big supporter of the club."

The jigsaw was completed still further when club historian David Mason put Founders' Trail organisers Iain and Gordon in touch with Elizabeth Pirie. David had worked with her son several years previously and believed there may have been a connection with Moses.

Iain said: "Very nervously I rang Elizabeth and, incredibly, within a couple of days Gordon and I found ourselves sitting in her Glasgow home for what was a jaw-dropping experience. Elizabeth's grandfather was James McNeil, brother of Moses and Peter, and became very successful in the drapery and lace trade, working for Stewart and MacDonald's in Buchanan Street.

"He is buried at Craigton, which Elizabeth didn't know, so Gordon and I arranged to take her on the Founders' Trail. We visited many locations, including four homes where her grandfather once lived, and she was able to pay her respects at the final resting place of James and some of her great uncles.

"To top it all, we contacted the club and she was invited to join the 140th anniversary celebrations at Ibrox in December 2012. She watched the match from the directors' box with her son and daughter."

The memory of that special day lived long in Elizabeth's memory. She recalled: "It was a joy to sit at Ibrox with so many people. I was treated like royalty in the Blue Room before the match and it was all a bit of a shock because I never realised how much Uncle Moses meant to so many people.

"I can still vividly recall travelling from our home in Prestwick as a child with my mother and aunt to visit him in Clynder. We would take the train to Helensburgh and then a small boat across the loch and walk along the coast to his home, where we'd spend many a weekend. He was a happy, kind man who would often take me for walks around the village and down to the local shops."

Moses, like most of the children of John and Jean McNeil, was raised in a world of wealth and privilege which, unfortunately, was not their own. John McNeil was born in Comrie, Perthshire, in 1809, the son of a farmer, also named John, and mother Catherine Drummond.

He came to Glasgow in the early part of the 19th century where he met Jean Loudon Bain, born in around 1815, the daughter of Henry Bain, a grocer and general merchant from County Down.

They married in Glasgow on December 31 1839. According to census records of 1841, John was a gardener at rural Hogganfield Farm, in the north-east of the fledgling city, which only expanded to swallow well-known districts of today such as Anderston, Bridgeton, North Kelvinside and the Gorbals into its boundaries as late as 1846.

The young couple's joy continued when daughter Elizabeth was born the year after they wed and they remained in Glasgow until 1842, celebrating the birth of their first son, John junior. In total, the couple had 11 children, including footballers Moses, Henry, William and Peter, but two boys did not survive infancy, a sad but all too common aspect of childhood at the time.

By the time second son James was born in 1843 the family were living in Rhu and had begun a relationship with the Gare Loch that would continue until the death of Moses almost a century later.

John, who was now a master gardener, had accepted an offer of employment from John Honeyman at Belmore House near Shandon, on the east side of the Gare Loch now occupied by the Faslane Naval Base.

The house, which still stands, had been built to modest dimensions in around 1830 by a local fishing family, the MacFarlanes. However Honeyman, showing an eye for architectural design that would later earn his son his fame and fortune, subsequently bought the house and set about remodelling it. Meanwhile, John took control of its sizeable gardens and brought to fruition his own landscape design skills and vision.

Honeyman was a corn merchant with a principal residence off Glasgow Green, but had bought Belmore as a weekend and summer retreat. The new steamer routes from Glasgow to the coast and, from 1857, the introduction of the railway to the nearby town of Helensburgh, had made the area more easily accessible for the growing business class.

Finance was clearly not an issue for Honeyman, with no expense spared on Belmore. The education of his son, John junior, was also the very best. He boarded at Merchiston Castle in Edinburgh and attended Glasgow University, before setting up an architectural practice in the city in 1854.

Honeyman junior joined forces with another designer, John Keppie, in 1888 and within 12 months a young, up-and-coming architect joined the firm's offices at No. 140 Bath Street in Glasgow city centre – Charles Rennie Mackintosh.

Back at Belmore, the McNeil family continued to expand with the birth of Alexander in 1845, Henry in 1848 and Isabella Honeyman McNeil in 1850 – the latter named in honour of the wife of John's employer.

William McNeil was born in 1852, followed by Peter in 1854 and, finally, in 1855, Moses. Not only was the family of John and Jean growing, so too was the community in which they were living as Glasgow's new, prosperous, middle classes sought a release from the city and the smog by building second homes on the coast, in towns and villages such as Shandon, Garelochhead, Rhu, Rosneath and Kilcreggan.

In 1856, Belmore House was sold to the McDonalds, that family of impeccable merchant class. They had been significant players in the Glasgow retail industry since 1826 when John McDonald, a tailor from Vale of Leven, joined forces with Robertson Buchanan Stewart, a soldier from Rothesay. Their company, Stewart and McDonald, would become such giants of the industry that by 1866 it was turning over a colossal £1 million a year.

Stewart and McDonald opened a wholesale drapery business in the upstairs of a tenement building at No. 5 Buchanan Street, taking a bold risk on the expansion of the city centre westwards from its main thoroughfare on Argyle Street.

It was a calculated gamble that paid off within three years when the Argyll Arcade, a glass-covered thoroughfare of jewellers and upper-class outfitters, which retains much of its elegance to this day, was opened and lured more and more shoppers to an area of the town that had hitherto been under-developed for the fashionistas of the age.

Stewart and McDonald expanded to meet the demand from the growing population and by 1866 it occupied a massive 4,000 square yards and its huge warehouses dominated Argyle Street, Buchanan Street and Mitchell Street.

The first Hugh Fraser was a lace buyer to the company and rose to become a manager in 1849. A series of buyouts and mergers over the next 100 years finally led to it becoming known as House of Fraser. The current Fraser's department store on the west side of Buchanan Street still occupies the building that was first constructed for Stewart and McDonald.

John McDonald died in May 1860 aged just 51 and the debt of gratitude Rangers owe is to his sons, Alexander or, most probably, John junior.

Alexander had been made a director of Stewart and McDonald in 1859 but passed away in his prime, dying of consumption during a tour of the Upper Nile in March 1869, aged only 31.

The family fortune, including Belmore, passed in trust to John, then aged only 18, but the McDonald family would help develop a football legacy with one act of kindness, revealed by John Allan in his early history of Rangers.

He wrote: "To William (McNeil) there fell the rare gift of a football from the son of a gentleman by whom his father was employed in the Gare Loch. The generous donor was a Mr McDonald of the firm Stewart and McDonald, in Buchanan Street."

It was the same ball Willie would stuff under his arm before storming off in a huff at the prospect of being refused permission to play for the newly formed Rangers, telling his brothers and their pals: "If you can't have me, you can't have my ball."

He was not allowed to wander far, as Moses admitted in later years: "Willie was the proud possessor of a ball so, although he was the veteran of the little company, it was indispensable that he should be a member of our team."

A 12ft tall Celtic cross still stands in honour of John McDonald junior at Garelochhead Parish Church. He lived long enough to see the club flourish from birth into one of renown but he did not survive into old age and died, after complications arising from flu, in June 1891, aged just 40.

The influence of Stewart and McDonald on the early years of Rangers was more than just an accidental donation of the club's first football and it is entirely reasonable to conclude that it was through the relationship with the McDonalds that Rangers also secured the support from their business partners, the Stewarts.

John Stevenson Stewart was another notable patron of the club and was listed as honorary president of Rangers in the Scottish Football Annuals across various seasons between 1878–85.

Born in 1862, he was still a teenager at the time, but would no doubt have been encouraged by his father, Alexander Bannatyne Stewart, to take an active role in public life and choose an association with the Light Blues, perhaps on the back of the growing reputation of the club as a result of their appearance in the 1877 Scottish Cup.

Certainly, it would not have harmed the reputation of the fledgling club to be so closely associated with two of the leading business figures in the city at the time.

By 1871 John, Jean and Moses, then 14, had moved across the Gare Loch to a cottage named Flower Bank, which still stands today above Rosneath. It is possible that John was still in employment at Belmore as it was an easy commute across the loch to the pier at Shandon.

The gardens in which John worked no longer stand in their past glory. At their peak, the grounds extended to 33 acres. The house left the McDonald family in 1919 and was sold on again in 1926 to biscuit manufacturer George McFarlane, before eventually passing into government control following his death in 1938.

Faslane was developed as a military port from 1942, a role it continues to fill to this day as the home of the UK's Trident nuclear defence programme. However, the Royal Navy had no inkling of the connection between Belmore House and Rangers and, intrigued to find out more, they invited organisers of the Founders' Trail to Faslane in September 2011.

Iain McColl said: "We couldn't have been made to feel more welcome. Their interest in our research and their hospitality was overwhelming. After giving the background to the link with Belmore House, the McNeil family and the story behind The Founders' Trail, we were presented with a plaque from The First Mine Countermeasures Squadron as a token of their friendship.

"We, in turn, presented them with copies of The Gallant Pioneers. I thought we'd be viewed as nothing more than geeky enthusiasts who would be allowed to take a few pics and then ushered back off the base quick style. I couldn't have been more wrong. It was a wonderful day and a chance to connect still further with the story of our wonderful club."

Undoubtedly, growing up in the area Moses had access to one of the best backyards in Scotland and he and his brothers clearly took advantage of the leisure spaces the Gare Loch and its surrounding countryside had to offer.

Shinty was a popular sport – his brother Harry was credited as a player – while Moses also found enjoyment in rowing and athletics.

A memento to his prowess as an athlete is to be found in the Ibrox trophy room still, an eight-inch silver goblet he won for finishing first in a half-mile race at the Garelochhead annual sports in 1876. It is the oldest trophy on display, but he had been setting the pace at the village sports meeting, held every New Year's Day, for several years before.

In 1873, for example, the Dumbarton Herald reported on him pipping close friend and fellow Ranger Peter Campbell in a quarter-mile race for the Under-16s. Moses made it a double when he teamed up with Tom Vallance to win the three-legged race, but there was no old pals' act in the 200 yards when Tom held off the youngest McNeil for first prize.

Undeterred, on January 1 1874 Moses returned home and this time triumphed in the half-mile race for the Under-20s. He then followed it up with success in the hurdles and 200 yards and repeated his three-legged feat from 12 months earlier with Tom.

The entrants' list at the Garelochhead sports read like a who's who of Rangers in the 1870s, with the Campbell, McNeil and Vallance brothers all to the fore.

Despite his escapades on the track that year, Moses still had more to offer 24 hours later on Friday January 2 when he, brother Peter and William McBeath scored the goals for Rangers in a 3–0 challenge match victory against wonderfully named local select side the Garelochhead Dollopers.

Still, it came as no surprise when Moses followed the well-worn path of his brothers and sisters to Glasgow, most likely towards the end of 1871. Employment was plentiful and his siblings, under matriarch Elizabeth, had established themselves in the Sandyford district, first at No. 17 Cleveland Street and then around the corner at No. 169 Berkeley Street.

Elizabeth, listed in the census as housekeeper, effectively operated a home from home for her younger brothers and their friends from the Gare Loch, including John and James Campbell, two great Rangers and brothers of founding father Peter. Indeed, Berkeley

Street would remain a base for the McNeils for at least the next two decades under the watchful eye of Elizabeth, who never married before her death in 1915 in Rosneath.

By 1881 their father and mother were being lured back towards Glasgow and lived at Old Kilpatrick with their other daughter, Isabella. John may have been 71, but even in his eighth decade he was still listed as a master gardener and employed three men.

By the end of the decade, John and Jean had moved back into the city, to the family hub at Berkeley Street. Jean died at the house in September 1890 aged 76, just five months after John had passed away in the same abode at the age of 82.

Fittingly, they were buried together at Craigton Cemetery in a lair that had been purchased 15 years earlier by their son Alex. Unfortunately, their graves lay unmarked and untended until the publication of The Gallant Pioneers, when Rangers fans stepped in to mark and tend the plots.

It was appropriate, not just in honouring the family, but in giving consideration to the pleasure a well maintained garden gave John McNeil through his long working life.

Moses, on the other hand, restricted his design skills to the football field – and what pretty patterns he could weave.

However, he was almost lost to the club he helped to form within three years when he was seduced by the covetous glances of Queen's Park, no doubt prompted by his brother Harry, who was already a Hampden stalwart.

Moses joined Queen's Park on October 5 1875 and it is surely no coincidence that it was just four days before his new club were due to face Wanderers at Hampden Park.

Wanderers were the first great powerhouses of English football; they were winners of the first FA Cup in 1872, once again in 1873 and triumphant in another three straight finals from 1876–78.

The Glasgow club had met Wanderers once before – in the semi-final of the English competition that first season – and their willingness to travel to London to face such mighty foes was considered a remarkable show of courage.

In actual fact the visitors' play was a revelation. Not for them a series of aimless dribbles up the park, more in hope than expectation, but an accurate passing game that had rarely before been seen outside of Glasgow. The game finished goalless but Queen's Park were forced to scratch as they could not afford to stay in London for the replay, especially as their fares to the capital had been paid from a public subscription in the first place.

Moses and Harry played starring roles on October 9 1875 as Queen's destroyed Wanderers 5–0 in front of 11,000 at Hampden Park. Opposition players such as C.W. Alcock and Lord Kinnaird, the first president of the FA, a Scotland cap and veteran of nine FA Cup Finals, could not get close to them.

One report read: "The brothers McNeil – Harry well backed up by Moses – made some beautiful runs, nor were they, in fact, ever away from the ball when it was in their part of the ground. Their English opponents too found it was no use knocking them over as they just rolled on to their feet again."

Moses returned to the arms of Rangers immediately after the return match in London, which was held on February 5 1876. Wanderers took their revenge, winning 2–0, to inflict on Queen's their first defeat since their formation in 1867.

Moses was scarcely mentioned in the match reports, although the correspondent of the North British Daily Mail lamented on the poor turnout of spectators: "The number, I believe, did not reach any more than 1,000. Londoners will not and do not crowd to see a football match." His crystal ball was as defective as the Queen's Park performance.

Still just 20, Moses came increasingly to the fore in the mid-1870s and he was confirmed as a Rangers player again on February 19 1876 when Glasgow travelled to Sheffield for their annual inter-city match, almost as important and high profile at the time as the yearly meetings between Scotland and England.

Moses and teammate Peter Campbell (the latter a last minute call-up) became the first Light Blues to earn representative honours as they helped their new city to a 2–0 win in front of 7,000 fans at Bramall Lane.

Moses also represented Glasgow against Sheffield in 1878 and 1880 and won two full caps for Scotland, the first in a 4–0 win over Wales at Hamilton Crescent in 1876, while the second came during a 5–4 victory over England at the first Hampden Park in 1880.

As a left-winger, he played with something of a dash for club and country – the SFA Annual in 1881 considered him: "an excellent forward, possessing great determination and pluck…a good dodger and dribbler, his long passing is at times very effective."

His brief hiatus at Hampden apart, Moses played for Rangers for a full decade from the birth of the club, playing somewhere in the region of 135 matches and scoring approximately 40 goals until he bowed out in a goalless draw at home to South Western on April 5 1882.

In contrast to his brother Peter, the politics and internal structures of football seemed to hold little interest for him. Peter undoubtedly compensated for his lack of skill and ability on the park by concentrating on the contribution he could make as an administrator off-field.

The opposite applied to Moses, who seemed to find fulfilment enough in playing the game at the very highest level possible. Certainly, the running of the club appeared to hold limited appeal – the most senior position he was awarded in office was the post of honorary treasurer in 1876–77.

Moses was a committee member of the club throughout the 1870s, but this appeared to be an honour bestowed on most first team players, courtesy of the high regard in which they were held for their footballing skills. Membership numbers would rarely climb above 70 in the early years, so founders and stalwarts from the early seasons would have been at an immediate advantage when it came to drawing up the club's portfolio of office bearers.

That his dynamism was reserved for the football field is also suggested in Moses' employment record throughout the latter half of the 19th and into the 20th century.

Moses, who never married or had children, spent most of his professional career in the employ of Hugh Lang junior, a commission agent who was based at No. 70 Union Street in Glasgow, not far from H. and P. McNeil's sports outfitters at No. 91.

Lang came from a famous family whose name has long been synonymous with Scotch whisky. Hugh Lang senior was a Broomielaw innkeeper in the first half of the 19th century, famed among sailors for the quality of his blends, which were sold in his bar, as well as in five gallon jars around the local area.

In 1861 three of his five sons – Gavin, Alexander and William – decided to take their father's whisky and market it more widely and the Lang Brothers brand proved so successful that by 1876 they bought over the Glengoyne Distillery at Killearn, which remained in the family's hands for over a century.

Hugh Lang junior was clearly close to his siblings and became a director of Lang Brothers when it was incorporated in 1897. He undoubtedly shared their passion for their popular brand but, in actual fact, census records between 1871 and 1901 clarify that the nature of his business was as a wholesale hosier.

Moses started working for him as a clerk and later became a commercial traveller – in effect, a travelling salesman, with a contact book of buyers that most likely included his brothers' shop along the road.

Moses worked for Lang for around two decades but by 1901 was living in a lodging house in Stanley Street (now known as Baliol Street, just off Woodlands Road in the West End) and still working as a commercial traveller, this time as a brush and oils salesman.

The specific nature of his employment is not known, but it is possible he had been found his new position by his nephew John McNeil, son of older brother Alex.

John started work as a commercial traveller with Craig and Rose, the renowned Edinburgh paint merchant who provided the paint for the Forth Bridge when it was constructed between 1883–1890. John was promoted through the ranks of the company after many years of distinguished service and eventually became managing director.

By 1911 Moses had moved again, this time to No. 16 Bath Street in Glasgow city centre, and he was still listed as a commercial traveller, this time selling soaps.

It is tempting to suggest that Moses distanced himself from the club he helped to create as his life progressed, but the evidence is too flimsy, its weight not heavy enough to sustain an argument for any length of time.

However, it is surprising, for example, that Moses, so recognised as an influential figure in the early years of the game, did not participate in the trailblazer reunions for up to 80 ex-players organised by Vale of Leven benefactor James Ferguson up and down Loch Lomond throughout the 1920s.

More intriguing was the decision by Moses to send an apology to excuse his presence from the gala dinner at Ferguson and Forrester's in April 1923 to mark the 50th anniversary of the club he helped create. The Evening Times reported: "Tom Vallance, one of the two sole survivors of the original team, was present. The other, Moses McNeil, wrote regretting that he was unable to participate in the reunion."

Teammate James 'Tuck' McIntyre, by then approaching his 80th birthday, was there to help lower Tom Vallance into his grave following the death of the club's first great captain in 1935, but Moses was not mentioned as being present at the funeral of one his closest childhood friends.

The other side of the argument is that Moses still played an active role in and around the club in the years immediately following his departure from first team football, even if he chose not to participate politically behind the scenes.

He was regular enough for the Rangers ancients and was listed in a team of Kinning Park old boys that took on the Cameronians at Maryhill Barracks in November 1885.

He did not play in the ancients against modern game in February 1887 that marked the closure of the old Kinning Park ground, but was pictured in the souvenir photograph taken on the day in a position of prominence in the second row, his trusty cane at hand and that dapper bowler on his head.

Brother Harry bowed out of football in September 1888 when a team of Queen's Park old boys took on a side of Rangers veterans at the exhibition showgrounds at Kelvingrove Park and beat them 2–1.

'Mosie' had been tipped to play by the Scottish Umpire but prematurely, although he was not alone in the no shows. Another McNeil brother, Willie, also failed to trap but the likes of Harry, William 'Daddy' Dunlop, George Gillespie, the Vallance brothers and 'Tuck' McIntyre kept the sizeable crowd entertained.

Of course, Moses was the source of much of John Allan's material in his 1923 jubilee history of Rangers and was also quoted at length in the Daily Record of 1935, talking about how he had helped form the club so many years before.

He was arguably still in contact with Rangers (if, as his neighbour suspected, he was drawing a pension) or at the very least with influential figures such as Allan, who was close to the Ibrox power-brokers at the time.

However, as life moved on he possibly preferred the pace of a quieter existence, especially after moving to Rosneath around 1930 after a spell in a flat at West Graham Street in the Garnethill district of Glasgow.

Moses was certainly company for his sister Isabella, who died in 1935 and whose own life had been touched with terrible sadness. She married master mariner Duncan Gray in 1884, but his life ended at Rosneath in 1907, with his death certificate ominously recording his passing as a result of a gunshot injury to the head. Those around at the turn of the 21st century with an intimate knowledge of the Grays' former marital home confirmed his suicide.

Perhaps it is inevitable, given the size of the family and the time in which they lived, that untimely deaths and tragic passings would so affect the McNeils.

Harry also knew his share of grief and lost his second wife, Margaret, in bizarre circumstances in November 1895 at the Royal Hotel, the establishment they had run together in Bangor, County Down, from May 1892 until Margaret's death on November 2 1895.

The Belfast Newsletter of Tuesday, November 5 told the sad story in grisly terms, reporting on the coroner's inquest that established Margaret's death was a result of an accidental overdose.

The court was told she had been struggling mentally after the loss of her first child in infancy following his birth in March 1893 and the hotel had even been put up for sale 12 months earlier, before a change of mind from the couple.

The Newsletter quoted the attending physician, a Dr Bolton, revealing how Margaret was left broken hearted at the death of her son and "grief, worry, anxiety and chloral were the sequence."

She had been put to bed that Saturday afternoon by Harry, as was her habit, and had taken a nip of brandy, some soup and a narcotic draught to help her sleep but unfortunately – and not for the first time – had taken twice the prescribed level of the drug, which she had been using for 18 months.

Harry checked on her at 5pm and all was well but two hours later, when he next looked into the room, she was struggling for breath and appeared to be choking on her false teeth. Dr Bolton was called, but could do nothing to prevent her untimely death at the age of just 32.

The coroner passed no blame and ruled her death was a result of narcotic poisoning, leading to paralysis of the heart.

Moses, the youngest McNeil child and the longest surviving, eventually succumbed to cardiac disease in April 1938 – and someone loved him enough to send a short notice recording his death to the Glasgow Herald and the Evening Times.

At the time of his death, the sports pages were dominated by the forthcoming Scotland versus England clash at Wembley. Scotland won the match 1–0, courtesy of a goal from Hearts ace Tommy Walker. Rangers also played that afternoon, with a solitary strike from Bob McPhail securing a slender win over Clyde in the League at Ibrox.

The passing of Moses did not merit a mention in the press that week. He was buried on Tuesday April 12 but it was not until six days later that 'Waverley' – aka John Allan – penned an obituary of sorts in the Record.

He wrote: "A famous player of a long past era in Moses McNeil has also departed. Moses was one of several brothers who helped to form the Rangers clubs [sic] in 1873 and he was the last of the old originals. He played against England in 1880. It is wonderful to think that one who was at the start of the Rangers 65 years ago should have been with us until a few days ago."

In recent years, as the final resting place of Moses has become more widely known among the community of Rangers fans, many have made a pilgrimage to Rosneath to pay their respects.

The Founders' Trail have also organised hugely popular days out to the village to walk in the footsteps of the gallant pioneers and Rangers, rightly, awarded Moses one of the first memberships in the club's Hall of Fame.

He gave us all the slip for too many years, left us trailing in his wake like a bemused 19th-century back trying to tackle him on the wing. Little by little, Moses McNeil has finally been pinned down. For all his achievements, he deserves nothing less than the widest public acknowledgement.

4

VALIANT, VIRTUOUS, AND VALE OF LEVEN

It says much for the camaraderie and friendships formed in the early years of Scottish football that reunions of its earliest pioneers were still being held half a century after they had first kicked leather.

Old scars were put on display and old scores playfully settled on a day cruise up and down Loch Lomond, held annually throughout the 1920s. The host was one of Vale of Leven's most fanatical supporters, James Ferguson, a successful colour and dye making merchant who built a thriving business in Merton, South London, that survived well into the 1960s, two decades after his death in 1941.

Those in attendance included former Vale skipper John Ferguson, no relation to James, a skilful forward who won six caps for Scotland, scoring five goals, and was an equally proficient athlete and former winner of the Powderhall Sprint.

The group, typically around 80 strong, "their tongues going like 'haun guns,'" would gather on Balloch Pier at noon before boarding the steamer for a trip to a hotel where a lavish lunch was served.

Drink flowed as freely as the anecdotes and on the journey back to Balloch speeches were delivered to the assembled throng. On the last get-together organised by James Ferguson, on Saturday September 1 1928, a year before the death of John at the age of 81, a familiar old foe stepped forward to speak – former Rangers president Tom Vallance.

Amazingly, video footage of the gathering exists on the news website, www.itnsource.com. It gives a remarkable glimpse into the close knit relationships that existed between players in those days, with pioneer Tom very much to the fore.

Opposite Tarbet, the signal had been given for the vessel, the Prince Edward, to cut its engines in order that the speakers might be more distinctly heard as Vallance, by then in his early seventies, stood up to propose the toast. His jovial address to the throng was a touching and heart-warming tribute that underlined just how highly respect and friendship were valued in the very earliest years of the game.

Vallance started by saying to those whom had played football that the years spent kicking a ball were the most pleasant of their lives. To loud applause he went on to say he never regretted the decade he committed to Rangers as a player.

"In fact," he revealed, "I mentioned this to my good wife, indeed more than once, and she had replied: 'You should be playing football yet,' and I did not know whether that was sarcasm or not, but thinking over what she had said, I went to the manager of Rangers and asked if he could find a place for me in the team."

There was laughter as Vallance admitted Bill Struth had asked him for a fortnight to consider his request and that several months on he was still waiting for his reply.

Vallance said it was a great joy to meet with old friends again and added: "The other day I read in a spiritualist paper that games were played in heaven and I earnestly hope that is the case, for a heaven without games would have little attraction for me. And if there was football beyond, then assuredly I would get the old Rangers team together and we would challenge the old Vale – and I could tell them the result beforehand: the Vale wouldn't be on the winning side."

Vallance reflected on a period soon after their formation during which the youthful nomads of Rangers finally established themselves on the map of the burgeoning Scottish football scene.

They were helped to a huge extent by the three games it took to settle the 1877 Scottish Cup final, and even if they eventually went down to the men from Leven's shores, they attracted an audience they have never lost since.

The 1877-78 edition of the Scottish Football Annual noted that "thousands of the working classes rushed out to the field of battle in their labouring garb, after crossing the workshop gate when the whistle sounded at five o'clock."

Rangers have played countless crucial championship, cup and European matches in their long and successful history but, even now, few games have been as important to the development of the club as those three encounters, two played on the West of Scotland Cricket Ground at Hamilton Crescent in Partick and the third and decisive head-to-head at the first Hampden Park.

As a fledgling club, effectively a youth team with no 'home' to call their own, Rangers were not invited and nor did they apply for membership of the Scottish Football Association in March 1873 when eight clubs came together at the Dewar's Temperance Hotel in Bridge Street, Glasgow, to form a sporting alliance.

Each club – including, of course, the mighty Queen's Park – contributed £1 towards the purchase of a trophy for a newly established Cup competition – the Scottish Cup. Rangers secured membership in season 1874–75 and in their first Scottish Cup tie, on October 12 1874, saw off a team called Oxford (from the east end of Glasgow) 2–0 on the Queen's Park Recreation Ground, with goals from Moses McNeil and David Gibb.

In the second round, played at Glasgow Green on November 28, Rangers drew 0–0 with Dumbarton but lost the replay a fortnight later 1–0 to a controversial winner.

The consensus in an era when goal nets were still a brainwave for the future was that the Dumbarton 'goal' had gone over the string bar, rather than under. However, the umpires and referee signalled the goal to stand and Rangers were out of the tournament – for the first time, but certainly not the last – in controversial circumstances.

The backbone of the team in the early years, of course, came from the Gare Loch connection – Moses, Willie and Peter McNeil, Peter, James and John Campbell, Alex and Tom Vallance, as well as other friends including William McBeath, James Watson (who became president of the club in 1890), John Yuil and George Phillips.

Queen's Park were regarded as visionaries and pioneers and regularly undertook tours across Scotland to teach the new game to interested participants.

However, the great Hampden outfit initially refused to face Rangers in its infancy, citing the new club's lack of a permanent home as the principal reason. They agreed instead to send their second side, known as the Strollers, but Rangers wanted all or nothing and refused their offer.

They wrote again to Queen's Park in July 1875, and this time the standard-bearers slotted in a game against them on November 20, with the £28 proceeds from the fixture, a 2-0 victory for the more senior club, distributed to the Bridgeton fire fund.

The charity pot had been established to help the eight families left homeless and the 700 workers left idle following a blaze at a spinning mill in Greenhead Street, which was recognised as the biggest ever seen in the city to that date. Amazingly, there were no casualties.

An official publication on the history of Queen's Park, from 1920, was adamant the big boys of the Scottish game were acting not out of malice in refusing a game, but out of concern for the well-being of the youthful club, fearful of crushing its spirit so early in its development.

The third season of Rangers' existence had offered glimpses of better to come, with 15 matches played in 1874–75 against sides long since gone, such as Havelock Star, Helensburgh and the 23rd Renfrewshire Rifles Volunteers.

Rangers won 12 games, losing only once. The issue of a more permanent base was addressed in time for the start of the 1875–76 season, when the club moved to recreational space at Burnbank, a site on the south side of Great Western Road near St George's Cross, today bordered by Park Road and Woodlands Road.

A move to Shawfield (near to, but not the ground later associated with Clyde) had been briefly considered and then rejected, no doubt as Burnbank was much closer to the homes of the founding fathers around the Sandyford and Charing Cross districts of the city.

Initially, Rangers shared the space with Glasgow Accies, the rugby club who were formed in 1866, although they later moved to North Kelvinside. In addition, the Caledonian Cricket Club, who also had a short-lived football team, played on the site, which was later swallowed by developers for tenement housing which still stands today.

Burnbank did its damnedest to stand as an oasis in an increasing desert of red sandstone and was also the home of the First

Lanarkshire Rifle Volunteers, who were raised in 1859 by the amalgamation of several existing Glasgow corps as a forerunner to the modern territorial army.

Among the members of the First Lanarkshire Rifle Volunteers and the Glasgow Accies was William Alexander Smith, who founded the Boys Brigade in Glasgow in October 1883. Smith was moved to form his Christian organisation in frustration at his difficulty inspiring members of the Sunday School where he taught at the Mission Hall in nearby North Woodside Road.

The youngsters were bored and restless, in stark contrast to the enthusiasm he came across as a young officer among the Volunteers on the Burnbank drill ground every Saturday afternoon.

Smith, who was born in 1854, would have been no stranger to Burnbank at the time Rangers were playing there: more than likely, at the same time, he was fermenting his ideas for an organisation that still boasts more than half a million members worldwide.

Rangers played their first fixture at Burnbank on September 11 1875 against Vale of Leven, who had quickly established themselves as the second force in the Scottish game behind Queen's Park. The match finished in a 1–1 draw, but Rangers were beginning to cause a stir.

Previously a draw among fans at Glasgow Green, their youthful endeavour and skill at the infant game was starting to attract strong and admiring glances in the west end of the city.

A Scottish Athletic Journal rugby columnist, The Lounger, looked back over a decade in 1887 and charted the growth of the fledgling club as he recalled: "When I used to go to Burnbank witnessing the rugby games that were played there I always strolled over to the easternmost end of that capacious enclosure to see the Rangers play, and I was never disappointed.

"They were a much finer team then than they are now. The Vallances were in their prime, Peter McNeil was at half-back, Moses – the dashing, clever dribbler of those days – was a forward and Peter Campbell and David Gibb (both dead, I am sorry to say) were also in the team."

However, a lengthy run in the Scottish Cup, the principal tournament, was to elude Rangers for a second successive season. In the second round, Rangers defeated Third Lanark 1–0 at Cathkin Park, but their opponents protested that the visitors had kicked-off both halves. The appeal was duly upheld and the game was ordered to be replayed at Burnbank, with Third Lanark winning 2–1.

This time it was Rangers' turn to appeal on the grounds that the opposition keeper wore everyday clothing and could not be distinguished from the crowd, that the winning goal was scored by the hand and that the game had been ended seven minutes early as a result of fans encroaching on the field of play. Their pleas fell on deaf ears. The result stood and Rangers were out.

Nevertheless, there was further cause for optimism as Rangers headed into season 1876–77 and a campaign that would not only seal their new-found reputation as a club of substance, but would also earn them their 'Light Blues' moniker that stays with them to this day.

Firstly, they secured a 10-year lease on a ground at Kinning Park that had recently been vacated by the Clydesdale club, who had first played cricket on the site in 1849. The cricketers originally rented fields next door from a Mr Tweedie for up to £9 per annum but they were evicted within a year (after playing only two matches) when they literally refused to allow the grass to grow under their feet, thus denying his herds valuable nutrition.

The Clydesdale lads had better luck when they approached a Mr Meikelwham for permission to build a club on the fields he was leasing in Kinning Park and the precious acres were to remain dedicated to sport until Rangers moved to the first Ibrox Park in 1887.

Land which was given over for agricultural use and sporting prowess in the 19th century now forms part of the M8. It is something for present day fans to think about as they crawl towards the Kingston Bridge from Ibrox in their cars and supporters' buses at the end of every matchday.

Rangers' move to Kinning Park in the summer of 1876 took them to the south of the city for the first time and it has remained their spiritual home ever since. For their part, Clydesdale had located to a new ground for their favourite past times of football and cricket further south at Titwood. Memories of football at Clydesdale have long since faded, although they boast the honour of playing in the first Scottish Cup final in 1874, a 2–0 defeat to Queen's Park.

The reasons behind Clydesdale's desire for a new home away from Kinning Park have never been recorded, but the creep of industry and demand for space across the south side of the city in the period is likely to have been a factor.

As late as the 1860s, the eminent Scottish sportswriter D.D. Bone reckoned: "Kinning Park was…a beautiful meadow surrounded by stately trees and green hedges, a pleasant spot of resort for the town athletes, away from the din of hammers and free from the heavy pall of city smoke."

In 1872 it sat in splendid isolation, but within 12 months the Clutha Ironworks had been constructed on its doorstep and by 1878 a depot for the Caledonian Railway had been built across the street. The dimensions of a cricket field being considerably larger than a football pitch, maps of the time show that Rangers occupied only a portion of the land originally allocated to Clydesdale.

Rangers had been boosted in the summer of 1876 by the arrival of several new players, most notably George Gillespie. A former player with the Rosslyn club based in Whiteinch, he was a back who later converted to goalkeeper and went on to win seven caps for Scotland between the sticks with the Light Blues and Queen's Park. He was never on the losing side in an international and luck appeared to be on his side in his debut season with his new club.

Rangers also strengthened their youthful squad with the addition of goalkeeper James Watt and forward David Hill and there were also two new additions to the forward line, William 'Daddy' Dunlop (of True Blue fame) and Sandy Marshall.

Watt and Dunlop came from the Sandyford club (Gillespie is also credited with once being a member). Players at Sandyford were well-known to founders of Rangers as they were part of the same community on the western fringes of the city centre.

The prospects for Rangers never looked better, particularly when they opened the new ground on September 2 in front of 1,500 fans, again with a match against Vale of Leven, and this time the boys from Dunbartonshire were defeated, 2–1.

Of the 16 challenge matches Rangers were acknowledged as playing that season they lost only three and their form in the Scottish Cup won them a new army of admirers among the Glaswegian labour class that they still maintain to this day.

Rangers could certainly not be accused of lacking enthusiasm, which endeared them to an audience that had been growing since those early kickabouts on Glasgow Green.

Scottish football was frightfully territorial in the 1870s. The club with greatest mass appeal, Queen's Park, had secured a fan base on the back of their all-conquering success of previous seasons, but at heart they were considered a club for the wealthy and their cloak of on-field invincibility was also beginning to slip as the decade drew to a close.

The time was right for a new challenger. Other clubs drew their audiences from the immediate areas in which they played – Pollokshields Athletic, Govan, Whiteinch, Parkgrove, Partick and Battlefield to name just a few.

To some extent, the nomadic status of Rangers in their early years worked to their benefit, as they moved from the east of the city to the west and then on to Kinning Park, representing no particular district but winning an audience with their exuberance on the pitch.

Such was the dedication of the players to their new home that stories abounded in the local community of eerie sounds and peculiar sights coming from the ground during the night. Soon, there were whisperings the place was haunted.

In fact, it was the zealous Light Blues, whose dedication to the new game and their new environment saw them consult astronomy charts to train late into the night under the full moon, leading to the nickname the 'Moonlighters.' It highlighted the tremendous commitment to their new club and the new sport by the young amateurs.

The picture that emerges of the time is of football as a thrilling new adventure for young men on the cusp of adult life. Moses McNeil fondly recalled 'tuck-ins' of ham and eggs and steak at a local eating house every morning after a 6am rise for a 10-mile training walk or a 90-minute session with the football in the build up to the 1877 Scottish Cup final.

Up to 11 plates were laid out for the famished players, with John Allan poetically recalling in his jubilee history: "It happened frequently that only six or seven players were able to sit down to the feast; still, the waiter never took anything back on the plates except the pattern."

Rangers were fortunate to have huge personalities in their squad to match their appetites. Gillespie, for one, was a renowned practical joker. In April 1879 Rangers accepted an invite to play a match at Dunoon to celebrate the birthday of Queen Victoria, but the players were ordered back to the city on the Thursday evening to prepare for a Glasgow Merchants' Charity Cup semi-final tie against Dumbarton at Hampden 48 hours later.

All the players took the last steamer home, with the exception of Gillespie, Archie Steel and Hugh McIntyre. Blatantly breaking curfew, they booked into the Royal Hotel for the night instead.

Steel and McIntyre, who were sharing a room, were awakened from their slumbers by a loud banging on the door and the frantic order from Gillespie to follow him to the pier as they had overslept and were about to miss the first boat across the Firth of Clyde.

Steel and McIntyre dressed at speed and dashed along the pavement outside their lodgings before they realised it was still the middle of the night. Gillespie had earlier returned to bed, where no doubt he chuckled himself back to sleep. The rude awakening did not perturb Steel too much, as he scored on the Saturday afternoon in a 3–1 victory.

Steel, writing in 1896 as 'Old International' in one of the first in-depth histories of the Scottish game, '25 Years Football', also fondly recalled Rangers teammate Sandy Marshall. He was tall and thin as a rake and it was claimed John Ferguson ran under his legs during one of the games in the 1877 final when the Light Blues player took a fresh air swipe at the ball.

Training at Kinning Park frequently ended with a one-mile run around the ground, after which the players were treated to a 'bath' of a bucket of cold water poured over their heads by the trainer as they stooped double, their fingers touching their toes.

One evening Marshall took up his usual angular pose and jokingly warned the bucket holder "see and no' miss me," and his comments induced such fits of giggles the water went everywhere except over the player's head.

The majority of the Rangers team were barely out of their teens when they kicked off the Scottish Cup, hoping for third time lucky, with a 4–1 defeat of Queen's Park Juniors at Kinning Park on September 20 1876.

Defender George Gillespie was just 17, while James Campbell, the only goalscorer from that match to be officially recorded, was 18. His older brother Peter and friends Moses McNeil and Tom Vallance were all 20 years old and William Dunlop was the oldest at 22.

Towerhill were swept aside in the next round 8–0 and Rangers also travelled to Mauchline and Lennox and won comfortably 3–0 on each occasion.

Surprisingly, even though fixture scheduling can charitably be described in the 1870s as haphazard, Rangers were given a bye at the semi-final stage. The kids from Kinning Park had made the Scottish Cup final for the first time in their short history – and Vale of Leven lay in wait.

The club from Alexandria is long gone as a senior outfit – they withdrew from the Scottish League in 1892 and limped on at various levels until 1929 – but Rangers still owe them a debt of gratitude, in part for their Light Blues nickname, which first came to the fore around the time of the final.

In his history of Rangers, written for the SFA's annual in 1894, a scribe operating under the name of 'Obo' claimed the club had been known as the Light Blues for the first 22 years of their existence as a result of the colour of their shirts.

However, his claims do not stand up to scrutiny when compared against the evidence provided by club officials for the earliest SFA annuals. All teams were required to list their colours and Rangers' shirts were frequently listed as blue (1876 and 1878) or, more commonly, royal blue (from 1879 onwards). Light blue was never mentioned. They also wore white knickerbockers and blue and white hooped socks.

It has been argued, with some merit, that the Light Blues refers not to the colour of the shirts but the dash of performers such as Moses McNeil and Peter Campbell when they pulled the cotton kit, most likely provided by H and P McNeil, over their youthful shoulders around the time of the 1877 final.

The Glasgow News of Monday March 19 referenced the "light and speedy" Rangers, while Archie Steel makes a compelling case for the Light Blues to be considered in the context of the tradition of Oxford and Cambridge universities.

Vale's colours were a very dark blue, almost black (although they wore plain white in the second of the three epic matches) and he claimed Vale were similar to the Dark Blues of Oxford in their appearance, while Rangers, in a hue of kit not as powerful, resembled the Light Blues of Cambridge.

To describe Vale of Leven as favourites to win the Scottish Cup on Saturday March 17 1877 is as much an understatement as saying football had caught the imagination of the general public ever so slightly.

True, the Vale had never lifted the trophy, but the previous season they had been considered unfortunate to be knocked out of the competition at the semi-final stages following a narrow 2–1 loss to Queen's Park, prompting the editors of the Scottish Football Annual that summer to conclude that the rest of the Scottish game, in particular Vale of Leven and Third Lanark, were quickly catching up with the Hampden giants.

The men from Alexandria had caused a sensation in the fifth round by handing Queen's Park their first defeat on Scottish soil after a decade of existence.

Furthermore, experienced players such as Alex McLintock, John McGregor, John Ferguson, John McDougall and John Baird had already been capped for their country – Moses McNeil and Tom Vallance were the only two Scotland players in the Rangers team at that time and the latter had only won his first two caps in the fortnight before the final.

Vale of Leven had age and physical presence on their side, not to mention that morale-boosting win over the greatest Scottish club of them all.

The rain had fallen ankle deep on the Hampden playing surface that historic Saturday afternoon of December 30 1876 as the visitors celebrated their 2–1 win over Queen's Park to take them into the semi-final. However, subsequent events threatened to dampen the feelgood factor of their sensational victory.

The following Tuesday, several Queen's Park members were strolling over the playing surface and noticed suspicious marks in the turf that looked as if they had come from spiked boots, which were strictly forbidden at the time.

As a result, Queen's Park wasted no time in dispatching a delegation of two officials to the lodgings of various Vale players with a request to see the footwear worn three days earlier. They first called upon the home of John Ferguson and although he was out, his wife invited the visitors into their home and produced her husband's boot bag.

As luck would have it – or, from the point of view of Queen's Park, bad fortune – the bag also contained the boots of teammate Bobby Paton and there was not a spike in sight.

Undeterred, they marched on to the home of another player, John McGregor. Initially, he mistook their arrival as a show of bonhomie to welcome the New Year and uncorked a bottle as the three men toasted the arrival of 1877.

However, when the true nature of their business became clear McGregor threw his unspiked boots at their feet in disgust and swore bitterly that he regretted ever offering a dram in the first place.

He was not alone in being incensed. The Vale committee pointed out that the holes on the Hampden pitch were various sizes and more consistent with marks from the tip of a shooting stick or umbrella, which had been carried by at least one umpire.

One newspaper correspondent mischievously suggested the markings were made by crows, which thrived in the district, and the game was forever after known as the 'Crows' Feet' match. There was no replay and Vale went on to meet Rangers following a 9–0 demolition of Ayr Thistle in the semi-final, adding to victories in the earlier rounds against Third Lanark, Vale of Leven Rovers, Helensburgh and Busby.

On the morning of Monday March 19 1877 newspapers went into overdrive to describe the final that had taken place at the West of Scotland Cricket Club in Partick 48 hours earlier. The North British Daily Mail even declared the game as "decidedly the finest match that has ever been played since the dribbling game was introduced to Scotland."

The teams lined up as follows and did not change over the course of the next three games – Rangers: J. Watt, goal; G. Gillespie and T. Vallance, backs; W. McNeil and S. Ricketts, half-backs; W. Dunlop, A. Marshall, P. Campbell, D. Hill, J. Watson and M. McNeil, forwards. Vale of Leven: W.O. Wood, goal; A. Michie and A. McIntyre, backs; W. Jamieson and A. McLintock, half-backs; R. Paton, J. McGregor, J. McDougall, J. Ferguson, D. Lindsay and J.C. Baird, forwards.

Headlines had been dominated that week by the acceptance of William Gladstone, who would soon become Prime Minister for his second of four terms, of the candidacy to become Lord Rector of Glasgow University.

A New Kilpatrick farmer was fined five guineas in the Glasgow courts for selling sour milk to the public, which contained 38 per cent added water; while in Dumbarton, the council turned on local MP Sir Archibald Orr Ewing and called on him to retract or disown statements he had made alleging excessive drunkenness in the district.

However, Vale of Leven players had other things on their minds than the slating of their neighbours by the man charged with representing their interests at Westminster because they knew, despite their tag as favourites, that their rivals from Kinning Park would be no pushovers.

Tradition dictated that a Scottish terrier, known as the 'Derby dog', was brought out before kick-off at 3.30pm to parade up and down in front of the fans in the pavilion at Hamilton Crescent. Snow, rain and sleet had fallen all week, although the weather had improved slightly in time for the kick-off and a crowd estimated at 8,000 was present.

In a breathless encounter, Vale took the lead when Paton nodded home from a McLintock cross early in the second half and the crowd awaited the inevitable onslaught. However, even with the wind in their faces the plucky youngsters from Kinning Park, inspired by skipper Tom Vallance, refused to be cowed and drew level with 20 minutes remaining when McDougall put through his own net.

A draw was acceptable to neither team as the action swung from one end of the field to the next, the air punctured with cries such as: 'Time to win the Cup yet, Rangers!' and 'Waken up and run through them, Vale of Leven.' Eventually, time was called with the score still locked at 1–1 and while a replay was scheduled it was the underdog Rangers who claimed the moral victory as their players were carried off the field shoulder high by their excited fans.

Both sides came together again later that evening, this time at the Athole Arms in Dundas Street, where every kick, pass and opportunity was examined over a glass of beer.

Three weeks passed between the final and the first replay, but time had neither dulled nor dampened the enthusiasm for the second match. If anything, a fevered excitement and anticipation hung in the air with the grey clouds above Partick that Saturday afternoon,

April 7, and even the rainfall would not keep the supporters away. Inside the ground, more than 8,000 fans huddled together against the weather, with just as many outside trying desperately to sneak a look over the fence at the action.

The Glasgow News of April 9 reported that "an enormous crowd assembled within the well known cricket enclosure of the West of Scotland Club and outside the railings and on the high ground to the north thousands of spectators took up positions.

"A dozen omnibuses, numerous cabs and other conveyances collected in the roads and from the top of these vehicles a large number of people enjoyed a much better view of the game than many who had paid for admission – the crowd around the ropes standing three and four deep.

"An estimate of the numbers present will be gathered from the fact – officially announced afterwards – that the receipts exceeded any previous amounts collected at any match in Scotland and it may be asserted without hesitation that Saturday's assembly was the largest ever seen on any football rendezvous in Britain."

The game kicked off at 3.30pm and within seven minutes Rangers had opened the scoring after William 'Daddy' Dunlop struck a well-placed shot between the posts. Vale, kicking downhill and with the wind at their backs, immediately searched for an equaliser but their attacks were repelled time and again by the ever reliable Tom Vallance and keeper James Watt.

Rangers enjoyed the advantage of the conditions as the second half kicked off but Vale scored within two minutes of the restart, although the roar of the crowd was muffled by peals of loud thunder as the heavens opened.

Moses McNeil passed up a couple of opportunities late on, while Vale also went close before the game swept into an extra-time period of 30 minutes. However, it was never completed as five minutes into the second period a shot from Dunlop caused chaos and sparked fierce debate among fans that lasted for years afterwards.

Rangers argued passionately that the ball had crossed the line from Dunlop's shot and bounced off a spectator before landing safely back in the arms of Wood, but the referee, SFA honorary secretary William Dick, was too far from the action to make a balanced call.

To add to the confusion, one of his umpires insisted the ball had crossed the line, while the other debated just as vigorously that no goal had been scored.

The spectator the ball was alleged to have struck was Sir George HB McLeod, regius professor of surgery at Glasgow University, who later offered to swear on oath a goal had been scored, but his offer was not accepted by the football authorities.

In the time it took to discuss the incident many fans, who had been craning their necks all afternoon for a closer glimpse of the action, burst on to the field and arguments broke out between them about the validity of Dunlop's 'goal'. It was a scene of utter bedlam and when the pitch could not be cleared the final whistle was blown 10 minutes early and another replay arranged for the following week at Hampden.

In the 21st century, football administrators are often criticised for arranging times and dates for matches that do not always suit the paying public but, as ever, the only thing new in life is the history not already known.

The third and final game between Rangers and Vale of Leven in the Scottish Cup kicked-off at the unusual time of 5.30pm at Hampden on Friday April 12 (rumours of a Rangers no show in disgust at Dunlop's disallowed goal in the previous match proved unfounded).

The attendance and gate receipt record from six days earlier was smashed again as 10,000 fans crammed into the first Hampden Park, sited at Crosshill, next to Hampden Terrace.

It was estimated that a similar number again sought every height advantage outside the ground to watch the match once more from the tops of cabs, buses and trees. The majority of the crowd were Rangers fans, although they were hardly partisan.

The Scottish Football Annual recalled: "In justice to the great majority of the people it is only fair to add that when a bit of brilliant play was shown on the Vale of Leven side it did not pass uncheered, and when the goals were taken on each side the scene baffled description. The hum of human voices was heard far and near and caps, hats, and sticks were waved overhead in thousands."

Among the crowd were two youngsters from Alexandria, presumably Vale of Leven fans, who would pay a heavy price for their attendance. The following Tuesday, April 17, the Glasgow Herald told how Hugh McArthur, 12, John Slowan, 11, had rushed to the final from their home town, but only after McArthur had stolen the princely sum of £3 10s from a chest belonging to his uncle to fund the adventure.

The two youngsters lived high on the hog during their trip to Glasgow and purchased, among other things, pipes, tobacco and "several luxuries". They duly appeared at Glasgow Sheriff Court and pleaded guilty to theft. McArthur was sent to prison for 30 days, his sidekick Slowan for 20.

If Rangers had the better of the first game and Vale of Leven showed their strength in the second then the third was more evenly balanced although not, according to match reports of the time, as much of a football spectacle, despite five goals being scored.

Vale of Leven netted through McDougall after only 15 minutes, making amends for his own-goal in the first tie. However, Rangers equalised in the second half when a tame Peter Campbell shot was missed by Wood, who made a feeble and unsuccessful attempt to kick it clear, and the Glasgow youngsters took a grip on the game 10 minutes later when Willie McNeil slotted home the second.

The mental strength of Vale came to the fore as John Baird snatched an equaliser only three minutes after McNeil had given Rangers hope that it might be their year.

There was clearly little appetite among both groups of players for a fourth match as the game reached an exciting climax, swinging from one end to the other. Sam Ricketts and Tom Vallance went close with shots for Rangers, while Watt was a sterling performer between the sticks.

However, it was Baird who had the final say when he knocked in the winner with 10 minutes remaining to give his side a 3–2 victory. Unsurprisingly, the game was more bad-tempered than the previous two fixtures and one unnamed Vale player was chastised for kicking out at Moses McNeil.

This time, the informalities of the Athole Arms were dispensed with as Vale of Leven headed to Alexandria to celebrate with their families, friends and fans, who had waited patiently at the post office in the town for news of the result, which finally arrived at 7.30pm.

The Vale of Leven players descended from the Glasgow train two hours later, by which time a crowd of 3,000 were waiting to greet them. The players were lifted shoulder high onto an open-top wagon and paraded around the town, with the Bonhill band leading the way.

Amid joyous scenes at the departure of the cup from Glasgow for the first time, The Glasgow News reported that "cannons were fired, pipers were discoursing Highland music and all the dogs of the district barked their part in the chorus of rejoicing over the famous football victory."

Rangers players, who had practised so long and hard at Kinning Park under the light of the winter moon, could only howl in frustration. However, these pups would soon have their day.

5

PETER MCNEIL

It is astonishing to think, 150 years after its formation, that a grandchild of one of the founding fathers is still around to witness the celebrations of the first major European club to reach this milestone mark.

Doreen Holland, grand-daughter of Peter McNeil, is a sprightly 90-year-old and lives near London and was unaware of her famous family connection until she was contacted as part of the research into the first edition of The Gallant Pioneers.

Doreen and her sister, Heather Lang, were feted by Rangers fans at a dinner at Ibrox in October 2009, organised by Gordon Bell and Iain McColl of the Founders' Trail. It was attended by 300 fans, including club legend Davie Wilson. Artist Helen Runciman presented a commissioned painting of the boys who formed the club and it is now on display at the top of the Marble Staircase.

Doreen said: "Helen kindly gave us a very limited print of her canvas and mine now has pride of place at the home of my son, Rory, in Barbados. A new generation of fans has been inspired among the ranks of our families.

"We didn't know about our grandfather's contribution to the formation of Rangers and it's a fantastic achievement we have happily shared with everyone we know. Their amazement is matched only by our pride and delight.

"Our grandfather would walk from his home in the Sandyford district on a Saturday morning and stake out a pitch at Glasgow Green, 'holding the fort' before the rest of the players arrived for kick-off by mid-afternoon.

"Peter, Moses, Peter Campbell and William McBeath had no money, no ball and not even a home in those fledgling months of the club. I'm absolutely thrilled to hear that very line has now become a staple of one of the most popular Rangers songs!

"We know the last couple of years have been the most difficult in the history of the club, but the fans have responded magnificently. Peter and Moses and their wonderful group of friends would be so proud of the loyalty shown by Rangers supporters."

Heather, sadly, passed away in February 2015 at the age of 87, but was delighted to have been told of the famous family line. Indeed, she helped pull the cord on a commemorative plaque at Glasgow Green in September 2009, marking the club's humble beginnings, with Sandy Jardine looking on.

Val Hedges, Heather's daughter, said: "It's fair to say we were all surprised and very excited to hear of our family connection to Rangers and ever since it's been our 'go to story' when asked to provide an interesting fact about ourselves. It's just a pity none us are famous, as it would make a great episode of 'Who Do You Think You Are?'

"Gary Ralston's research brought to light a lot of interesting details about Peter's life and we're very pleased and grateful he took the time to share the story with us. We're all very proud of our footballing heritage and wish Rangers all the best for their 150th celebrations."

Heather had reflected on the grandfather she never knew in an interview at the Mitchell Library in the summer of 2008 for The Gallant Pioneers. Appropriately, as she spoke she was sitting in the cafe that overlooks Cleveland Street, where Peter first lived when he moved to the city from Garelochhead around 1870.

She said: "The news came as an absolute shock, a bolt from the blue. Doreen was speechless on the telephone when I told her about our connection with Rangers. We didn't know a thing about it."

Peter McNeil long had the back of Rangers in the early years and so it was entirely fitting that the club's support decided to look after one of their own when the story of his sad plight came to light for the first time in the pages of The Gallant Pioneers.

Peter was one of the founding four of Rangers and, while his temperament may have been even and his judgement as a football administrator regarded as sober, his personality was clearly underpinned by a tenacious streak of stubbornness.

It was to stand the club in good stead during its first season at Flesher's Haugh as he fought – no doubt, sometimes even literally – to preserve for Rangers the most favourable playing corner of Glasgow Green, thus allowing the club to forge its early reputation among the casual observer as one worth watching.

There is no escaping the high regard with which early pioneer William 'True Blue' Dunlop held the contribution of Peter to the formation and growth of the club in its infancy.

He wrote: "Peter McNeil, with characteristic self-denial and zeal for the best interests of the club, used to journey to the most desirable part of the Green about twelve noon, and set up the now noted standards (early goalposts). But it was not enough to set them up. He had, at first, either to watch them himself or pay a boy for doing so until the classic hour in the afternoon was reached."

Time fades, however, and as the 20th century gave way to the 21st, Peter's selflessness in establishing the club that would go on to scale such great heights was in danger of being overlooked.

His final resting place at Craigton Cemetery was a sad metaphor – unmarked, unheralded, overgrown, consumed by the passage of time. Subsequent events indicated this should come as no great surprise.

However, Peter's contribution to the club has now been fully recognised, thanks to the sterling effort of fans and the support of the Founders' Trail.

It was the Light Blues legions who raised the funds to commission that portrait of Peter and his friends by artist Helen. The sorry state of Peter's final resting place was also put right by fans, again led by Gordon Bell and Iain McColl of the Founders' Trail.

There was a poignancy about the occasion in June 2013 when new memorial headstones were unveiled during one of the visits by fans as part of the hugely popular Trail experience around Glasgow and Ibrox Stadium.

Two young lads, part of the tour with their families, were asked, instinctively, to place a wreath on the graves of Peter and his brother James as the other supporters looked on. The boys, only a couple of years shy of the age of Peter when he helped form the club, immediately stepped up to the challenge – just as Peter had done at Glasgow Green on behalf of the club all those years earlier.

Peter is laid to rest in one of two previously unmarked plots that also include his mother Jean, father John and brothers William, James and Alexander.

Fittingly, a fine view is afforded from Craigton Cemetery towards Ibrox Stadium and on sunny days its famous red-brick facade glows ruby rich in the brilliant bright light.

For those with an interest in Rangers' history Craigton Cemetery has, until now, been better known as the final resting place of legendary manager Bill Struth, the Ibrox colossus who led the club from 1920–54, winning 18 league titles, 10 Scottish Cups and two League Cup finals.

Until recently his grave lay badly neglected. Admirably, the issue was raised by fans at a club AGM and Rangers agreed to assume responsibility for the restoration of the headstone and future upkeep of the plot. The only problem, cemetery staff point out with a smile, is that Mr Struth lies with his back to the club he helped establish as one of the most famous in the world.

Sadly, however, there are few moments of humour in the story of Peter, who was shredded of his dignity in the latter stages of his life by the tragedy of mental illness.

Peter McNeil was listed as aged 42 or 43 at the time of his death on March 30 1901, although earlier census records indicate his date of birth was more likely to have been around 1854, making him four years older.

He was a small man, standing a little over five feet four inches tall, but he possibly had bigger vanities as his wife, Janet, was at least eight years his junior and may have been reluctant, in his eyes, to enter into a courtship with a man of more advanced years.

The picture that emerges of McNeil is of a man of modesty, order and principle, characteristics that would serve his fledgling club well as it grew in power and influence in the Scottish game throughout the 1870s and early 1880s.

He arrived in Glasgow from the Gare Loch, where he was born, around 1870 and was in his mid-teens when he made his way to the city. He lived at No. 17 Cleveland Street and No. 169 Berkeley Street in Charing Cross with oldest sister Elizabeth, among other family members, and quickly set up with brother Harry in the business of H and P McNeil, listed as 'hatters, hosiers, glovers and shirtmakers' but better known as the 'leading athletic outfitters in Scotland.'

They had premises at No. 21 and No. 23 Renfield Street before moving to a new shop at No. 91 Union Street in Glasgow city centre in 1883. They were regular advertisers in the sporting press at the time, including the Scottish Football Annuals.

Their banner displays called out 'to all the principal clubs in Scotland, also to the Scottish, Sheffield, Ayrshire and Welsh football associations' and they were 'outfitters for all amateur athletic sports' and promised 'association footballs specially made.'

Football quickly became the McNeils' sporting obsession and any early disputes on the right of Rangers to play in their preferred corner of Glasgow Green were, according to Dunlop, soon replaced by a widespread acceptance that this was a special team of young players.

They were as worthy of their right to indisputably own a patch of public ground for a few hours every week as they were the support of working class football fans for whom a trip to Hampden Park to watch Queen's Park was either too far or too expensive.

Dunlop added: "Peter's commendable zeal was not taxed to the utmost…the rapid strides with which Rangers had acquired (their) reputation constrained the followers of the ball to look, wonder and admire.

"As a consequence, the desirable part of the Green was, with something like mutual agreement, regarded by all as sacred to the Rangers. And if players looked, didn't spectators come and stare? The sacred spot became the Mecca of the Green, the god Football being there worshipped by thousands of devotees whose piety would not bear either a journey to Hampden Park, or the necessary subscription… Football was their Allah and the Rangers, if not at that time the prophet, were at least their prophet."

Peter played alongside brothers Moses, William and, occasionally, Queen's Park stalwart Harry, and was one of the club's early captains, a reflection of the respect with which he was held at the new club for his powers of organisation.

As a player he featured regularly for the Light Blues in the early years and took part in the club's first match against Callander in May 1872. He held down a regular first-team place until 1876, when the position of honorary secretary would have at least lessened the blow of being overlooked in favour of more capable performers on the pitch.

He served the committee well and was secretary from 1876 to 1883, the equivalent position of the modern team manager, and vice-president of the club from 1886–88.

In addition, he was one of the earliest treasurers of the SFA, beating off several other candidates to win the vote of football's governing body in April 1879, a further reflection of the admiration in which he was held, not only at Rangers but throughout the infant game.

After he stepped down in April 1883, the Scottish Athletic Journal noted: "The meeting expressed their sense of the worth of the 'genial Peter' and he must have felt proud at the reception accorded him when he stood up to acknowledge the vote of thanks awarded him."

However, his tenure as treasurer at the SFA was not without it challenges, as the new regulatory body struggled to find its feet financially in the early years of the game.

Peter resigned as treasurer at the association's AGM in 1883 to concentrate on his own business affairs, but it was a time of frustration at the inability of the SFA to balance its books.

Nevertheless, his contribution was noted in the minutes of the time and Peter also received a formal vote of thanks for his efforts. The minutes stated "that the association regret that Mr McNeil has resigned the office of treasurer and that this association feels deeply indebted to him for his great services in the past."

Andrew Carnegie himself would have struggled to make sense of the game's financial figures, which relied heavily on the money raised at the gate every second year from the fixture against England.

By October 1883 the SFA's debt had risen to a daunting £120, secretary John K McDowall had not been paid for nine months and was owed £80 and even Scottish Cup winners Dumbarton had still to be reimbursed for the £15 they had spent on medals for their players.

However, the situation improved as the decade progressed, in part as a result of a move from premises at well-to-do Carlton Place into Waterloo Street, halving the SFA's rent at a stroke (the SFA returned in September 1889 and bought the Carlton Place premises outright, moving in after refurbishment by 1892).

For much of the 1870s and 1880s, and even into the early 1890s, McNeil appeared to lead a prosperous life. In March 1885 he married Janet, who came from Cathcart, and within five years they had two children, John Fraser and Gertrude Grace (the mother of Doreen and Heather).

At that time, H and P McNeil were still regular fixtures in the Post Office Guide, an early Yellow Pages in which relatively well-to-do citizens paid to advertise their business and home addresses.

By 1891, according to the census, Peter, 34, (but probably 37 or 38) and Janet, 29, had moved with John Fraser (5) and Gertrude Grace (1) and a domestic servant to No. 37 Bentinck Street in Glasgow, a stone's throw from the West End Park, later renamed Kelvingrove, where the idea of forming a club had first been mooted in 1872.

From the outside, the family clearly boasted trimmings of wealth, but it was a veneer masking the grim reality of Peter's slow decline in mental health, although his psychological sensitivities were hinted at in earlier newspaper articles.

The 'Echoes' columnist of the Scottish Athletic Journal noted in February 1883: "I am sorry to learn that Mr P McNeil, through pressure of business, has been compelled to resign his position as match-secretary of the Rangers."

Three weeks later the same columnist wrote: "Publicity is given to a rumour that Mr Peter McNeil will, at the coming general meeting of the Scottish Football Association, retire from the position of treasurer. The cares of an increasing business, I know, have been weighing somewhat heavily on him for some time past and for that and other reasons he would, I believe, like to relinquish all connection with the Association. The idea to get up a testimonial is a splendid one and I hope it will be taken up heartily by all the clubs."

No testimonial was ever granted, but it was not without further promptings from 'Echoes', as the Scottish Athletic Journal columnist clearly felt that Peter could have done with a financial boost as he prepared for his marriage.

Writing a month before Peter's wedding in March 1885, he implored: "I would like to revive a little matter that should never have been allowed to drop. When Mr P McNeil resigned the treasurership of the Scottish Football Association there was a universal feeling that he should be the recipient of some mark of respect for the great service he had rendered that body.

"At the time the Association was in financial difficulties and it was thought advisable to wait for a little while. Well, three years [it was actually two] have gone and nothing has yet been done, which I think is a little ungrateful. But what has remained so long undone can now be done and I call upon the present committee of the SFA to move in the matter.

"Mr McNeil is to be a conspicuous figure in a very interesting ceremony which is to take place shortly [his wedding] and it has occurred to me that the present would be the most fitting time to honour one who devoted ungrudgingly so much labour to devising means that would result in enriching the Association."

There was to be no SFA dowry, however, and by 1896 H and P McNeil's had disappeared completely from the Post Office Guides, their business premises at No. 91 Union Street taken over by a seedsman, William Leighton. Peter was also a member of the Clydesdale Harriers for at least five years in the 1890s and was a regular advertiser in their annual handbook. By the 1896–97 edition he was no longer listed as a member and H and P McNeil's were no longer advertising.

Significantly, their place as official outfitters to the Harriers had been taken by a Robert Scott ('late with H and P McNeil'), who had premises at No. 232 Buchanan Street. Clearly, Peter's business or personal life had taken a wrong turn with devastating consequences – bankruptcy, perhaps, or a family feud that dissolved the partnership?

Certainly, he would never again be in business with Harry – his older brother left Scotland in the mid-1890s to take over the running of the Royal Hotel in Bangor, County Down, where their mother had been born.

Peter's character may have been stubborn (witness his determination to secure a sacred acre of Glasgow Green on which he and his friends could play games in the early years of the club) but it probably acted as camouflage for a more sensitive soul (the Scottish Athletic Journal referred to him as the 'genial' Peter).

Irrespective, soon Peter's mental health issues could no longer be ignored.

The day before Queen Victoria's death on January 22 1901 two doctors, Gilbert Campbell and James Hamilton Campbell, certified the insanity of Peter McNeil as a result of financial worries after his wife, Janet Fraser McNeil, had applied under a sheriff's order to have him sectioned at Hawkhead Asylum in Paisley.

The Govan District Asylum at Hawkhead was built for the Govan District Lunacy Board – the brutal, callous language was typical of the time – and opened in 1895, with a capacity for 400 patients.

The story of Peter McNeil's hospitalisation unfolded more than 100 years later using information from public records gleaned from sources such as the NHS and National Archives and also the Govan Poor Law Relief applications of the time, held at the Mitchell Library in Glasgow.

He died on Saturday March 30 1901 and his two-line death notice, which appeared in the Evening Times and Glasgow Herald, made reference only to his name, address and cause of passing as "a lingering illness".

In the same week, smallpox outbreaks were reported in the press, along with regular bulletins on the ailing health of the Prime Minister, Lord Salisbury, and the news that a new railway had opened, taking passengers along one of the most scenic routes in the world, from Fort William to Mallaig.

The decline in the quality of life of the McNeil family had been evident as the 19th century drew to a close. By May 1897 they had downsized through necessity, from Bentinck Street to a four-apartment flat at No. 32 Gibson Street in Hillhead ('three up, first door, name on door').

Soon, Peter began to display the signs of the mental distress that would kill him within four years. In his health records of January 1901 from Hawkhead, which was renamed Leverndale in 1964, it states he had suffered "growing (mental) paralysis for three years."

By the time he was sectioned he had been insane for six months and although he was not listed as suicidal or epileptic, he was considered dangerous.

He weighed only eight stones 13 pounds, stood five feet four and a half inches tall and had grey hair, brown eyes and a pale complexion. He was listed as being in fair nutritional state and his first check-up at the asylum disclosed "a large scar on the front of the left leg." An old reminder of the rough and tumble from his playing career with Rangers, perhaps?

McNeil was admitted to the Hawkhead Asylum only after being granted Poor Law Relief by the Govan Parish, of which Hillhead was a part in the early 20th century.

He was described as 'wholly' disabled as a result of 'insanity' and his wife was struggling so badly to pay the rent of £25 a year she had resorted to taking in lodgers.

Fraser, 14 by this time, had already been put to work as a clerk earning five shillings a week, while Gertrude was approaching her 11th birthday and still at school. The family was described as having 'no means, no society' and, unsurprisingly, their application for relief was approved.

On arrival at Hawkhead, it was recorded that none of McNeil's relatives were known to be insane and the reason for his admittance, as stated earlier, was 'paralysis induced by financial worries.'

The records states his 'speech was thick and hesitant and incoherent. Tongue tremulous, gait uncertain and pupils pin-point. Furthermore, it noted: 'Wife says he is very irritable and at times excited. He has no idea of where he is or what time of year it is'.

The records added: 'On admission, patient was somewhat excited and resisted when his clothes were being removed, but he soon became quiet and went to bed without further trouble. Patient has a difficulty in his speech. His words are pronounced in a thick and hesitating manner.'

The following day, January 22, McNeil seemed to have calmed and adapted to his new situation. The records noted: 'Patient…submits readily to examination. His pupils are contracted and there is a suspicion of cardiac disease.' The next entry from doctors, on February 6, read: 'Patient is up every day. He is very happy and contented and thinks that he is staying in Dunbartonshire. He takes his food well and sleeps well.'

On February 12: 'Patient now recognises that he is staying in a hospital. He is able to be up every day. He takes his food well and sleeps well. Patient appears to be very contented and happy.'

A fortnight later, on February 26: 'Patient remains in much the same condition. He answers questions readily but does not know very well where he is or what he is talking [about]. He is happy and contented and eats and sleeps well.'

The following week, March 4: "Patient continues in the same happy and contented condition."

However, within four weeks McNeil's condition had changed dramatically as his life drew to a close. On March 30 his records stated bluntly: 'Patient became much worse since last night and gradually sank, dying at 6.20pm today. No PM (post mortem) allowed.'

Janet Fraser McNeil married again two years later to potato merchant James Fulton. She died on April 18 1932, her age listed as 74, at a Glasgow nursing home, having outlived both her husbands.

Gertrude Grace married in 1925 to a William Stewart Chapman at Pollokshields, who worked as a trader in East India. Until recently, little was known of the life of Peter's son, John Fraser McNeil.

Four days after his death, on Wednesday April 3 1901, Peter was laid to rest at Craigton Cemetery, where he was buried in the family plot with his parents John and Jane McNeil. The plot, in the name of James N.B. (Neil Brodie) McNeil, the second-oldest McNeil brother, was opened for the last time on August 19 1908 when brother William, who gave sterling service as a Rangers player until 1878, was buried following his death aged 53.

In plot I502, again unmarked, lie the bodies of James Neil Brodie McNeil, listed as aged 64 when he died in November 1909, his first wife Lucy Ann McNeil, aged 42 when she passed away in March 1895 and also a Brodie McNeil, most likely the son of James and Lucy Ann, who died aged 32 in May 1914.

In plot I500, marked with a handsome headstone, lies Alexander McNeil, the third oldest brother of Peter and Moses, who died in 1914 aged 66, and three of his family members.

Beyond the formation of a great football club, the personal stories surrounding the four founding fathers cry out for a happy ending – and they found one in the shape of Heather and Doreen and the happy, prosperous families they raised and whose branches have, in turn, spread out fruitfully across the UK, the US and even the Caribbean.

The two daughters of Gertrude Grace and her husband William Chapman were the closest descendants of the founding four. Now it's an honour held by Doreen alone. The lineage of Peter and Janet McNeil has been in strong, firm hands these last 100 years.

Sadly, Doreen and Heather's uncle John Fraser – Peter's son, known in the family as Fraser – did not survive World War One. A second lieutenant with the Royal Field Artillery Regiment, he made it to within two months and two days of the Armistice before he died in France on September 9 1918, aged 31.

He is buried at the Ligny St Flochel British cemetery in the town of Averdoingt, near Arras. Fraser was a keen golfer and his name is still acknowledged on the memorial board for fallen heroes at the local club where he was a member, Ranfurly Castle in Bridge of Weir. He is also remembered on the memorial board at the Western Baths in the west end of Glasgow, a swimming and fitness club, where he was a member with Harold Vallance, son of Tom.

Heather said: "We knew about Uncle Fraser and his death in World War One, although little about his background and employment until that point. I'm rather pleased, knowing what we do now about the sad circumstances of my grandfather's death, that Fraser did not seem to be affected by his father's financial worries as he moved into adulthood.

"My mother didn't inform us about any details of her father's death. The only explanation I can think of is she must have been very distressed and upset about the whole thing and not wanted to talk about it. Of course, we knew about Fraser and also my grandmother's second marriage – my mother was 13 when grandmother remarried.

"Mother lived until the age of 93 and was always very guilty, when asked about her father and other events of her family past, of saying: 'Och, I can't remember.'

"We were absolutely never aware of a football connection in the family, though maybe that was because there were no boys, only Doreen and me. The favourite sport in our family was tennis – mother became quite a star at her club in Pollokshields and also played with my father when he came back on leave from his job in the east.

"Mother never once said to us: 'Let's go and have a look at where I used to live,' even though we moved back to the west of Scotland in 1940. I vaguely remember the death of my grandmother Janet, Peter's wife, in April 1932.

"When Moses died in 1938 I don't even think mother knew anything about it. By that time, father was working in the Far East and mother was with us at Westcliff-on-Sea.

"As far as I know, we were never in touch with any other members of the McNeil family and, to be honest, didn't even know they existed. It's amazing to think both sides of the family had a connection with Garelochhead and we didn't even know about one another.

"My father's mother ended her days at Whistlefield, which is a stone's throw from Garelochhead, and I still have pictures from a holiday there in 1934. It's incredible my great-uncle Moses was still alive then and living only a few miles along the road in Rosneath.

"I'm sure Peter would be very pleased with the way his family has turned out. I was glad to see his decline and eventual death came over a very short period of time. It all happened so quickly in the end, only a few months, and that's at least a crumb of comfort.

"It's such a pity we didn't know more about the McNeils before now, but I'm very proud of my grandfather's achievements, even though his life ended so sadly. Rangers Football Club is quite a legacy to leave behind."

6

SWEET CHARITY

If charity begins at home then good causes in and around Glasgow never had to stray far for support in the early years of Scottish football.

The game echoed the benevolent paternalism of Victorian society at large and Rangers were never found wanting, with their generosity of time and spirit to boost fundraising efforts for a whole range of groups.

They asked for nothing in return, but received thanks of a kind in 1879 in the shape of the fledgling club's first piece of silverware – the Glasgow Merchants' Charity Cup, which made some amends for the loss of the Scottish Cup final that same year following another controversial showpiece against Vale of Leven.

Since its formation in 2002, the Rangers Charity Foundation has given £6 million in financial support and assistance to a range of grateful groups, but the Light Blues have been willing contributors to a host of good causes from their very earliest days.

Their first game against Queen's Park, played in November 1875, raised £28 for the Bridgeton Fire Fund. They played on a public park on Rothesay in August 1879, once more against Queen's Park, in support of local good causes.

They moved swiftly to set up a benefit game against Scottish Cup holders Dumbarton in July 1883 when the Daphne went down following its launch at Alexander Stephen's Linthouse shipyard on the Clyde with the loss of 124 lives.

They regularly played fundraisers at Kinning Park to boost the coffers of the local unemployed in days long before the safety net of social security was available to protect the most vulnerable. One such match, against a Glasgow select side known as the Crusaders, raised £18 in 1886.

Those who have carelessly linked Rangers to uber-Protestantism since its formation in 1872 may be surprised to learn that the club fought out a 2–2 draw against Hibs at Easter Road in May 1903, in a game played to raise funds for the Leith Roman Catholic School Building Fund. The Star of the Sea RC School was built in the grounds of the Stella Maris Church in Constitution Street in Leith as a result.

The Glasgow Merchants' Charity Cup, which survived as a competition until 1961, raised over £10,000 between 1877 and 1890 for various good causes and its formation came as a result of the interminable squabbles that characterised the early years of the sport, this time between Queen's Park and Vale of Leven.

The Glasgow giants had taught the men from Alexandria how to play the new game in 1872 and initially relations between the clubs were good, but things soured when the SFA, under influence from Queen's Park, refused to give Vale of Leven permission to compete in the first two Scottish Cup tournaments.

Cancellation of subsequent fixtures between the clubs led to a claim from Vale of Leven that the trailblazers of the Scottish game were running scared. They seemed to have a point, as Vale of Leven handed Queen's Park their first defeat by a Scottish side, 2–1 in the quarter-final of the Scottish Cup, in season 1876–77.

The victory, in turn, led to those contentious allegations from the Hampden club that the Vale of Leven players had used spikes on the soles of their boots, strictly forbidden in those days.

Glasgow merchants put up the new trophy in the hope it would heal the gaping wounds between the clubs, but Vale of Leven refused to enter the competition in its first year. Rangers did play, however, as defeated Scottish Cup finalists, but were dismissed 4–0 at Hampden by Queen's Park.

They fared little better the following year when they were knocked out by Third Lanark in the early stages, 2–1 at Hampden. However, season 1877–78 was memorable in many other ways. It was during this campaign that Rangers played their first game in Edinburgh, against Brunswick (a 2–1 win), in England, against Nottingham Forest (a 4–2 victory), and also secured their record victory, twice (13–0 against Possilpark and repeated against Uddingston, both games in the Scottish Cup).

Nevertheless, the charitable work on the football field paled into insignificance in comparison to the fundraising efforts that had been undertaken off it in Glasgow as Rangers set off on a season that would yield their first success after seven years in existence.

In October 1878 the failure of the City of Glasgow bank was considered to be the greatest disaster to hit the business community in Britain and would find echoes in the credit crunch of the modern era.

At its annual general meeting in June 1878 the bank, a haven for small investors, revealed the number of branches had risen to 133 and deposits stood at £8 million. All appeared well and although rumours of its instability had been expressed as early as 1857, there was still genuine shock and dismay when the directors announced they were closing the doors.

The business community of the city was paralysed and many merchants faced ruin as auditors estimated the bank's losses to total £6.2 million. One business after another went to the wall, while the 1,200 shareholders had a call made on them by liquidators of £500 for every £100 of stock owned in a bid to raise £5 million.

Civil unrest was predicted, but Lord Provost William Collins raised a fund of £400,000, primarily from big-hearted Glaswegians and, astonishingly, within two years creditors were paid 18 shillings in the pound.

The directors of the bank did not escape punishment and were sent for trial at the High Court in Edinburgh in January 1879. It was revealed that large unsecured loans had been made to insolvent companies with which some of the directors were involved. Two directors were imprisoned for 18 months and others were sent to jail for eight months with the public, unsurprisingly, unsympathetic to their plight.

The debate on the financial uncertainty of the city that dominated the front pages was vigorous, and if worried investors hoped they would escape controversy in their leisure time by following their favourites from Kinning Park they would be sadly mistaken.

For the second time in three years Rangers made the Scottish Cup final, conceding only three goals in six games en route to a re-match with Vale of Leven.

The Alexandria club had won the Cup for the first time in 1877 and also knocked Rangers out of the tournament in the fourth round in 1878 with a comfortable 5–0 replay win in Dunbartonshire following a goalless draw at Kinning Park. They subsequently went on to win the trophy for the second season in a row with a 1–0 victory over Third Lanark.

Another record crowd was attracted to Hampden on Saturday April 19 1879 to see Rangers play Vale of Leven. Included in the throng, the Glasgow News was delighted to note, were "a number of ladies."

Not all fans were happy, however, and in a letter to the North British Daily Mail on the Tuesday after the Cup Final a reader by the name JMW championed the advent of all-seater stadia over a century before the Hillsborough disaster was a catalyst for such a move.

JMW wrote: "It is anything but fair that the public should be asked to pay such a sum as a shilling each to be allowed to roll on each other as we are compelled to do, if at all inclined to see the game as it goes on?

"It is not to be wondered that thousands of the people prefer to stand outside rather than be crushed as we were on Saturday last, not to say one word of the inconvenience to the traffic and annoyance to the people of the district.

"I am sure it cannot be for the want of funds that better accommodation is not provided as three or four hundred pounds, I think, would go a long way in providing seats all round, which would add not only to the comfort to the sightseers but profit to the coffers of the club."

Rangers had six survivors from the side that had lost over the epic three games only two years earlier – Tom Vallance, Moses McNeil, William Dunlop, Peter Campbell, David Hill and George Gillespie, although the latter had switched position from back to goalkeeper in the interim period, while Vale of Leven contained five of the team that took part in the final in 1877.

The 1879 line ups were: Rangers – Gillespie, goal; T. Vallance (captain) and A. Vallance, backs; H. McIntyre and J. Drinnan, half-backs; W. Dunlop, D. Hill, W. Struthers, A. Steel, M. McNeil, P. Campbell, forwards. Vale of Leven – R. Parlane, goal; A. McLintock and A. McIntyre, backs; J. McIntyre and J. McPherson, half-backs; J. Ferguson, J. McFarlane, P. McGregor, J. Baird, J.C. Baird, J. McDougall (captain), forwards.

The match kicked off at 3.30pm and as Rangers had the better of the early exchanges it came as no surprise when William Struthers opened the scoring with a shot from close range after only 12 minutes.

However, then came the moment on which subsequent events centred. Peter Campbell and Moses McNeil worked the ball down the wing and when it was sent into the middle an exchange of headers resulted in Struthers knocking another effort between the Vale posts.

Vale appealed against the goal for offside and the referee R.B. Colquhoun from the Havelock club disallowed the effort. According to the Glasgow News it was "a decision which, as might be expected from the strong partisanship displayed by the crowd, evoked a storm of hisses and counter-cheering."

Vale immediately pressed for the equaliser, but Rangers maintained their lead to half-time and looked as if they would hold out as the clock ticked down on the second-half action, despite pressure from the cup holders.

Vale fans had all but given up hope of three-in-a-row when, with only two minutes remaining, a shot from Ferguson squirmed inside the post, with Gillespie mistakenly believing the ball was heading past.

The crowd had no sooner dispersed from Hampden anticipating a replay than Rangers announced they were appealing the result on the basis that the second 'goal' from Struthers should have stood.

They were given short shrift at an SFA committee meeting on the Monday evening. Astonishingly, referee Colquhoun chaired the discussion in his position as vice-president of the SFA and the association ruled an appeal could not be heard.

Colquhoun argued that Rangers' claim was being made against a decision of the referee, whose word was final, so the argument was invalid. Rangers were ordered to play the replay at Hampden the following Saturday.

Rangers dug in their heels and 24 hours before the replay was due to go ahead at Hampden the Glasgow News announced the game would not be played as the Kinning Park club were refusing to take to the field until their appeal had been heard.

It further revealed that Rangers were happy to play a replay if the decision of the appeal went against them. Queen's Park, fearing lost revenue, quickly arranged a game at Hampden against Glasgow University.

Vale of Leven duly arrived at the ground in time for kick-off the next day, along with the referee and his two umpires but, as expected, Rangers were nowhere to be seen.

Vale pulled on their kit and remained on the pitch for several minutes before the officials declared them cup winners by default, a decision ratified by the SFA at a committee meeting the following Monday. Meanwhile, a telegram was sent to Alexandria informing the eager public of the news. There was general feeling of satisfaction, mingled with disappointment.

Rangers officials were persistent, and in the week after the replay that never was Tom Vallance, in his position as club captain, and former goalkeeper James Watt, the ex-president who was by then honorary treasurer, demanded to address the AGM of the SFA at the Trades' Hall in Glasgow on Tuesday April 30.

Some of the exchanges were pointed and personal, but Vallance and Watt clearly had their supporters from other clubs in the assembled throng as Colquhoun was forced to defend himself against one of the earliest recorded allegations of match-fixing:

Vallance: Why, in face of precedents, was the Rangers protest not opened for discussion at the last committee meeting? Last year, Vale of Leven lodged a dispute following our cup tie with them and it was heard, even though it related to nothing but a question of the play. (Shouts of 'hear hear'.) Colquhoun: Stick to the facts.

Vallance: If the Vale of Leven's protest was given consideration, so ought to have the one from Rangers. (Applause.) We are entitled to have our case heard.

Watt: The Vale of Leven team did not, after having claimed and received from the umpire the offside allowance, take the free-kick from where the offside took place. This is becoming personal, but there has been a lot of personal talk in the matter. One of the judges informed a Vale of Leven player near the end of the game he had five minutes left to save his team's honour. (Applause.) Is it possible for judges to be neutral in such circumstances? (Cheers.)

(Rangers then demanded the protest should be considered by the meeting, but Colquhoun refused, claiming it was out of order as the SFA committee had already disposed of the matter the week previously.)

Watt: How can Vale take possession of the Scottish Cup when they haven't won it?

Colquhoun: Because Rangers did not appear when the committee of the association ordered them to play.

Watt: Well, it was impossible that the game could be played anyway when a match between Queen's Park and the University had been arranged on the Hampden pitch that day. (Laughter.)

Colquhoun: Our secretary, Mr Dick, had secured the ground for the cup tie and had Rangers turned up they would have played at the hour advertised. On the issue of precedent on the grounds of the Vale protest last year, it was actually considered because the incident related to an interpretation of the rules. Rangers have received the utmost fair play. I'd also like to address rumours that I had money on the game but I declare on behalf of myself, the other umpire and referee there were no bets placed on the match whatsoever. As for telling players how much time was left to play, I informed members of both sides when asked. This has been my practice in the past and will continue to be my practice in future.

Colquhoun sat down to a burst of applause and, following further discussion, Watt was told to take any proposal to play the match again to another committee meeting which, unsurprisingly given the time that would have then elapsed, he never did.

However, Rangers clearly had the goodwill of the majority of the Glasgow public on their side if the letters to the Glasgow News in the weeks that followed were anything to go by.

There was anger that the SFA had ratified the decision of the referee and umpires to award the trophy to Vale of Leven when Rangers refused to show on point of principle.

One particularly irate reader, named only as J.C., thundered: "With respect to this match there is only one conclusion to which anyone present at the association meeting can come – namely, that, come what may, the committee were determined that the Rangers should not get the cup."

A writer named 'Olive Branch' called on Vale of Leven to offer to play the game again in a gesture of true sporting spirit.

He said: "As a witness of the contest on Hampden Park, I have followed the progress of the dispute along its devious course to the present point, and deplore the depth to which the game of football has sunk in the estimation of those who are its exponents.

"It is difficult to see how the Vale of Leven club can enjoy possession of the cup even under the plea that it has been awarded them by the association.

"It would be a magnanimous act on their part, and help to raise them in the good opinion of all who like fair play, were they to say to one another, 'Well, we don't want to lie under the stigma of holding a cup we have not won and, although the association have vindicated our legal title to it, we are ready to play the Rangers afresh and abide by the result.'"

No more than 24 hours later, reader 'Mackenzie' went straight to what many considered the nub of the issue when he asked: "Why did the Vale kick from goal instead of from offside? And the decision of committee not to consider the protest, while they had considered similar ones?

"It was apparent to disinterested spectators of the match that the umpires and referee had 'lost their heads,' and I am afraid this opinion will gain ground in regard to the association also."

Immediately 'An Old Half Back,' surely with leanings towards Vale of Leven, took J.C. and Olive Branch to task for their points of view.

He hit out: "J.C.'s remarks seem to me to be the outcome of disappointed spleen. The Rangers, by their high-handed and unjustifiable proceedings in regard to the decision of the committee, have debarred themselves from any and all chances they had to secure the cup and the committee, in handing it over to the Vale of Leven, adopted the only course open to them.

"The childlike statements of Olive Branch are also, to say the least, very nonsensical. To expect the Vale of Leven club to offer to play the Rangers for possession of the cup is absurd."

That argument cut no ice with the wonderfully named 'Hard Nut', who cracked in a fiery letter to the Glasgow News on the Saturday morning and demanded his favourites resign from the SFA all together.

He wrote: "Before An Old Half Back assumes such a bold tone against the Rangers let him answer the following pertinent questions: Can the disputed goal be proved a 'no goal' when the umpires and referee could not tell which player was offside?

"Assuming it was 'no goal', is it fact that in resuming play the Vale men did not kick from the offside, but kicked from goal, thereby infringing the rule?

"Is it the case that one of the umpires at the match, Mr. R.B. Colquhoun, occupied and retained the chair when the Rangers protest was decided in committee, and, if so, when a man sits in judgement upon his own action what is the usual result?

"Let Old Half Back crack these nuts and then supporters of the game can decide as to the justice or injustice of the committee's decision. If this cannot be done satisfactorily (which I fear it cannot) then the Rangers have certainly not had justice afforded them, and they would do right, as suggested, in withdrawing from an association that sanctions such questionable proceedings."

Things were bubbling up nicely for the Charity Cup final on May 20, which Rangers had reached following a 4–1 defeat of Third Lanark two weeks previously.

Preparations were underway throughout Scotland on the day of the final to celebrate the birthday of Queen Victoria 24 hours later, with many shops and businesses preparing to close for the day.

In Kilmarnock, for example, excursions were being arranged to places such as Carlisle, Greenock and Arran, although the Evening Citizen reported that "as usual, the Provost issued a caution to those likely to be outrageous in their methods of celebrating the holiday."

In the pavilion at Hampden the atmosphere was more sober as the two captains turned to face one another. Vale of Leven's John McDougall looked Tom Vallance in the eye and said: "Well Tom, this is the conqueror." Tom replied: "It is."

In total, 10,000 fans crammed into Hampden to watch teams so evenly balanced they had each also claimed a win at home against the other earlier in the season, 2–0 at Vale of Leven and 3–0 to Rangers at Kinning Park.

Vale stunned Rangers after only two minutes of the final when McDougall, playing the skipper's role to perfection, nodded his side in front. However, the game was level on 15 minutes when Struthers, repeating his scoring feat of the Scottish Cup final, headed home an equaliser that could not be disputed.

Rangers pressed after the interval for the winner and the ball was finally scrambled over the line for a clincher so ugly the scorer has never been recorded. Still, it was a thing of beauty to Rangers as they celebrated lifting silverware at last.

With so much tension hanging in the air for several weeks it was hardly surprising the game ended in a bad-tempered fashion.

Players traded punches and even the Rangers fans jostled their rivals as they left the pitch. Bob Parlane, the Vale of Leven keeper, was accused by the North British Daily Mail of deliberately kicking an unnamed Rangers player as he lay on the ground, sparking the furious reaction from the crowd.

Parlane, however, vehemently denied any wrongdoing and wrote to the paper claiming he travelled home on the bus with the player he was alleged to have assaulted.

It seemed all the best battles took place off the field that season, rather than on it.

7

PETER CAMPBELL

The family of Peter Campbell undoubtedly reflected on fate as a fickle mistress when the Rangers founder was forced to give up his life to the sea in the spring of 1883 at the tender age of 25.

It was a cruel end to a life robbed short. Perhaps it was a gnawing guilt that finally led Dame Fortune to deliver one of Peter's most prized possessions back into the safe hands of the Rangers support after more than 125 years.

In 1967, 11 year-old Stephen McCafferty was walking from his home in West Mains, East Kilbride, to Duncanrig Secondary School.

Dragging his heels, as schoolboys are wont do do at the thought of double maths and science, his head was down as he tried instead to focus on the thought of a game of football with his pals later in the day.

Suddenly, as he trudged across a piece of waste ground in the district of Westwood, his eye caught a sliver of gold glistening off the sun through the weeds and grass.

Reaching down to pick it up, he turned it over gently in his hands, hardly believing what he had found. It was an old, gold medal – and not just any medal, but one awarded to a player from his favourite team, Rangers.

Half a century later, Stephen is still amazed at the combination of fate and good luck that led him to find and cherish the first medal any Rangers player ever won.

It came from the Glasgow Merchants' Charity Cup final of 1879, the club's first trophy success following its formation seven years previously. More than that, the winner's badge from the 2-1 victory over old foes Vale of Leven at the first Hampden Park belonged to Peter Campbell, one of the club's founding fathers.

Stephen said: "I struggled to come to terms with what I had found at first. I thought: 'This must be a fake,' but quickly realised it was so well made it had to be an original.

"There was no way I could keep it so my parents and I contacted the police and handed it over in the hope it could be returned to its rightful owner. What was it doing there on that piece of waste ground? I wonder still.

"There was a link attached to the medal, as if it had been on a chain, and it was quite worn. Initially, I thought it must have been lost but 12 months later the police made contact again. No-one had claimed the medal and so, legally, it belonged to me. I was invited to the station to pick it up.

"I can only think it must have been stolen at some point in time past and therefore couldn't be claimed. Why else would anyone abandon it?"

It quickly became one of Stephen's most prized possessions, but the issue of ownership continued to gnaw at him and he even contacted then Rangers boss David White in the hope it could be returned to Peter's family.

Stephen added: "I still have the letter from Mr White. He replied on official Rangers notepaper, admitting he knew only brief details about the life of Peter Campbell and wasn't aware of any relatives we could contact, so the medal stayed in my family for many years, in a box at my mother's home.

"I actually took it to Christie's twice, in the 1970s and 1980s, with the thought of putting it up for auction. They quickly verified its authenticity and calibre of gold, 24 carat, and it was of such high quality I barely needed to shine it.

"All those years and it wasn't even tarnished. They couldn't believe it had survived a couple of major depressions, because players often cashed in on their medals by melting them down at times of financial difficulty. However, they couldn't put a value on it as they had never seen anything to compare it against."

"I admit there have been times in my life when the money from a sale would have come in handy, especially the early years of my marriage when finances were tight.

"But on both occasions I pulled back from putting it up for auction. Something at the back of my mind told me not to sell it, that fate would take its course. The medal was never mine, I only found it. Deep in my heart I knew it belonged within the Rangers family and that it had to be shared and not kept hidden away in a box at my home."

Stephen told the story a few years ago to workmate and fellow Bluenose William Mason, who took it upon himself to find out more about Peter's life.

The details were fleshed out still further in the pages of The Gallant Pioneers and soon Stephen was in touch with Sandy Jardine and presented the medal to Rangers, who framed it to hang proudly in the Blue Room.

Stephen said: "The medal deserves more than just a select few to take enjoyment from it. It is unique and the story on how it came to be in my possession is surreal. I'm glad it's on general view. I'd love to find out more. Perhaps now it's on show people will see it and start to talk about it and we can clear up the mystery of how it came to be in East Kilbride that morning in 1967. It would be good to know."

The story of Peter's death was tragic as the ship on which he was a seaman, the St Columba, capsized and sank in the Bay of Biscay, south of Nantes in 1883.

The news was confirmed on March 2 1883 with a message to the Registrar General of Shipping and Seamen in Cardiff, which was blunt and to the point.

It read: "Reliable information received here direct from Marennes stated some wreckage from steamer St Columba washed ashore near Marennes, Bay of Biscay. She left Penarth Dock, January 28, for Bombay."

Tears were shed up and down the country for loved ones lost, particularly at Glasgow and Garelochhead as relatives and friends of Peter came to terms with his untimely passing.

Peter McGregor Campbell was born at Craigellan, a villa in Garelochhead, on March 6 1857, the son of John McLeod Campbell, a steamboat master, and Mary Campbell, who came from Kirkconnell near Dumfries.

Of all the gallant pioneers, Campbell's early life was easily the most privileged. He was raised in a substantial sandstone property his father had built on land feued from the Clan Campbell chief, the Duke of Argyll, in 1850.

It still stands today on the shores of the Gare Loch, next to an almost identical home constructed at the same time by Peter's uncle, Alexander.

The houses were built after the Duke began to allocate lucrative parcels of his extensive land holdings to allow the construction of sizeable properties, many of them weekend and summer retreats for the Glasgow mercantile classes.

John McLeod Campbell became a man of means and influence throughout a life spent mostly on the Clyde, where he thrived as a successful steamboat captain and shipping entrepreneur.

He married into a family of substance when he wed Mary Jenkins at Rhu in 1846 – her brother, Sir James Jenkins, was honorary surgeon to the Queen and a graduate of medicine from Glasgow University who had entered the Royal Navy in 1841.

The Jenkins family, as the name suggests, hailed originally from Wales, but settled in Upper Nithsdale in the latter half of the 18th century, where they were widely respected for the benevolence shown to the poor at the family farm, Nivinston, at Kirkconnel.

A local history, The Folklore and Genealogies of Uppermost Nithsdale, almost beatifies the family for their charitable disposition, which included turning over one of the farm buildings to vagrants and itinerants.

Their country hospitality even extended to setting up a makeshift infirmary for the homeless wanderers who fell ill "so that among the outcast, the name of Jenkins became the synonym of all that was good."

Peter Campbell had two sisters, Jessie, five years his senior, and Mary, five years his junior. In the 1871 census, taken when he was 14, the family also included older brothers Alex, 23, and William, 22, both engineers, and John, 15, James, 12, and Allan, 11.

Sadly, the lives of the three oldest sons would prove tragically short, as was the life of another daughter, Margaret, who died within a year of her birth in 1852.

Two years before Peter's death, William drowned in an accident in the harbour of the German port of Geestemunde. Alex also died young, aged just 28 when he passed away in October 1876 of tuberculosis.

The story of the Campbells is the story of the Clyde itself, as the family's history and fortunes flowed with the tides of time, lapping the banks of the river at Govan long before the legacy left by Peter and his friends on Edmiston Drive came to compete with the cranes of the shipyards for dominance on the skyline of the city's south side.

John McLeod Campbell, born in 1815, and his brother Alexander came from a line of ferrymen and fishermen who made their living on the waters of Argyll, from the west side of the Gare Loch through to Loch Goil, Loch Long and the Holy Loch.

It was inevitable that their careers would intertwine with the new steamship industry, which began to flourish from 1812 when the paddle steamer Comet was commissioned and built at Port Glasgow and became the first successful commercial vessel of its type, running daily services between Greenock and Glasgow.

Astonishingly, before then, the shallow nature of the Clyde allowed journeys along the river only at the top of each tide and, depending on the vagaries of the wind, it took up to 12 hours to complete a trip – miss the high water and an overnight stay at Bowling became a hastily scripted part of any traveller's itinerary.

John became a ship captain as early as 1835 when he took charge of a vessel named the James Dennistoun, followed by the St Mungo the following year. Soon he was a regular on the Glasgow-Gare Loch route in command of ships such as the Sovereign, the Monarch and the Fire Queen.

He served his apprenticeship working for ship owners such as Henderson and McKellar and James and John Napier but, time-served, by the mid-1850s he and Alexander began to set out on their own lucrative journey.

The expansion of Glasgow as an industrial centre gathered pace throughout the 1850s and the Gare Loch was to feel its benefits in many different ways.

For a start, the wealthy urban elite began to look for weekend retreats away from the grey backdrop of the industrial revolution and suddenly picturesque corners of the Argyll countryside became accessible by steamship and affordable through the rapid economic advancement of the lucky few merchants and business owners.

However, the working classes also derived benefits from the advance of the steamship trade. The Glasgow tradition of going 'Doon the Watter' began in the 1850s and the Campbells were at the forefront of transporting the poorer citizens back and forth from often wretched living environments to resorts where the lungs could be cleared of the gritty reality of industrial living, even if only for a few short hours.

The regular commuters may have looked down their noses at the passengers they disparagingly referred to as 'excursionists', but they were to play a vital part in the economic success story of the Campbells.

Unsurprisingly, perhaps, passenger motives for a trip on the steam ships were not always so well intentioned. The Forbes McKenzie Act of 1853 had forbidden pubs from opening on a Sunday, but pleasure craft were conveniently excluded from the legislation and so began the trend for booze cruises, leading to the popular west of Scotland slang term for overindulgence as 'steaming'.

The Campbells clearly had an entrepreneurial bent that allowed them to trade successfully in ships and develop new markets.

Amazingly, this included an important role in the American Civil War for one of their vessels, the Mail, built in 1860 but sold three years later for the princely sum of £7,000 after its speed attracted the attention of Confederate agents looking for blockade runners in the Bahamas port of Nassau.

The US Navy had been ordered to halt all maritime traffic in and out of Confederate ports, which caused the armies of the south considerable hardship.

As an economy based mostly on agriculture, the southern states relied heavily on Europe for their essential military and medical supplies. As a result, Nassau and ports in Havana and Bermuda were used as staging posts, where supplies were loaded on to blockade runners such as the Mail and taken to the Gulf of Mexico, where they were distributed to those areas most in need.

The Mail had been guided across the Atlantic in June 1863 by the Confederate conspirators and although she was captured by Union forces in 1864, dismissed as a prize and sold, she was actually bought by undercover agents again and once more returned to work as a blockade runner.

The last purchase involving John McLeod Campbell and Alexander Campbell was the Ardencaple in 1869, which ran on the Glasgow to Dumbarton route, with afternoon excursions to Greenock and Garelochhead.

However, by the latter half of the 1860s the Campbell brothers had begun to progressively withdraw from the business they had founded, allowing their nephew Robert Campbell, 'Captain Bob' of Kilmun, to take it forward. In the case of John McLeod Campbell, poor health undoubtedly contributed to his decision to step back and allow Captain Bob to assume fuller control.

Peter's father died on May 13 1871 in Glasgow after a brief illness, aged only 56. His obituary in the Dumbarton Herald the week after his death described him as "one of the best known and most popular steamboat captains."

It went on: "Few of any of the Firth stations were better liked by passengers and brother professionals than John Campbell. Shrewd, well-informed, careful, courteous and honourable, he merited the estimation in which he was held."

John left almost £1,300 in his will and the family continued to live at Craigellan for many decades, including his wife Mary, who died there on May 12 1912, aged 89.

Even after the death of his father, Peter Campbell was clearly close to his cousin Captain Bob and his application for his certificate of marine competence in 1882 listed his address as No. 2 Parkgrove Terrace in Glasgow, the city residence of the steamship entrepreneur, who died in 1888.

A year earlier, Captain Bob's sons Peter and Alec had relocated the company to the Bristol Channel, their eyes having been opened by the financial possibilities of a business in a corner of England that had a sizeable population, but few passenger services of note.

The company P and A Campbell dominated for decades, seeing off all competitors and in some cases buying out their fleets. It survived until the early 1980s when rising fuel and maintenance costs and an inevitable drop off in demand as the vogue for foreign holidays increased put paid to its existence.

The success and longevity of P and A Campbell, borne from the entrepreneurial zeal of John McLeod Campbell and his brother Alexander, made the death of Peter at the age of 25 all the more tragic, as fate denied him the opportunities afforded his relatives.

The history of the Campbells of Kilmun makes no reference to Peter of Rangers fame – naturally, perhaps, as he played no role in their Clyde operations.

However, the impact he had on Scottish sporting culture has lasted longer than the considerable maritime achievements of his other family members.

Peter was present at the birth of Rangers, but brothers John and James also gave the club sterling service in its early years and the family links with the McNeils remained strong in the second half of the 19th century.

The 1881 census, for example, listed James as living with Moses, Peter and William McNeil and their sister Elizabeth at No. 169 Berkeley Street in Charing Cross, Glasgow.

Peter had arrived in Glasgow a decade earlier and was the youngest founder of Rangers, having just turned 15 when he embraced the idea of organising a team with his three friends, not least as a release from the toils of the work on the Glasgow shipyards where he was employed.

His employment records, accessed from the historical vaults at Greenwich, show he spent five years as an apprentice with the oldest shipbuilding company on the Clyde in Glasgow, Barclay Curle, at Stobcross Engine Works between 1872 and 1877.

John Barclay had started shipbuilding on the Clyde in 1818 and his yard lay half a mile outside the city boundary, on a patch of land near to the present-day Finnieston Crane, surrounded on three sides by open countryside.

Facing the Stobcross Shipyard, on the south bank of the river, was the estate of Plantation, with the huts of the river's salmon fishermen standing back from the river bank.

It is almost impossible to imagine the site in the present day, where the Squinty Bridge now connects north and south of the river, alongside the Mecca bingo hall and Odeon cinema that make up one of the city's best-known leisure parks.

In today's post-industrial era the shipyards of the Clyde often struggle to compete, financially at least, with other areas of the world but in the 1860s, shortly before Peter began his apprenticeship with Barclay Curle, 80 per cent of British shipping tonnage was constructed on the Clyde.

He would have worked in an industry at its peak in the 1870s as bigger and faster ships were built up and down the river. They included the exotic, such as the Livadia, built in 1880 at Fairfield for the Czar of Russia, and government contracts, not only in Britain, but estimated at half the maritime nations of the world – including Japan, who took control of the Asahi from the Clyde in 1899.

Throughout most of the 19th century the shipyards of Glasgow proudly held the record for the speediest transatlantic crossings, with the firm grip of a rivet in an iron hull as Clyde-built ships were successful from 1840 to 1851, 1863 to 1872, 1880 to 1891 and 1892 to 1899.

By the end of the century, Fairfield-built vessels Campania and Lucania could make the journey in five days and eight hours. In the 20th century great liners would maintain the reputation of Clyde shipbuilding, including the Lusitania, Queen Mary and Queen Elizabeth.

Peter stayed an additional two years with Barclay Curle as a journeyman from 1877–79 before leaving for at least seven spells at sea on board the London registered merchant ship Margaret Banks, ranging in time from a fortnight to over six months.

His apprenticeship served on the Clyde in Glasgow, he was clearly keen to extend his education to the waters of the wider world. As part of the process he sat engineering exams in March 1882, at Greenock and Glasgow, but failed each time on a poor grasp of arithmetic before passing at the third attempt the following month, on April 12.

Even the most mathematically gifted would surely have offered long odds on his death within 12 months, but betting on an extended life at sea has always been a dangerous gamble.

Peter's passion for the water was matched by his enthusiasm for football and he was an inspired supporter of Rangers, not to mention one of its most outstanding players throughout the 1870s, playing for the team in its very first match against Callander in May 1872 until he bowed out in a 5–1 Scottish Cup defeat to Queen's Park in September 1879.

He also spent part of a season at Blackburn Rovers from 1879 and was one of the first Rangers players to cross the border, at a time when the English game was being criticised for its 'shameful' move towards professionalism.

Peter was also a keen shinty player and was recorded by the Southland Times newspaper on May 15 1876 representing the Vale of Leven club in a game against the Glasgow Camanachd, who featured Harry McNeil in their ranks.

The Vale of Leven Shinty club were the forerunners to the football club – Queen's Park taught them the game in 1872 – and within a few short years the sticks had been retired for good as the leather ball was grasped with glee.

The game, a 3-0 defeat for Glasgow, was played at Burnbank and many of those who featured for Vale of Leven would go on to represent the club in the Scottish Cup final the following year against Rangers.

However, football was his true sporting passion and Peter and Moses McNeil had become the first Rangers players to win representative honours when they turned out for a Glasgow select against Sheffield at Bramall Lane in February 1876, helping their adopted city to a 2–0 victory.

Campbell was twice chosen to represent Scotland, scoring a double in a 9–0 demolition of the Welsh at the first Hampden Park in March 1878 and following it up in April the following year with a single strike in a 3–0 victory against the same opposition at the Racecourse in Wrexham.

He was also named vice-captain of the club in its earliest years and was renowned as a forward player of some repute, earning praise from Victorian sports historian D.D. Bone as "the life and soul of the forward division."

In the Scottish Football Annual of 1876–77 Campbell was described as a "very fast forward on the left, plays judiciously to his centre-forwards and is very dangerous among loose backs."

Three years later, the same review book gushed: "Peter Campbell: one of Scotland's choice forwards; has good speed, splendid dribbler and dodger and is most unselfish in his passing."

Sadly, the last mention of Campbell in the Scottish Football Annual of 1881–82 featured him in a list of 'Old Association Players Now Retired'. It read simply: "Peter Campbell: one of Scotland's choice forwards; has good speed, splendid dribbler and dodger and is most unselfish in passing; gone to sea."

Peter's love for football and Rangers was passed to siblings John and James, who played for the club in its earliest years before they sought a new life in other parts of the world.

In February 1884, James left Glasgow for Australia to take up a post with the Union Bank of Melbourne. He lived to a ripe old age, dying in Brisbane in 1950. His younger brother Allan had also joined him in Australia and died in the same city in 1932, aged 72.

John Campbell also emigrated, this time to the United States, and died in Middletown, New York, in 1902, aged approximately 46. Jessie Campbell lived until her late 70s before her death in 1931. The Campbell connection with Craigellan remained strong until 1939 when youngest daughter Mary, then aged 78, passed away at the family home.

Peter set off on Sunday January 28 1883 from Penarth in South Wales on his second voyage with the St Columba, a 321-foot-long steamer of over 2,200 tons, which had been built on Merseyside in November 1880 for Liverpool company Rankin, Gilmour and Co., although the roots of the firm were Glaswegian.

The St Columba was bound for Bombay with a cargo of coal, but it never got beyond the dangerous waters off the west coast of France and, with hindsight, it should never have left its berth near Cardiff Bay in the first place.

The weather that weekend was dreadful and merited mention in the press at the time, as several disabled vessels ran into Plymouth harbour for shelter.

The St Columba clearly entered a maelstrom and God only knows the horrors suffered by the crew in those final moments as the waves lashed the vessel, cruelly whipping them into the sea and certain death.

The report sent from Cardiff five weeks later confirmed the terrifying circumstances and stated: "The missing steamer…was under the control of Captain Dumaresq and there is no doubt she was overpowered by the terrible weather which prevailed in the Bay of Biscay at the commencement of February."

The passing of Peter did not go unnoticed in the Scottish game and 'Scotsman', writing in national publication 'Football: A Weekly Record of the Game', paid a particularly warm tribute.

He wrote: "To most of us it is allotted that our virtues are not discovered till we cross the narrow isthmus that separates us from the great majority, but in the case of Mr Campbell, although our appreciation of his never failing amiability, his unchanging kindness, his tact as a club official and his brilliant play on the field may be intensified owing to the dire calamity.

"In our midst he was so universally beloved that even his opponents on the field could not for a moment harbour any angry thought about him.

"It was he who, along with Thomas Vallance and Moses McNeil, nursed the Rangers in its days of infancy and brought it to the position which it held so honourably, and since business engagements forced these players to retire, the once famous and popular "Light Blues" have had rather an uneven career.

"Mr Campbell played for Scotland against Wales and for Glasgow against Sheffield, but he retired before representing his country against England. Memory is said to be short but it will be long – aye, very long, ere one of the truest and best of fellows shall be forgotten by his many friends."

In August 2017, a plaque in Penarth honouring Peter was unveiled by members of the Cardiff True Blues, accompanied by Iain McColl and Gordon Bell, who were instrumental in persuading the local council of its significance.

The plaque, sited in the Italian Gardens on the promenade, overlooks the Bristol Channel. Across the water, the English resort of Weston Super Mare, where fellow founder William MacBeath owned a hotel, shines.

The warm tributes paid to Peter on his passing by the likes of 'Scotsman' contrasted sharply with company owner Rankin's words in a vanity publishing tome from the turn of the 20th century, 'A History of Our Firm', which, no doubt unwittingly, managed to read as disregarding and uncaring.

His somewhat indifferent tone shone through as he discussed the company's penchant for naming its vessels after saints in the 1880s. He rattled through the alphabet, from St Alban to St Winifred, before adding: "On our adverse experience of the letter 'C' we have not repeated St Columba and St Cuthbert, whose losses were both accompanied by some loss of life. My brother always favoured Saints' names taken from his favourite Sir Walter Scott."

In a later chapter, however, he reflects on the company's low points. He wrote: "I draw a veil over the ghastly period wherein the ships St Mirren, St Maur and St Malcolm disappeared with all on board. It was a terrible time.

"At a later date the St Columba under Captain Dumaresq was never heard of. I may have been overwrought, but a vivid dream wherein I saw her sinking is often times with me still. I pray that we may never have again to pass through such a time.

"Captain Davey, who has revised these notes, told me Mrs Dumaresq had a similar dream, of which she informed Mrs Davey at the time. If I have written mostly of disasters it is to be said they have been relatively few. Successful voyages have largely predominated, but these are usually uneventful."

Back in East Kilbride, Stephen McCafferty nods in agreement with Rankin's words.

He said: "Like Peter, I was in the merchant navy as a young man. I spent six years at sea and quit at the age of 25, the same age as Peter when he died on the St Columba. You know, I've sailed the Bay of Biscay many, many times and must have passed over the spot where his ship went down on several occasions.

"Maybe fate determined I would find that medal as a boy and return it to Ibrox. It seems too strange a coincidence, doesn't it?"

8

THE END OF THE INNOCENCE

Rangers had found order and consistency towards the end of its first decade in existence but little new blood to sustain the momentum built throughout the 1870s.

Sadly, the five years after their second Scottish Cup final appearance in 1879 would be recognised less as the start of the big push and more as the end of the innocence.

There was a worrying decline towards financial crisis and an unpopularity that could never have been predicted in 1877 when so many thousands of Glasgow's citizens first thronged to Hamilton Crescent and Hampden to embrace their new association football favourites.

Success on the field, then as now, brought with it problems associated with their new-found popularity.

Rapacious English football agents plundered the Light Blues in the aftermath of their two Scottish Cup final appearances, not least because the game was growing at an increasing pace south of the border.

Peter Campbell ultimately left for Blackburn Rovers, who had been formed in 1875, as did Hugh McIntyre, who became landlord at the Castle Inn in the town. McIntyre was an upholsterer by trade, but it was the Lancashire club who were undoubtedly feathering the nest of his future financial prosperity with the offer of a profitable pub. McIntyre, who also went on to gain notoriety as one of the earliest Mr Fixits, was widely criticised for accepting the move to the English club.

Bolton added to Kinning Park woes in 1881 when they persuaded Archie Steel, William Struthers and John Christie to join. Not surprisingly, the following season, for the first time in their short history, a Rangers side shorn of its most talented stars lost more matches than they won.

The departure of Campbell and McBeath left only the McNeil brothers and Tom Vallance as the original pioneers, but changes were afoot that, in the short term at least, would loosen the bonds between the club and the band of teenagers who had brought it into existence.

Firstly, Tom Vallance accepted a position on the tea plantations at Assam and left Glasgow in February 1882. Such was the affection in which he was held that he was presented with 50 sovereigns by the club at his farewell reception at the Bridge Street Hotel and as he boarded the train for London the platform was thronged with well-wishers.

Moses McNeil had been a committee member from the beginning of the club's existence until as late as 1879, but the nature of his relationship with the team he helped to form had begun to change as Rangers entered the 1880s.

He remained a regular in the side until February 1881, when he played his last game of the season in an 8–2 defeat of Partick Thistle. It would be another year before he would pull on the Rangers shirt again, for a 3–2 defeat at Aston Villa on March 25 1882.

Moses played his last first-team game for Rangers a fortnight later, on April 5, in a goalless draw with South Western. In subsequent years he would feature for the 'ancients', an old boys' XI who frequently played charity and exhibition matches around the country, but his days at the sharp end were over.

It is entirely likely that Moses was sidelined or usurped by others keener to grab the club's key executive positions. Apart from a 12-month stint as honorary treasurer in 1876, he became a bit-part player in the running of the club. Few would argue against the fact that in helping to create Rangers in the first place he had made more than a sizeable contribution.

The club was also thrown into a state of flux in the early 1880s by events outwith its making. Firstly, in November 1882 club president Archie Harkness tragically died from typhoid fever at the age of just 26, leaving a widow whom he had wed less than five months previously.

He had been suffering ill health for several months, but still insisted on taking training at Kinning Park on summer evenings and was acknowledged as an influential member of the club he had first joined in 1874 as a friend of the McNeils.

Secondly, the club lost one of its longest serving officials when Peter McNeil was forced to step down from the post of honorary match secretary as a result of business pressures at the end of the 1882–83 season. The sports outfitting store owned by Peter and his brother Harry had moved from its original premises to a new building at No. 91 Union Street and the switch necessitated a focus on their business enterprise at the expense of the club the McNeils had helped to form. Peter also stood down from his post as treasurer of the SFA at the same time.

At this stage Rangers were rudderless and this was reflected in the end of season stats, which showed only eight matches won and 16 lost from 29 games played.

The club played the season in white and blue hoops. Their faces were almost permanently red. It came as no great surprise when they ditched the shirts at the end of that solitary campaign.

In its end-of-season review the Scottish Athletic Journal was moved to warn: "One has always to be particularly cautious in forecasting the form of such a shifty, uncertain set of players as the Rangers. Today they do something extraordinary and tomorrow they exhibit such a falling off that one is perforce compelled to write them down a very ordinary lot indeed."

Sarcasm dripped from the pages of the Journal like the self-confidence from the very soul of the club. A few weeks earlier, a reader had written to the newspaper asking for details of the club's defeats over the previous months. They replied mischievously: "It is impossible to give the exact number of defeats as these have been so numerous. In fact, it is only an average of once a month they get what is popularly called 'a look in' and when that happens it is generally against second rate clubs."

Financially, the club was in a precarious position. By the summer of 1883 the praise of four years earlier, when the club was described as "flourishing" and lauded as the biggest and strongest in the country, rang hollow.

The club were £100 in debt, despite a £30 bail out from new president George Goudie, who had replaced Harkness. Membership numbers had stalled as little attention was paid to the recruitment of those who could have brought fresh ideas and impetus to the Kinning Park set-up. Throughout the second half of the 1870s membership numbers had remained stable at between 70 and 80 per season, but there was a fine line between close knit and clique.

Admittedly, it would have troubled few on the back of two appearances in the Scottish Cup final in the space of three years and that Charity Cup success, but it would prove problematic to those who wisely took a more long-sighted view of the club's sustainability.

In 1880, for example, Queen's Park attracted 97 new members and their numbers exceeded 300. Indeed, the Hampden club were so popular that they were forced to restrict membership numbers to 350, while season-ticket holders were limited to 600.

The financial crisis of 1883 brought to a head the need to widen the sphere of influence around Kinning Park and a recruitment drive proved so successful that by the start of the 1884–85 season Rangers boasted 180 members, a record number.

It had become clear that there was a void at the heart of Rangers and that the club needed a radical restructure, which duly took place at the annual general meeting in May 1883 at the Athole Arms.

Tom Vallance was back from India. He had suffered poor health in Assam, forcing his early return, and his playing career had been compromised as a result. However, he was too valuable an ally not to be welcomed to Kinning Park again with open arms.

He was quickly named president, with the club's delicate finances placed in the hands of treasurer Robert White. The post of captain was deleted from the list of office bearers and instead a 10-man committee was appointed to oversee team selection. It was a break with tradition for the Light Blues, but acknowledged at the time as a wise move and one that had proved successful for other clubs in Scotland and England.

The situation had improved markedly by the time of the six-monthly meeting in November 1883. The new treasurer had stemmed the losses and his report to members was greeted with enthusiastic applause.

All debt had been paid off, the Scottish Athletic Journal reported, bar some "trifling sums". It was forecast the club would soon be in credit again after forthcoming matches against Queen's Park and Dumbarton at Kinning Park.

Nevertheless, this period of transition had also left the club open to opportunists keen to use the good name Rangers had built over the previous decade to their own advantage.

John Wallace Mackay shares his first two names with one of Rangers' best known bosses, but jungle fighter Jock would surely have given short shrift to the match secretary from the 19th century, who manoeuvred himself into such a position of dominance that it quickly threatened to destroy the very reputation the club had worked so hard to forge among its contemporaries. Singlehandedly, he almost emptied the reservoir of goodwill and respect Rangers had built in their first years of existence.

Mackay first came to prominence at the club in 1882 when he was named honorary secretary and by the following summer he had stepped up to fill the role of honorary match secretary, replacing Peter McNeil. The Scottish Athletic Journal welcomed his appointment at the time, claiming him to be an amenable figurehead with whom other clubs could do business, but within two years they had performed a complete volte-face.

Three months hadn't even passed after his appointment as match secretary in May 1883 than Mackay was attracting scorn for his handling of the aftermath of the charity game played between Rangers and Dumbarton for the families of the victims of the Daphne Disaster.

It still stands today as the greatest tragedy in Clyde shipyard history (memorials to the victims were erected in Elder and Victoria Parks in Glasgow as recently as 1996). There had seemed little amiss when a bottle was broken across the hull of the 449–ton Irish Sea ferry on the morning of July 3 1883 and it slipped gently into the Clyde from its mooring at the Linthouse shipyard of Alexander Stephen and Co.

However, within five minutes the Daphne capsized to port and 124 men and boys, who had been working inside its hull, died in the murky waters of the river, dragged to their deaths by the weight of the equipment they were wearing and by blind panic as they gasped for breath in the pitch darkness.

One woman, a Jane Drysdale from Tranent, lost her husband and son and for almost a fortnight afterwards turned up at the shipyard gate in the vain hope that they had survived.

Another victim left a wife with eight children, including a son with mental health issues and a daughter paralysed from the waist down. His wife was forced to sell her own clothes to survive and the children were given two bowls of porridge a day to eat. Accounts from the time tell of the poor mother rushing home after hearing the news of the ship's capsize to find her children screaming and the clock on the mantelpiece, which had been in perfect order until that point, stopped forever at the time of her husband's death.

A Disaster Relief Fund was established, which provided regular but modest payments to those who needed it most. It should have been bolstered by a sum of £73 11 shillings and ninepence from the football game, played in front of a crowd of 2,500 at Kinning Park and which Rangers won 4–2.

However, to the astonishment of almost everyone involved, most especially those Dumbarton officials who provided their time and team for free, Mackay took game-day expenses for Rangers.

The sorry state of affairs first came to light when a letter was sent to the Lennox Herald in Dumbarton, which was re-published in the Scottish Athletic Journal. Dumbarton officials denied sending the information to the press, although they confirmed the facts were substantially correct.

The letter started: "A case of smartness combined with shabbiness on the part of a football club has just come to light which deserves publication." It went on to explain the belief and expectation that both clubs would take care of their own expenses, as Dumbarton had demanded and which was an example, as intimated in the Glasgow press, Rangers were expected to follow.

However, the Kinning Park committee deducted £10 three shillings and threepence for costs. Appalled, club officials at Dumbarton immediately forwarded half the sum, £5 one shilling and eightpence, to the Daphne Fund from its own coffers to add to the £68 eight shillings and sixpence sent by Rangers.

Angered by the bad press, Rangers immediately withdrew its advertising account from the Scottish Athletic Journal, which hit back by thundering: "The Rangers are wrong if they think our opinions are to be purchased in this way. All along we have been independent, which is the secret of our success. Perhaps there is no club that has benefited so much by our free criticism as the Rangers."

For his part Mackay wrote an irate letter to the Journal and – changed days indeed – effectively complained that it was all right for big clubs such as Dumbarton to show such largesse, which was beyond the means of the cash-strapped Light Blues, still mindful of their delicate financial position.

Mackay said: "From the very first I made it clear to Dumbarton that... we could not, as a matter of prudence, undertake to bear a part of the expenses involved in the arrangements for the match... While pleased to know that the Dumbarton intend sending in their share of the expense of the match I have, at the same time, to regret that they should insist by such action, generous though it be, in placing the Rangers in unfavourable contrast to them in this respect, but I am sure were the Rangers in the same enviable financial position as the Dumbarton are at present in, they would not soon be outstripped in generosity."

In addition to the Daphne fund debacle, Mackay also attracted fierce criticism for the 'Cooking the Books' scandal that beset their Scottish Cup ties with Third Lanark throughout October 1884.

The second-round tie finished at 2–2 but Thirds lodged a complaint over the involvement in the Rangers team of their former player Sam Thomson, who had been playing as a professional with Preston. Professionals were banned from playing for Scottish clubs and, furthermore, only registered players who had their names lodged with the SFA before the tie could play for their clubs.

Mackay rode roughshod over the rules on both accounts and was fortunate the SFA demanded only a replay of the game. The second match, played a week later in front of 5,000 at Kinning Park, finished goalless and bad feeling was such that it ended in a brawl.

To compound matters still further, Rangers fielded another professional, Bolton star Archie Steel, but Thirds threw in the towel on the idea of protesting again and under the rules of the time both sides progressed into the third round.

As fate would have it, the same sides were drawn from the hat to play again in the next round and this time Rangers won comfortably 3–0 at Cathkin, with goals from Lawrie, Morton and new signing Tommy Cook.

However, the latter's involvement aroused suspicion in the Thirds ranks, who suspected he belonged to another club. Closer examination of the books indicated, indeed, that a T Cook had been registered with Rangers, but not in time to turn out in the game.

Another player with the surname Cook, first initial 'J', was also associated with Rangers at the time and would have been eligible. A clumsy attempt had been made to cover the club's path as the 'J' was doctored to make it look like the letter 'T'.

The Scottish Athletic Journal accused Mackay in all but name of sneaking into the office of SFA secretary John McDowall and making the change. As an SFA committee member, he would certainly have had access, literally, to the corridors of power.

Astonishingly, Rangers dodged the bullet of cup expulsion or, worse still, expulsion from the association, but their actions were succeeding only in making the club look increasingly tawdry.

In the next round of the cup they lost 4–3 at Arbroath, but they dared not lose with dignity and as soon as the game had finished Kinning Park officials appeared with a tape measure and, after running it across the pitch, declared the playing surface a yard short of regulation width.

The protest went in. After a discussion, the SFA agreed to a replay and Rangers won 8–1. They eventually tumbled out of the competition at the quarter-final stage following a 5–3 defeat at Renton. The Scottish Athletic Journal jibed four days after the defeat: "So far there has been no protest from Rangers."

Mackay clearly felt himself to be untouchable, but he was occasionally called to task by club members, not least when he berated Third Lanark for their role in the Cook scandal and suggested Rangers never play them again for their insolence in protesting.

His call, at the half-yearly meeting of the club in November 1884, was dismissed, as most members claimed Rangers would have done exactly the same.

At the same meeting he was also scolded for claiming Queen's Park were in the financial grubber as a result of costs associated with the construction of the new Hampden Park (the second Hampden. The current national stadium, the third, was opened in 1903).

The mighty amateurs had refused Rangers a game at Kinning Park the previous season, unless they were presented with half the gate and stand money. Generously, Rangers gave them the money from the terraces, which amounted to £60, while they banked the takings from the pavilion, a more modest £10.

The prudent financial management of Queen's Park meant they were on course to pay off the cost of construction of their new ground within 12 months of it opening. The Scottish Athletic Journal, ever alert, admonished Mackay: "Those who live in glass houses shouldn't throw stones… Mr Mackay is not the Rangers club, nor the Rangers team."

Mackay also had a nefarious influence over the players, which saw a revolt against Tom Vallance on the way to play a game at Dumbarton in October 1883. The players refused to sanction the popular president as their umpire (one in each half in those days, each chosen from the ranks of the competing teams to assist the referee) because he was too honest. Vallance resigned in disgust, only to be talked back the following week following a grovelling apology from his squad.

However, Mackay continued to referee and his lack of balance and judgement soon forced other clubs into appointing their own partisan officials, with the result that games became increasingly bad-tempered.

Rangers reached their nadir, at least according to Mackay's arch enemies at the Scottish Athletic Journal, in September 1885 following a 3–2 defeat at Queen's Park. Indiscipline on the field led to rowdy scenes off it and at one point it was feared the pitch would be invaded.

There was more than a hint of sarcasm in the Journal's coverage as it revealed: "The rowdy element from Kinning Park hooted and yelled in the style most approved in that aristocratic suburb and the usually serene air of Hampden Park was a perfect pandemonium."

The scenes so sickened the editor of the Scottish Athletic Journal that he condemned the Light Blues in print and, the following week, issued a public challenge to Rangers in general, and Mackay in particular, to clean up their act.

He hit out: "My remarks last week on the match between the Rangers and Queen's Park have created no little sensation and the 'light blues' are smarting very sorely under the lash. I do not trim my remarks to suit any club or any individual and I am as indifferent to threats as I am to cajolery.

"I stated the Queen's Park as a club are composed of gentlemen and the Rangers as a club are not. I stated the Rangers are not now socially the same set of fellows they were when Tom Vallance and Alick Vallance commanded them, and I stated they are no longer a first class club.

"I stated the game was the most unpleasant ever played between two clubs of standing. All this I repeat with emphasis. I take this opportunity of laying before the public the reason why I give the Rangers on every occasion their exact desserts. The social decadence of the Rangers may be dated from the day Mr Peter McNeil resigned the match secretaryship and JW Mackay took it up. Then began that system of trickery which has brought the club to its present low level."

Players and officials were also criticised for their boorish behaviour at club smokers, where alcohol was more than prominent.

Rangers were even chided by the Journal for their lack of concern for good causes following a Charity Cup tie against Queen's Park. The Hampden club refused to turn up at a social in the Athole Arms afterwards, where food and drink had been arranged, because they felt it was an unnecessary expense and against the spirit of the tournament's fundraising ethos. Rangers agreed to differ and "turned up to a man and, aided by some friends, disposed of the viands."

The war of words between Mackay and the Scottish Athletic Journal had long since grown personal and severe criticisms became a feature of the newspaper's coverage as it delved into the Rangers official's background, including his church membership.

It revealed Mackay had once been a part of the Christian Institute, but resigned after being caught using "unchristian language". It added: "Coward-like, rather than face the indignant and grave seigniors, he sent in his resignation and beat an undignified retreat, thus saving himself from expulsion."

Then came the twist of the mighty pen: "This, together with the fact Mackay failed to pass an examination which any fifth standard schoolboy could manage, has left him what he is – a working compositor – and ruined his aspirations forever. His conduct over the Daphne match proves charity is not in his composition." The article was delivered on the pages of the Journal on January 5 1886. A Happy New Year indeed.

However, criticism of Mackay in the pages of the Scottish Athletic Journal must be seen in the context of the loss of advertising revenue from the Kinning Park club in the aftermath of the Daphne fiasco and also the involvement of the Rangers official with a rival publication, the Scottish Umpire, which was published for the first time in August 1884.

It had been set up by those, including Mackay, who were disgruntled at the occasionally scurrilous tone of the Journal, which had been on the go since September 1882.

Ultimately, by 1888 the two papers had merged to form the twice weekly Scottish Sport. However, the personal nature of the criticism aside (the Journal, in reference to its new rival on the news-stands, frequently referred to Mackay and his publication as the 'Vampire'), many of Mackay's actions were still worthy of being called to account.

Mackay's hypocrisy extended to the thorny issue of professionalism. He was moved to bring up the issue surrounding the plundering of Scottish teams by English outfits at an SFA meeting in April 1884.

The report read: "Mr Mackay said…when in England the other day his team was besieged by professionals and every effort was made to induce them to join English clubs – not only that, but they were followed home to Scotland by certain players who had left Glasgow some time before and who made every effort to find out the address of some of the Rangers team.

"These fellows went about in Lancashire with their hands in their pockets, apparently doing nothing but living on the money they received from football. Mr Mackay spoke very warmly and the committee were entirely in sympathy with him."

However, little more than a week after his report on the evils of professionalism which had elicited nods of support and understanding, Rangers were welcoming an ex-pro, John Inglis, back into the fold.

The move was, at the very least, against the spirit of the times in which Scottish clubs – outwardly anyway – railed fiercely against the payment of players.

As the Scottish Athletic Journal wryly commented: "The Rangers are a strange lot. In a fit of virtue the other day they ejected Inglis from their club because he chose to assist the Blackburn Rovers in their cup ties rather than play for his own club. Mr Mackay, too, delivered a virtuous speech on professionalism at the last meeting of the SFA committee. The virtuous fit did not last long and Inglis has been taken back into the fold again and played against Thistle for his old club last Saturday."

Clearly, Rangers were no innocents on the issue of professionalism and, as early as October 1885, they were lobbying other Scottish clubs to follow the route of the English towards the paid ranks.

With the aid of hindsight, the opposition to their plans to have professionalism even discussed appears quaintly romantic, but it was a burning issue of the football age and, typically, the Scottish Athletic Journal took no prisoners as it thundered against the Light Blues for earlier breaches of rules and etiquette.

Its 'Echoes' columnist rapped: "The pseudo-opposition to the recent edict of the SFA which is being organised by the Rangers is sufficient to damn it in the eyes of the public. A member of the Rangers' committee has sent out circulars to the clubs asking them to attend an anti-amateur meeting tonight.

"The Queen's Park and other leading clubs will not be represented. No wonder the Rangers desire professionalism. The club has before now paid its players and one of its present office bearers has been dependent on the bounty of the club [no doubt they meant Mackay]; while Hugh McIntyre does not deny he and other members of the team received 10 shillings a week as training expenses.

"(Sam) Thomson of Lugar Boswell got 15 shillings a week for expenses from Lugar to Glasgow. He is now a Lancashire professional and so is McIntyre. The recent action of the Rangers in trying to induce players to join them has caused no little scandal. Tonight's meeting will fall through, like its predecessors."

In fairness to Rangers and Mackay, under-the-table payments were rife in Scottish football at the time, with Hearts the first club to feel the ire of the SFA following an 11–1 victory over Dunfermline in the Scottish Cup in October 1884.

The Pars protested the result, claiming the Jambos had two paid professionals in their line up, Maxwell and McNee. Maxwell was employed at the Fountainbridge Rubber Works on a salary supplemented by the club's fans, while McNee was paid 25 shillings a week from the man with whom he lodged, George Barbour, who received the cash in the first instance to pass on from a grocer friend of the club.

It was difficult not to feel a pang of sympathy for Hearts, who had lost arguably their greatest-ever player, Nick Ross, to Preston North End at the age of just 20 only 12 months earlier.

Ross was already skipper of the club – a role he went on to perform with the Invincibles – and had recently married an Edinburgh girl when the English outfit came calling.

It was claimed he would have stayed at Hearts for 10 shillings a week and the estimation in which he was held at Tynecastle was symbolised by the expensive clock he was gifted by the club when he married. He vowed never to leave the Edinburgh side, but when he was offered 30 shillings a week under the guise of work as a slater in Preston, he moved south, much to the chagrin of the fans.

Dunfermline's original Scottish Cup protest was upheld and they were awarded the tie. Maxwell and McNee were banned for two years and Hearts were suspended from the SFA. Nevertheless, they continued to play while under suspension and when the erring Hearts committee was disbanded and other club members took their place they were quietly welcomed back into the fold.

The formation of Celtic in November 1887 also hastened the advent of professionalism in the Scottish game as they quickly became one of the powerhouses of the sport.

There was nothing serendipitous about it – Celtic raided Hibs for players with the promise of greater riches and left the Easter Road club, champions of the world only three months earlier following their 2–1 defeat of Preston at Leith, in a depressed state as the mantle of foremost Catholic club in the country was seized by the canny businessmen in control of the east end of Glasgow.

To highlight the farce of the situation, Celtic players even threatened to go on strike in 1891, two years before professionalism was introduced in Scotland, if their wages were not raised to the levels of new signings recently secured from the English League.

The Parkhead players were paid a bonus of £3 and presented with a new suit for winning the Scottish Cup in 1892 and three years earlier it had been noted that Celtic donated £432 to charity at the same time as captain James Kelly, a young joiner from Renton, had bought a pub for £650.

The Athletic News posed the relevant question: "Where did he get the money?"

Hibs had also been under investigation for payment to their star player Willie Groves after Vale of Leven hired a private detective following a Scottish Cup tie to investigate his dubious amateur status amid allegations he was being paid up to four times his salary as a stonemason in 'broken time'.

Clubs were permitted to make these 'broken time' payments to players who missed work shifts to prepare for or play in important matches, but Queen of the South Wanderers took it a stage too far when they were caught making payments to two of their players – both of whom were unemployed.

In addition, clubs frequently kept two sets of books, only one of which was displayed with a flourish whenever SFA auditors came knocking and whose fictional figures had been created with all the craft of a Hans Christian Andersen fairytale. Cowlairs and St Bernard's were caught out and suspended. The Scottish Sport newspaper estimated in 1892 that one unnamed club had paid out £1,150 in salaries the previous year.

However, the commercialism of the sport was becoming less of a trickle and more of a torrent. Celtic secretary John McLaughlin, who, coincidentally, acted as pianist and accompanist at the Rangers Glee Clubs for many years in those more innocent times, famously declared: "You might as well attempt to stem the flow of Niagara with a kitchen chair as to endeavour to stem the tide of professionalism."

His observation could not be disputed – Rangers announced a profit of £500 when they won the first Scottish League championship in 1890–91 and the Light Blues and Celtic were regularly turning over £5,000 a year by that time. The Glasgow Charities Cup alone helped raise £10,000 for the needy of the city from 1877–1890.

The popular newspapers of the time disliked the idea of clubs paying their players and Scottish Sport summed up press feelings best when it carried an editorial on rules for professionalism which had recently been introduced by the Scottish Football League. The Sport loftily declared: "Our first and last objection to them is that they exist. The entire rules stink of finance – money making and money grabbing."

Rangers were included in this mix, of course, but there was more than the financial expansion of the game causing unrest about the way the Kinning Park club was running its business. Mackay, in his position as honorary match secretary, had become exceedingly unpopular. His politicking had made him a major player at the club but not without winning enemies elsewhere, particularly within the pages of the Journal.

The farce of the situation, not to say the depth of control he held over others at the club, was highlighted at the annual meeting in May 1885, held at Ancell's Restaurant on Glassford Street.

The income of the year was listed at £804, with an expenditure of £604. Astonishingly, approximately one sixth of the expenditure was paid to Mackay for printing costs associated with the club – bills, members' tickets and advertising. In comparison, the printing and stationery bill at Queen's Park that year was only £29.

His 'Vampire' nickname was never more appropriate, as the Journal said: "Mackay proves his capacity for blood sucking by bleeding the Rangers to the extent of about £100…honestly, of course – all in the way of trade! It is a very profitable thing to be match secretary of the Rangers when it brings grist to your own mill."

The excesses of Mackay may have been less of a talking point had Rangers continued their success of the late 1870s into the new decade, but further trophy success proved elusive.

Admittedly, the low of only eight victories in 1882–83 was not repeated, but the campaigns that followed were far from vintage. In 1883–84, for example, Rangers won 22 of 36 games played and in 1884–85 there were 24 wins from 40 matches, most of which took place at Kinning Park.

Crowds of only 500 were not uncommon at home matches the following year, with modest opposition such as Battlefield and Fifth Kirkudbrightshire Volunteer Rifles. As president, Tom Vallance had promised at the start of the season that the Scottish Cup and Charity Cup would be on the table by the end of the campaign. For once, he proved not to be a man of his word.

Eventually, the pressure told and by the summer of 1886 Mackay had resigned, 12 months after he had been knocked off the executive committee and on to the general committee of the club.

Rangers turned to a familiar face to steady the ship as Peter McNeil returned and assumed the role of vice-president, his first period of office at the club since business pressures had forced his resignation three years earlier.

The Journal noted the return of McNeil on June 8 with great warmth and claimed it was "delighted…this denotes a change. I hope the new committee will inaugurate a new policy now that they have got rid of JW Mackay…if the old policy is carried about, bankruptcy awaits them."

However, the Journal could not resist one final dig.

"By the way," it added "who is to represent the club on the Glasgow Association Committee? JW Mackay has been appointed treasurer without a club and, of course, the printing bill is a substantial sum as he can fix his own prices. Should the Rangers or any other club father him, they know the consequences. If he cannot get a club, he must give place to a less notorious man."

9

WILLIAM MCBEATH

The hammer that fell on the auction house lots at Butter Market in Lincoln in April 1906 represented a death knell for the comfortable and respectable life that William McBeath once knew.

In the Lincolnshire Echo, auctioneer Caleb Smith listed everything for sale from No. 5 Vernon Street, without reserve. Oil paintings and water colours were made available, along with household furniture in walnut and oak, spring mattresses, feather beds, even a commode and a stock of high class cigars.

Sadly, the lot also included a pram. The advert was unsympathetic to the point of brutality: "The auctioneer has great confidence in recommending this furniture, as the greater part of it is equal to new."

William's descent to the lowest rung was confirmed three-and-a-half years later when the local press published a story in December 1909 that was shorn of Christmas cheer.

William's wife, Sarah Ann, had appeared from custody at the local court with two black eyes after being arrested on December 13 for being drunk in the High Street. She had earlier visited the Lincoln Arms, "to pay a debt" but had been refused service. It was her first time in front of the magistrates, police revealed, but alcoholism had clearly taken hold.

The black eyes, she explained, were "the result of a fall I sustained in the house a week ago." She denied being drunk in the Lincoln

Arms but the arresting officer, PC Skelson, revealed that "owing to her drunken habits the people with whom she had lodged had tried to get rid of her." She was fined 10 shillings, with an alternative of 14 days imprisonment.

William followed her into the dock after being arrested the previous night for persistently knocking on the door of No. 57 Cranwell Street, where he had once lived with Sarah Ann. He believed he still resided there, revealed the arresting officer PC Bailey, who added that he'd received complaints before about William's behaviour from the people now staying in the property.

The local chief constable summed it up: "This case was as sad as the last one. Prisoner once held a respectable position, but had gone to the dogs through drink." William was also fined 10 shillings, with an alternative to seven days behind bars.

Unfortunately, it was not the first time William had fallen foul of the law as a result of alcohol abuse. The Lincoln, Rutland and Stamford Mercury reported nine years earlier, in November 1900, that he had been charged with being drunk and incapable in St Mary's Street in the town. He was fined five shillings, with costs.

William Shakespeare wrote in Hamlet that sorrow comes not as single spies, but always in battalions. However, it could equally have been written about MacBeth. Or McBeth. Or McBeath. Or McBeith, or any one of the many derivatives of the surname used throughout the life of the founding father about whom least has, until recently, been chronicled.

If William had proved as adept at evading tackles on the field of play as his historical footprints have been at slipping the best efforts of researchers off it he would surely have followed in the path of fellow pioneers Moses McNeil and Peter Campbell and won representative honours for Scotland.

Unfortunately, the faint tracks he did leave, which have required expert genealogical assistance to help trace back in time, lead along a sad path of poverty and the poorhouse, alcoholism, mental decline and the tag of 'certified imbecile'. He was married twice, although his relationship with Sarah Ann was almost certainly bigamous, and he faced at least one other criminal charge in his life, for attempted fraud.

His final resting place in a pauper's grave, in a lair shared with a total stranger, lay unmarked for almost a century, literally under a holly bush in scrubland at the forgotten fringes of a Lincoln cemetery before it was discovered as part of the original research into the first edition of The Gallant Pioneers.

William's life had remained such a mystery to Rangers historians previously that the first known image of him only came to light in 2014. Gordon Bell of the Founders' Trail was undertaking research at the Mitchell Library and came across a profile of William in an early newspaper, 'The Chiel', which carried a sketch drawing of William in an edition from March 1885.

The Ibrox historical equivalent of the Holy Grail was reached in August 2021 when Val Hedges, great grand-daughter of Peter McNeil, came up trumps for author Gary Ralston.

Val's mum, Heather Lang – Peter's grand-daughter – had long ago inherited a leather bound photo album of family snaps from the Victorian era, but the identities of almost all of those within the weathered pages were a mystery even to her, particularly as they were not captioned front or back.

Heather was a kind and generous contributor to the original Gallant Pioneers project and handed over the family album to Gary, with pictures of early players such as Moses, Peter and Harry McNeil, as well as the Vallance brothers, quickly identified for use in the book before the album was returned to safe family keeping.

Heather sadly passed away in February 2015, aged 87, but Gary re-connected with Val in researching this edition and she was delighted to provide an update on the McNeil family line, expressing the enjoyment they had all taken from finding her great grandfather had been a founding father of one of the world's great football clubs.

Gordon Bell prompted Gary to ask again about the old album, hoping the identity of one or two of the mystery figures could be resolved a decade down the line. Eureka. Val sent a cropped black and white picture, immediately identified, even down to the flower in the lapel in his jacket, as the image of William that had inspired the sketch drawing in The Chiel.

The sketch artist at the newspaper even credited the photography studio that provided the image of William as his inspiration – Collis of Torquay. Seeking copper bottom verification, Gary quickly asked: "Val, is there a studio credited at the foot of the picture you just sent?" Her reply was instantaneous: "Yes, a company called Collis of Torquay."

William was first mentioned in reference to Rangers in 1872 as a family friend of the McNeils and one of the four founding fathers of the club. However, he played his last game for Rangers in November 1875 and disappeared from club records soon after.

He was forced to take to his bed for a week after the club's first game against Callander towards the end of May 1872, so exhausted was he by the effort required to participate in the developing sport. However, like Peter McNeil, he clearly enjoyed the respect of his peers for his organisational skills and WD McBeath was the first president of the club, listed in the roll of office bearers for the 1874–75 season.

One of the last recorded mentions of William in connection with Rangers came in the pages of the Scottish Athletic Journal in April 1884 when he was honoured by the club at its half-yearly meeting for the role he played in its conception.

The paper reported: "William McBeath was presented with a beautiful gold badge by a few of those who were intimately associated with him in the management of the club when he was one of its active members. The presentation was made by Tom Vallance… Mr McBeath replied briefly and after thanking those who had been good enough to honour him, said that he looked upon the days when he played for the Rangers as the brightest and jolliest of his life… Many of his old friends will be happy to learn he is doing well and is still cultivating those tastes for high art which made his company so pleasant to the more scholarly of his companions."

William's love for art, like team-mate Vallance, would see him exhibit his paintings in local shows when he moved to England around 1881. The Cornishman newspaper, in March 1881, mentioned his work at one such event and his Highland roots were recognised in his choice of 'Rob Roy's Cottage' as a subject, along with 'Cattle at Brook'. His love of art clearly continued throughout the 1880s and in December 1886 The Bristol Mercury also noted he was a contributor to a show at the local Fine Arts Academy.

Unfortunately, relating the life story of William is more akin to painting by numbers than flourishing wide brush strokes on a canvas coloured by rich memory, warm anecdote and bountiful documentation because, quite frankly, very little exists.

However, a fuller picture has finally emerged from the faint sketches of yesteryear on which research for this chapter has been painstakingly drawn. Confidence about the conclusions here remains absolute, even if there is a wish for a happier tale to tell than the sad story that developed over the 61 years of his life.

William McBeath was born in Callander, Perthshire, on May 7 1856. He was the son of Peter McBeath, a draper and general merchant born in Callander in 1803, and Jane Duncanson, 16 years his junior (his second wife). She too was also born in the pretty village that provided the opposition for the first Rangers game at Flesher's Haugh in the spring of 1872.

Callander FC have long since been confined to the archives of Scottish football history but they were a popular enough club at the time. They grew out of an earlier Glasgow Green team known as The Thistle and were, unsurprisingly, formed by the men who came from the village from which they took their sporting name.

On the face of it, the McBeath family appeared to lead a comfortable enough existence at their home on Callander's Main Street. The family's general store and their home upstairs is occupied today by the Waverley Hotel. Peter was 52 when William was born, a brother for Jane, aged seven, and Peter, aged nine. Another child, a boy, was born after William, but did not survive beyond infancy.

Unfortunately, Peter McBeath did not live long enough to profit from the soaring popularity of his birthplace through the Victorian tourist trade as he died of heart disease in November 1864, aged 60.

His wife and two of their children, William and Jane, moved to Glasgow soon afterwards to start a new life, drawn away from their countryside roots towards the rapidly expanding industrial heartland of Scotland, a million miles away from the picture postcard image Callander was beginning to portray to the wider world.

In Glasgow, the teenage William would make the friendships that would earn his name a place in Scottish sporting history. By the time of the census in 1871 William was 14 and working as an assistant salesman. He lived with Jane, a 21-year-old saleswoman, and his mother, 50, who was listed as a housekeeper and head of the family home.

They lived at No.17 Cleveland Street in the Sandyford area of the city – a street that still stands today, running parallel with North Street, a stone's throw from the Mitchell Library.

In the same tenement lived five members of the McNeil family, including eldest daughter Elizabeth, 30, the housekeeper, eldest son James, 27, a commercial traveller, brothers Henry, 21, a commercial clerk, William, 19, a seedsman, and Peter, 16, a clerk. Moses was still residing at home on the Gare Loch.

The birth of Rangers would have represented a period of mixed emotions for a boy who was still two months short of his 16th birthday. At the same time he and his friends were planning their new adventure in association football, William's mother died, aged just 53, in March 1872 from chronic bronchitis.

It was undoubtedly a crushing blow to young William to lose his second parent so early in life and, sadly, death was a spectre that was to shadow his existence throughout the second half of the 19th century.

The most distressing tale of all the McBeaths, including even William himself, was the terribly tragic short life of sister Jane, who must have felt she was preparing for decades of happiness when she fell in love and married shipping clerk Daniel Lang in Glasgow in June 1873.

However, by December of that year Daniel, aged just 22, had died from consumption. In July 1879, when she was only 28 years old, widower Jane also passed away, killed by the scourge of tuberculosis at her home in Kirk Street in the Perthshire cathedral town of Dunblane, a few miles from the original family home in Callander.

The year before, William had moved across the Clyde to Kelburne Terrace in the Crosshill district of Glasgow, following his marriage to Jeannie Yates (or Yeates) Harris, 21, who had been born in the Govanhill area of the city, the daughter of a hosier, David Harris, and his wife Agnes.

The marriage certificate noted the groom's full name as William Duncanson MacBeth, which is significant for two reasons. Firstly, as far as can be established, William's middle name of Duncanson was acknowledged for the first time on official documents and his mother's maiden name was possibly adopted by a loving son following her death six years earlier.

Secondly, a slip of a registrar's pen consigned the name of McBeath to the annals of history. William would never again be known, in official documents at least, by the name with which he was born.

Initially, the marriage of William and Jeannie MacBeth seemed to follow a happy and familiar pattern. Two years after their wedding Jeannie gave birth, in April 1880, to a son, also named William Duncanson MacBeth.

However, within 12 months the family left Scotland and set up home in Bristol. Almost certainly the demands of William's job as a commercial traveller took the family south, initially to the St Paul district of the city, at No. 16 Albert Park (the street still exists), where they remained until at least 1886.

The family was expanded still further in 1882 with the birth of a daughter named Agnes Isabella and another son, Norman Douglas, in 1890. Business must have been going well for William because the family had taken an upwardly mobile step by 1889 when they moved to a more upmarket address, No. 2 Chestnut Villas in the Stapleton area of Bristol.

It is impossible not to read the entry for the MacBeths in the census of 1891 and conclude anything other than the family, like man of the match William against Callander in 1872, were at the top of their game. Their residence at Chestnut Villas was well established and William and Jeannie were affluent enough to employ a domestic servant, 15-year-old Somerset girl Lillie Field.

However, some time after 1893 (the last known date linking them with their home in Stapleton) the family unit collapsed in such a spectacular style that it would never again be reunited.

What devastating episode would eventually force them to send young Norman northwards to live with his grandmother in Glasgow? What caused the breakdown of the relationship between William and Jeannie? Agnes would eventually find refuge working as a nursery governess in Torquay, but what became of her after 1901, when she seemed to fall off the face of the earth? What became of William junior, who has also proved impossible to trace beyond his 10th birthday in the 1891 census?

William's life appeared to hold good until 1896, when he had established the MacBeth Hotel in Victoria Square, Weston-Super-Mare, with Jeannie, who was listed as proprietress.

The Weston Mercury newspaper of May that year revealed William had offered a meeting room at the hotel to the members of the local

Commercial Travellers' Association. It reported he made the offer as he was a former commercial traveller himself, as well as being a life governor of the Commercial Travellers' Schools.

Unfortunately, by the spring of 1897 William was trudging from one boarding house to another around the town and other favoured holiday resorts that fringe the Severn Estuary including Clevedon, Clifton and Portishead.

That February, he had been reduced to selling advertising space for a publication known as Emmott's Seaside Advertiser. For 10 shillings a week and a 25 per cent commission it was the duty of William, most often accompanied by his newspaper's publisher, John Burgoyne Emmott, to persuade hoteliers and boarding house owners – many of them, surely, his friends – to advertise in the weekly journal.

The MacBeth Hotel continued to advertise in the local press until September 1898 but William's shock change of career indicated a breakdown in the relationship with his wife, with disastrous consequences.

Potential clients of Emmott's Seaside Advertiser were assured the paper was widely distributed each week to 5,000 households throughout the north of England and the Midlands, from where the bulk of their holidaying guests arrived throughout the year.

A standard advertisement usually cost at least five shillings for six months, but on immediate payment of cash it could be secured for half the price. On the face of it, a good deal seemed to have been secured, but nagging doubts soon surfaced among those who had paid up front – and they were confirmed when William and Emmott were arrested in Portishead under suspicion of securing money under false pretences.

The full story was recounted in May 1897 in the pages of the Bristol Times and Mirror and the Western Daily Press. It exposed William as a weak, naive and impressionable character – sadly pathetic, driven (most probably as a result of recent events in his family life) to accept a job working for a convicted criminal who had sweet-talked over 1,000 gullible souls out of up to £600 in the previous 18 months.

It was alleged William and Emmott obtained money by false pretences from a string of guest house owners and hoteliers by misrepresenting the circulation of Emmott's Seaside Advertiser, which was never published or distributed in the numbers claimed by the salesmen. They had clearly aroused suspicion in the local community and it came as no surprise when they were arrested by a PC Sharpe in Portishead on May 1 for the alleged offences, stretching back two months.

In a pitiful plea, William claimed: "I am only an agent for Mr Emmott, receiving so much per week, and he owes me now over £6 in wages. I did not know (anything) but this paper was printed every week in Birmingham and circulated in Birmingham, Manchester, Derby, Liverpool, Nottingham and several other places. I can't see how I can be convicted."

Charitably, Emmott damned William with faint praise, telling police: "I wish to say that he is innocent of the charge. He has worked for me faithfully for the last three months, though not successfully. He has handed over all monies, or accounted for them, which he has received."

Surely, justice was done the following month when William was acquitted, but Emmott found guilty of dishonesty. Emmott admitted a previous conviction at Liverpool, for felony, and was sentenced to 21 months of hard labour.

By the end of 1898 William had escaped to live in Bradford, but clearly ran the risk of falling foul of the law once again when he married for the second time, to a Sarah Ann Lambert, with whom he was sharing an address at No. 28 Marshall Street in the Horton district of the Yorkshire town.

There is no doubt that the marriage solemnised at the Register Office in Bradford on Boxing Day of 1898 involved William of Rangers fame – the wedding certificate noted his age as 40, his profession was given as commission agent and his father's name was listed as Peter MacBeth (deceased), whose occupation had been a 'stuff merchant'.

Intriguingly, however, William listed himself as a widower when there is no documented evidence to suggest that his first wife Jeannie had even died. In fact, it seems she continued to live until 1915, at which point she passed away in Bristol from ovarian cancer.

The evidence to suggest William's second marriage was bigamous is persuasive, not least for the lack of any official confirmation of Jeannie's passing in the first place. Indeed, in the 1901 census she appeared to have adopted the more anglicised Christian name of Jennie and was living in a boarding house in the town of Rochford in Essex.

This Jennie MacBeth also listed a middle initial of 'Y' (as in Yeates or Yates, Jeannie's unusual middle name). To add to the weight of evidence, her birthplace was confirmed as Glasgow, just like William's first bride. She listed herself as a widow who was 'living on her own means' and this marital status is likely to have been a front to maintain respectability.

It is no surprise she was not listed as living with any of her three children – William disappears completely from the records after 1890, while, in 1901, Agnes would have been 19 and was working as a nursery governess in Torquay. Norman, then aged 11, had been sent north to live with his grandmother, also Agnes, and aunts Jessie and Mary in Cathcart.

(As an aside, it appears that Norman lived the majority of his life in Scotland until his death in 1973, aged 83. A customs official, he never married and died at his home in the west end of Glasgow, a stone's throw from the former Rangers ground at Burnbank).

Following the trail of Jeannie to her sad death in 1915 also adds strongly to the belief she was William's estranged wife. Significantly, Jeannie had returned to Bristol from Essex in the early years of the 20th century and died on January 23 1915 at No. 18 Canton Street in the St Paul district of the city, only a few streets from the home at Albert Park where she and William had first moved around 1880.

If William was hoping for greater happiness from his second marriage, however questionable its legitimacy, he would not find it, as his life deteriorated towards a sad conclusion in 1917 when he died in the workhouse at Lincoln; penniless, forgotten and most likely the victim of alcoholism and dementia that led him to being officially cast as a 'certified imbecile'.

Sarah Ann's life, like her husband's, was also fated to be spent in poverty, with several spells in and out of the workhouse at Bradford and Lincoln.

Initially, however, all had seemed well in their lives and by the time of the 1901 census they appeared to be happily settled at 34 Vernon Street in Lincoln, a row of modest terraced houses still standing today.

The Lincoln Post Office Directory of the time, published every second year, listed William's occupation as insurance agent and by 1903 the couple had moved along Vernon Street to No. 5, where they lived until at least 1907.

By 1909 their address was published as No. 57 Cranwell Street – the scene of William's drunken demands for entry – four streets parallel to Vernon Street and only a mile from Lincoln town centre. From 1907 William's occupation was listed simply as 'agent', but after 1910 the name of MacBeth disappeared from the index of addresses for good.

Unfortunately, as he approached his 55th birthday, William was heading down to the lowest level of society, where the only succour for the needy and infirm was provided by the Lincoln workhouse, which had been established in 1740.

William was admitted in January 1910 and it is not only his age, listed as approximately 15 years out at 39, that raises an eyebrow. The Creed Register for Lincoln Workhouse, held at the Lincoln Archives, notes the 'name of informant' on William's entry records as simply 'prison warder'.

Workhouse historian Peter Higginbotham called on his experience to back the suspicion that William may have spent a short spell in gaol around this time, most likely for his failure to pay his 10 shilling fine for drunkenness the month before.

The Creed Register discloses that William was discharged from Lincoln Workhouse on June 3 1911, 18 months after he first entered, but he was back behind its gates within seven days. This time, on June 10 1911, the records reveal he was 'brought in by police'.

It is difficult to escape the conclusion, particularly on the back of evidence from later workhouse records, that law officers were fulfilling a social work function by directing William to a more suitable environment, particularly if alcoholism had taken its grip.

William's personal decline appears marked and it is clear he could not look to his equally troubled second wife for support. Sarah Ann had admitted herself into Lincoln Workhouse on December 6 1910 and was discharged six months later on May 12 1911 (a month before William, which may have prompted her husband to return to the outside world).

The relationship was clearly not loveless and at least once in August 1912 Sarah Ann made an unsuccessful attempt to secure her husband's release. The Lincoln Workhouse minutes from August 6 noted: "Mrs MacBeth appeared before the board and asked for her husband, who is a certified imbecile, to be discharged from the workhouse into her care and the question was deferred for a report by Dr McFarland upon MacBeth's state of mind."

A fortnight later, on August 20, the minutes noted a second request, adding: "Mrs MacBeth...asked for her husband to be discharged from the Imbecile Ward into her care and it was agreed to allow Mrs MacBeth to take her husband if the Medical Officer would certify him as fit to be discharged from the Imbecile Ward."

The Mental Deficiency Act of 1913 officially defined four grades of mental defect, listing an imbecile as someone "incapable of managing themselves or their affairs." The term 'imbecile' originally came from French via Latin, where it was defined similarly to the condition we now recognise as Alzheimer's, a dementia in which sufferers mentally regress towards childhood.

Certainly, the minutes of the Lincoln Workhouse indicate the inhabitants of the imbecile ward could not have been treated less like Oliver Twist. The notes of May 15 1915, for example, sympathetically recorded: "The clerk was directed to invite tenders for taking the imbeciles for drives during the summer months, as in previous years."

Sarah Ann gravitated back to Bradford some time after 1911, confirmed by the Lincoln Workhouse minutes from March 30 1915. They revealed: "A letter was read from the Bradford Union (workhouse) alleging the settlement of Sarah Ann MacBeth, aged 56, to be in this union. The clerk reported that her husband had been an inmate of this workhouse for several years and the settlement was accepted."

In effect, Bradford turned Sarah Ann over to the workhouse where she had previously spent some time, claiming Lincoln was responsible for her care because her husband was a long-term resident there, which was acknowledged.

Unfortunately, the creed register does not recall how long Sarah Ann spent under the same roof as her husband, but it would not have been much beyond two years, as William died in the infirmary at the Lincoln Workhouse on Sunday July 15 1917. The official cause of death was "cerebral softening", which indicates a stroke or brain haemorrhage, probably relating to his mental state or alcoholism.

His death certificate recorded his age at 46 (it should have been 61), his previous address as No. 2 Vernon Street (he lived at Nos 5 and 34) and his occupation as commercial traveller. The informant of his death on the certificate was Jesse E. White, the acting master of the Union Workhouse, Lincoln.

Sarah Ann was at least granted greater longevity of life, despite her equally tragic circumstances. She lived until June 1939, her age given in the records as 56 when she died in the Bowling Park Institution, one of the Bradford workhouses.

The Lincoln Workhouse has long gone. The workhouse system was abolished in 1930 and although the Burton Road site was used as an old folks' home for more than three decades it was demolished in 1965. However, little has changed in the physical appearance of Vernon Street and Cranwell Street beyond the ubiquitous modern-day sight of cars parked bumper to bumper down the length of each road.

Unsurprisingly, William was buried without ceremony on July 19 1917, four days after his death. The rights to plot A2582 where he lies were never privately purchased, which means they were owned by the council and he was given a pauper's burial. He rests on top of a total stranger, a Catherine Brumby, buried two decades before his death.

The man who helped give birth to a club that spawned Meiklejohn, Morton and McPhail, Woodburn, Waddell and Young, Baxter, Greig and McCoist, lay until recently in that pitiful, indistinct plot, under a holly bush in the forgotten fringes of the burial ground, unmarked and unrecognised behind a neatly tended resting place to a William Edward Kirkby, who died in September 1694, aged 26.

Back in 2008, the skilled assistance of cemetery staff and their dog-eared burial chart over a century old were required to even find the site where William was buried – and it was no treasure hunt.

Picking a way back on the path, fine views are afforded up to Lincoln Cathedral, which dominates the horizon for miles around in this flat corner of England. However, Rangers fans came to honour their own towering figure.

Shortly after The Gallant Pioneers was first published a group of Rangers fans launched a public appeal to purchase a 50 year lease from Lincoln Council and within days fans had rallied and sufficient funds had been pledged for the burial plot and a handsome stone.

In July 2010 a group of 30 gathered at Canwick Road Cemetery in remembrance of William, with a touching tribute to the founding father paid in the local press, as well as to those who had made the 300 mile trip from the west of Scotland.

Fan John McCrae said: "Only some of the group had met before, not everyone knew each other. We ranged in age from our twenties to our sixties. We varied in background, in hobbies, in upbringing. But from the first minute, there was a bonding, a kinship, a oneness. We all shared the same glowing pride at being there.

"Flowers were laid, we chatted. I stood around, trying not to feel like some sort of idiot, having cried. Men don't cry, do they? Well, almost every one of the bears there did."

For William, their tears were justified.

10

THE FA CUP – FROM FIRST TO LAST

The FA Cup has attracted many sponsors in recent years, but the commercial worth of the tournament remained unexploited throughout the latter half of the 19th century.

If English football bosses sought financial inspiration from the raucous exploits of the Rangers squad in the only season in which they participated, back in 1886–87, they could surely have attracted a bidding war for competition rights between Alka Seltzer and Andrew's Liver Salts.

These were more innocent times (thankfully for Rangers, that also included the media) as they kicked off their campaign at Everton amid accusations of over-drinking and ended it at the semi-final stages against Aston Villa at Crewe surrounded by allegations of over-eating.

The Football Association Challenge Cup has enjoyed a long and distinguished history from its first season in 1871–72, when 15 clubs set out to win a competition that quickly developed into the most democratic in world football, where village green teams can still kick-start a campaign in August and dream of playing at Wembley against Manchester United the following May.

Queen's Park were among the first competitors, alongside others whose names reflected the public school roots of the tournament, not to mention its southern bias – the Spiders and Donington Grammar

School were the only sides who came from north of Hertfordshire that first season.

The first FA Cup trophy cost £20 and Queen's Park contributed a guinea to its purchase, a staggering sum for a club whose annual turnover at the time was no more than £6.

Wanderers Football Club, based near Epping Forest, won the first tournament against the Royal Engineers 1–0 at The Oval, but only after Queen's Park scratched their semi-final replay.

In a portent for the zeal with which football would soon be greeted in Glasgow, the inhabitants of the city raised a public subscription to cover the cost of sending the Spiders to London to face the Wanderers, but they could not afford to stay in the capital for a second match and returned home unbowed and unbeaten.

In addition to their failure to see through to the end their first FA Cup campaign, there would be other losers as a result of their participation in the competition – keen students of association football in the Borders.

Queen's Park were forced to abandon a week-long tour of the Tweed, where they had promised to undertake their fine missionary work in the towns and villages, in order to play in the FA Cup competition. They never did make their visit and association football lost out to the oval ball game in the affections of a public in an area where the culture of rugby remains strongest still.

In the beginning of the game, all British clubs were eligible for membership of the Football Association, their calling card for the FA Cup, so it was no surprise to see sides such as Queen's Park from Scotland and the Druids and Chirk from Wales lining up against sides from the counties and shires of England.

However, for the most part Scottish club sides resisted the temptation to turn out in the first decade or so of the competition, particularly as cost was such a significant factor. Indeed, throughout the 1870s Queen's Park regularly received byes to the latter stages of the competition in a bid to keep their expenses low, but either scratched or withdrew as the financial realities restricted their ability to travel.

The FA, responding to the increased popularity of the tournament, particularly in the north of England, began to organise ties on a geographical basis as the 1870s gave way to the 1880s and suddenly Queen's Park returned to the fore to an English audience.

In 1884 and 1885 they reached the final, only to lose narrowly on each occasion to Blackburn Rovers. Until that point, Queen's Park were the only Scottish team to have made significant strides in the FA Cup but, perhaps buoyed by the success of the Spiders, by the third round of the 1886–87 competition there were four Scottish teams who had won through from an original entry of 126 clubs – Partick Thistle, Renton, Cowlairs and Rangers.

In actual fact, the Rangers name had been represented in the FA Cup as early as 1880, when they advanced to the third round before being humbled 6–0 at The Oval by the 1875 tournament winners, the Royal Engineers, but the information is misleading.

The Rangers team who competed in 1880 and 1881 were an English outfit who included in their ranks an F.J. Wall, who would later become secretary of the Football Association. He seemed none too disheartened to be on the end of such a heavy defeat, particularly against such illustrious opponents as the Royal Engineers, and later admitted fortifying himself for the game "with a splendid rump steak for lunch."

It was not – at that stage anyway – the state of the pre-match meal that concerned the Rangers as they prepared for their first game in the competition against Everton on Saturday 30 October 1886, but the demon drink.

Excitement must have been high among Rangers players during the 1886–87 season at the prospect of playing in the FA Cup as they boarded the train at Glasgow, bound for a game in a competition in which they had only once before come close to competing.

Rangers had decided to take up membership of the Football Association at a committee meeting in June 1885 and Walter Crichton, who would soon be named honorary secretary of the club, was listed as its delegate to the FA.

Subsequently, Rangers were drawn to face Rawtenstall in the first round of the Cup, but Rangers refused the match on the basis that the Lancashire club had paid professionals among their ranks of registered players.

Professionalism had finally been legalised within the English game at a meeting of clubs in July 1885, but with strict conditions for participation in the FA Cup, including birth and residence criteria, with all players also subject to annual registration demands.

Of course, at this stage the payment of players in Scotland was still a strict taboo – publicly at least – and the SFA frowned upon games played against English teams who knowingly employed professionals.

The FA fined Rangers 10 shillings 'for infringement of rules', although stopped short of telling the Kinning Park committee which rule had been broken. Rawtenstall were subsequently banned from the competition after playing out a 3–3 draw against near neighbours Bolton in the next round, apparently for breaches of the strict FA conditions in their cup competition relating to the employment of professionals.

Tensions had eased slightly 12 months later as Rangers arrived in Liverpool in high spirits for a game against the underdogs of Everton.

The previous campaign had been a miserable one for the Kinning Park regulars, with an early exit from the Scottish Cup at the hands of Clyde following a 1–0 defeat and an indifferent series of results against often mediocre opposition. Tom Vallance, who had just been returned for his third year as president, had promised three trophies at the start of the season – the Scottish Cup, the FA Cup and the Charity Cup.

However, the club's hopes of winning silverware proved as elusive as their bid to turn a profit – Rangers lost £90 that season, mostly as a result of their early Scottish Cup exit, although the Kinning Park bank book still held funds of almost £130.

Still, the Scottish Athletic Journal could not contain its glee as it threatened to present Vallance with three teacups to parade to members at the club's next annual general meeting.

The start of season 1886–87 promised better to come, despite the spectre of relocation from Kinning Park hanging over the club as its lease on its third ground neared its end, but the squad would not be fortified with the Assam blends so familiar to Vallance following his time in India.

There was certainly mischief in mind when Rangers travelled to Merseyside the evening before the game against Everton, who had been knocked out of the FA Cup the previous season 3–0 by Partick Thistle.

The Kinning Park squad arrived in Liverpool the worse for wear for a game in which they were overwhelming favourites. These days, the former Compton Hotel in the city's Church Street houses a branch of Marks and Spencer, but it was bed and not bargains on the mind of the bedraggled Rangers squad as they trooped in there on the morning of the game after being thrown out of their original digs.

The columnist 'Lancashire Chat' noted matter-of-factly in the Scottish Umpire of November 2 1886: "The Rangers arrived (in Liverpool) soon after midnight and roused the ire of the hotel proprietor in their night revels. In fact, the Rangers squad were bundled out bag and baggage without breakfast and took up their quarters at the Compton Hotel... They dressed at the hotel and the game was started pretty punctually."

In the 21st century the media would enjoy a field day with the story, but in those more innocent times observers of the fledgling football scene were less inclined to saddle up on moral high horses at a lack of professionalism among players who were entirely amateur, or purported to be so.

Historically, the Victorian era has been regarded as one of austerity and respect for place and position but, in truth, anti-social behaviour was never far from the fore in the Scottish game, which is hardly surprising when by 1890 it was estimated that one third of the total national revenue in Britain came from alcohol.

In 1872, the year of Rangers' formation, 54,446 people in Glasgow were apprehended by police for being drunk, incapable and disorderly. Social commentator Sir John Hammerton painted a vivid and horrifying picture of a drink-soaked society which, sadly, does not appear to have improved much in the century since his publication of 'Books and Myself'.

He wrote: "In 1889 Glasgow was probably the most drink-sodden city in Great Britain. The Trongate and Argyle Street, and worst of all the High Street, were scenes of disgusting debauchery, almost incredible today.

"Many of the younger generation thought it manly to get 'paralytic' and 'dead to the world'; at least on Saturday there was lots of tipsy rowdyism in the genteel promenade in Sauchiehall Street, but nothing to compare to the degrading spectacle of the other thoroughfares, where there were drunken brawls at every corner and a high proportion of the passers-by were reeling drunk; at the corners of the darker side streets the reek of vomit befouled the evening air, never very salubrious. Jollity was everywhere absent: sheer loathsome, swinish inebriation prevailed."

Football then, as now, mirrored society and Rangers players occasionally let themselves down. In March 1883, a columnist in the Scottish Athletic Journal commented: "High jinks in hotels by football teams are becoming such a nuisance that something must be done to put an end to the gross misconduct which goes on.

"I was witness to a ruffianly trick in the Athole Arms on Saturday night. A fellow – I will call him nothing less – as a waiter passed with a tray full of valuable crystal deliberately kicked the bottom of the tray and broke a dozen of the wine glasses to atoms. In the crowd he escaped notice, but the Rangers will, of course, have to pay for the damage. I cannot see any fun in a low act of this kind."

Of course, Rangers were not alone in drawing criticism for their alcohol related antics on and off the field. Dumbarton won the Scottish Cup after a replay in 1883, for instance, but only after it had been hinted by football columnist 'Rover' in the Lennox Herald that one or two of their players had partaken of whisky before the first match, which finished 2–2.

After the second game, a 2–1 win over arch rivals Vale of Leven, a group of Dumbarton players headed for a few days' celebration at Loch Lomond with assorted wives, partners and pals. Returning home on two wagonettes on the Monday and "boldened by excessive refreshments" they took no time to remind locals of the weekend scoreline as they lurched through Vale of Leven. Predictably, a rammy ensued, during which two buckets of slaughterhouse blood were thrown over the Dumbarton party.

Public houses were regularly used as changing rooms for teams, particularly in Ayrshire, and while the Highlands are synonymous with hospitality, it was another matter in Angus as Forfar treated their players to a half bottle of whisky and a bottle of port after every game, while visitors were restricted to a pie and a pint in 1890.

One club, the Pilgrims, vowed never to visit Dundee again after the Strathmore club tried to entertain them after a game on the derisory sum of only five shillings and sixpence. Reporting on the Pilgrims' point of view, the Scottish Athletic Journal lamented: "Can one blame them?"

Not even Queen's Park, the grand standard-bearers of the time, could escape the negative influence of alcohol when two players were fined 20 shillings each by Nottingham magistrates for being drunk and disorderly after a match in the town in January 1878.

For the non-professional Scots, trips to England generally took place at holiday times, with New Year and Easter particular favourites. Football often came a poor second to the festivities and the attitude of the press was as schizophrenic as the nation's relationship with alcohol itself.

Therefore, the Scottish Athletic Journal reasoned early in 1885 that "a New Year holiday trip does not come every day and youthful blood must have its fling…the honour and glory of Scottish football is cast to the winds and the present is only remembered."

This was a complete reversal from its stern editorial two years previously when it noted: "Generally, when any of our association teams go to England they run riot with everything and everybody they come across. They stick at nothing, not even dressing themselves in policeman's clothes and running pantomime-like through the streets with roasts of beef not of their own. This was what the frolics of one of our leading teams consisted of when in Manchester last Christmas."

By sheer coincidence, Rangers were in Lancashire at that time for a game against local club Darwen.

In these days of Premier League billions it is perhaps surprising to learn that Rangers were strong favourites in the first round against Everton, even though the home side had recently won the Liverpool Cup and had been undefeated all season.

In a burst of patriotism, the Scottish Umpire declared in its preview to the game: "Dobson, Farmer and Gibson are not eligible [for Everton]. And without them they have not much chance of winning… without the three named, Everton cannot possibly defeat a decent team of the Rangers."

The match was played at Anfield and the Scottish Umpire remarked that the ground was not a very good one, particularly as it was situated a couple of miles from the nearest railway station. However, football in Liverpool at that stage was, according to the newspaper, "leaping and bounding".

Rangers were handed the tie before kick-off – unsurprisingly, delayed 15 minutes to give the players time to arrive at the ground after shaking off their excesses – when Everton 'scratched' the tie to give their three ineligible players the chance to play and make the encounter more competitive.

The game almost did not start as a result of a morning deluge that had turned the playing surface into a mudbath, but the skies cleared to blue by lunchtime and soon the crowds were rolling up in their thousands.

The match report from the Liverpool Courier gives an idea of how established Rangers had become in the 14 years since the club's pioneers had first taken to the game at Flesher's Haugh.

The Courier reported: "The visit of the Glasgow team to the popular Anfield enclosure on Saturday excited such a large amount of interest that there could not have been less than 6,000 persons present to witness the play.

"Not only were the capacious stands well filled but every available point of vantage was early taken possession of, so long before the game commenced the enclosure presented an animated scene. The game was undoubtedly one of the best that has been witnessed on the Anfield ground during the present season.

"It was fully a quarter of an hour after the advertised time before the teams put in an appearance. When they did so the Rangers, by their fine physique, gained many friends, but this could not diminish confidence in the ability of the Evertonians to uphold the credit of the district."

Rangers won the game courtesy of a one-yard tap-in from striker Charlie Heggie after 20 minutes. Everton fought valiantly to get back into the game, but Rangers held out and even had a second goal disallowed late on.

In the Scottish Umpire, 'Lancashire Chat' later recalled: "Tuck McIntyre was in a happy mood and seemed to enjoy himself, whether knocking an opponent over or kicking the ball. [Afterwards] the Rangers drove off to the Compton and [then] returned to the Everton headquarters, where a pleasant evening was spent.

"The Glasgow men were accompanied by about half a dozen of their supporters and Hugh McIntyre came down to see his old comrades perform. Tom Vallance made a pretty speech, the remarks of the handsome international being received with great cheering. The smoking concerts have evidently improved the vocal attainments of the team and [John] Muir made a very successful debut at Everton. The Liverpool club's vice-president turned out in full force to welcome the Rangers, who left well pleased with their outing."

The club's subsequent early round cup ties, all played at Kinning Park, were to prove less eventful than the trip to Liverpool. Three weeks after the defeat of Everton another English outfit, Church, were put to the sword in a 2–1 victory, with two goals from Matt Lawrie, a dribbling winger who had been signed from Cessnockbank in the summer of 1884.

Lawrie found the net again on December 4 when Springburn side Cowlairs were knocked out 3–2 at Kinning Park, with Bob Fraser and Matt Peacock also scoring for the Light Blues. Rangers were guaranteed to be playing FA Cup football into 1887 when they received a bye in the fourth round and were drawn, again at home, to Lincoln on January 29.

On the face of it, the 3–0 victory over the English side that set the Light Blues up for a quarter-final crack at Old Westminsters seemed academic.

A swirling wind made playing conditions difficult at Kinning Park, but Rangers scored twice in the first half courtesy of strikes from Fraser and new boy Joe Lindsay. He was a Scotland forward who had previously played at Dumbarton and had been tempted to Kinning Park during the festive period of 1886 as it was closer to his workplace in Govan.

The third goal from Peacock sealed a comfortable win and Donald Gow so impressed Lincoln with his performance in defence that he was immediately offered a weekly wage of £2 10 shillings, a king's ransom at the time, to move south.

Gow refused the offer, but the English press were far from happy at the presence of Lindsay in the side and chided the amateur Rangers for alleged professionalism, which was still a strict no-no in the Scottish game under the terms of the SFA, even in the FA Cup.

The Midland Athlete newspaper bemoaned the fact that Lincoln City had to meet "a team called Glasgow Rangers, but an eleven that would never be allowed to compete for the Scottish Cup under that name… the Rangers have called in extraneous aid for their national cup ties."

An editorial in the Scottish Umpire hit back in a fit of nationalist pique: "The Light Blues played on the occasion referred to a team that could, if strong enough, have done duty in the Scottish ties without let or hindrance. Be sure of your fact, friend Athlete, before you launch out. It is awkward to be caught on the hop."

Nevertheless, the Midland Athlete had shone the spotlight on an issue that was becoming an increasing concern in the Scottish game, which would not embrace professionalism until the AGM of the SFA in 1893, eight years after England.

Of course, payment of players had been around even before then, with Glasgow shipyard worker James Lang acknowledged as the first professional player in the history of the game when he left Clydesdale and accepted a financial offer to turn out for Sheffield Wednesday in 1876. Lang literally had one eye on a moneymaking opportunity – he lost the other in a shipyard accident but somehow managed to keep his handicap hidden from his new employers.

In his latter years, Lang was a regular in the main stand at Ibrox and delighted matchday regulars with details of his ground-breaking claim to fame.

The bountiful orchards of Scotland yielded a harvest of impressive players ripe for export over the border. Many of them were from the industrial heartlands of the central belt and hungry to advance up the economic ladder, but there were still those who were attracted to the game as a leisure pursuit and could afford to adopt a more laid-back attitude to otherwise tempting inducements.

Pollokshields Athletic forward Frank Shaw, for example, delayed replying to an offer in 1884 of a handsome salary of £120 a year from English club Accrington after he had come to their attention at an earlier game. He wrote in reply that he could not give the matter his full attention until "my return from a fortnight's cruise among the Western Isles, on my yacht."

English clubs quickly began to burst at the seams with the 'Scots professors', skilled players from north of the border who played and educated their new paymasters with all the zeal of tartan missionaries. The last time England had seen such an invasion of Scots was in the previous century when the Jacobite forces of Charles Edward Stuart marched as far south as Derby. This time, however, the Scots did not turn back, but stayed on and conquered, spreading their influence further across the country.

The Liverpool team established by former Everton landlord Houlding, for example, kicked-off its first league campaign in 1893 with 10 Scots in its line up.

The first goal scored in English League football was by a Scot, Jack Gordon, who would never have felt homesick at Preston North End. The greatest-ever Preston team, known as the Invincibles, won the first English League title (the brainchild of Perthshire draper William McGregor, the grand patriarch of Aston Villa) in 1888–89 without losing a match, retained the championship the following season and also won the FA Cup in 1889 without conceding a goal.

The spine of their great team was Scottish, including brothers Nick and Jimmy Ross and internationals David Russell, John Gordon and George Drummond, while former Ranger Sam Thomson also played for the club. Scots also dominated in Sunderland's 'Team of all Talents', who won the English title in 1892, 1893 and 1895 and were even founded by a Scot, teacher James Allan, in 1880.

Undoubtedly, Rangers suffered at the hands – and wallets – of the English clubs, who set up raiding parties that would have been the envy of any 16th-century border reiver.

First to go in 1880 was Scottish international Hugh McIntyre, older brother of Tuck and a member of the Cup Final team of 1879, who quit for Blackburn Rovers after they bought him a pub in the town. He went on to win three FA Cup-winners' medals in successive seasons with his new side in 1884, 1885 and 1886.

He was followed to the Lancashire club by founding father Peter Campbell and, although he played several times for Blackburn, he never moved to the area. Rangers lost another stalwart of the 1879 team, William Struthers, who signed for Bolton Wanderers in 1881, quickly followed to the same club by halfback John Christie, no doubt lured by the promise of riches extolled by his former team-mate.

The finger lingered around the influence of Hugh McIntyre, in particular, in convincing young Scots to ply their trade in the south because then, as now, there were lucrative finders' fees up for grabs.

Agents were despised and routinely beaten up and one GL Harrison from Nottingham had cause to wish he had never wandered down the Copland Road on August 1 1889, when he arrived in Glasgow in a bid to lure defender John Hendry, an early darling of the Light Blues legions, south of the border.

Harrison's plan was cunning, as he roped in then Scotland striker Jimmy Oswald (who later went on to play for Rangers) to accompany him to Ibrox on the promise of a £5 commission if they persuaded Hendry south.

They had already trawled the player's home town of Uddingston in a vain bid to track him down, but the fear of losing their top talents was so strong among many of the leading Scots clubs, including Rangers, that they regularly formed vigilance committees to keep their non-professionals (in theory at least) away from the paid ranks of the English game.

Word quickly spread around Ibrox, which was hosting an amateur sports that Thursday evening, of the danger in their midst. Panic ensued and Hendry was quickly shepherded away from the dangerous suitors while Oswald, who played for Notts County, was led to safety, surviving the baying mob only because of his standing in the game and the presence of a team from the Rangers committee around him.

Harrison was not so lucky as he attempted to sneak from the ground and down Copland Road, only to be accosted by two irate Bears. The full story then unfolded in the Scottish Sport, filed by 'an eye witness' with more than a hint of eager pleasure.

"You are looking for someone?" politely enquired the smallest of the two, as they came up with their prey.

"No-no," replied the tall, handsome swell – for with all his audacity he looked a swell – but he did so with a look and hesitancy which identified him at once.

"We were told you were looking for someone," insisted the sly, self-possessed questioner.

"Oh, no. There…there must be some mistake."

"Were you not wishing to see John Hendry of the Rangers?"

An enquiring glance at his tormentors and a faltering "no" was the reply.

Then the second party spoke, but it was aside, and as if to his companion. "What's the use o' makin' a clown o' me. I thocht it was a good thing. I'll awa' back to Oswald," and he cast a withering look at his apparently perplexed companion.

The trick had fairly trapped the agent however, for in answer to a last attempt to draw him, his wily inquisitor was at length assured, in a half apologetic tone, that he did want to see Hendry and that he had at first denied his real mission because of the fear he had of the club's supporters, whose attentions were evidently not of the most reassuring.

"Well, this is Hendry," said the sly one, after a little more cross questioning, and pointing to his companion who, I need hardly say, was only a cruel impersonator playing a part in the interests of his club.

The "swell" became reassured, looked more like his audacious self, and prepared to do business.

"Do you want me to go to England?" inquired the bogus Hendry after being duly introduced and informed of the terms. "Yes, I want you to go to England."

"Are you perfectly sure you want me to go to England?"

"Yes."

"Well, take that!" and before anyone could say Jack Robinson the seducer was sent sprawling on the ground with a lick which could scarcely be described as a baby-duster.

"The elongated representative of the ascendant element in English football was not long in getting to his feet, but there was no fight in him. He took to his heels and, as if pursued by an evil spirit, careered down the road at the most undignified speed imaginable. Unfortunately for him, a crowd of unsympathetic Rangers were coming up the road as he was frantically tearing down and they, taking the situation at a glance, cruelly intercepted him and he was once more in the remorseless hands of the Philistines.

"There is no use in prolonging the sequel; sufficient to say that, after a good bit of running in as earnest an obstacle race as was ever ran, he reached Princes Street, about half a mile away, where he was mercifully taken in by a young Samaritan married couple, and allowed to sufficiently recover from his baptism of fright and fists to be able to be sent to his hotel [St Enoch's] in a cab.

"When I saw the bold adventurer lying low upon a couch, blanched, speechless, and sick unto death, with several well known members of the Rangers holding his low lying head, and timing his quick beating pulse, I did think that the way of transgressors is hard. Probably GL Harrison will not again put his prominent features within a mile of Ibrox Park on a similar errand."

The Scottish Referee was more sympathetic to Harrison's plight, if not his career choice: "We have only one opinion of the treatment which was extended to a professional agent at Ibrox on Thursday night," it thundered.

"Namely, that it was a dastardly and brutal assault. If a man has legitimate business and indulges in that business legitimately it is monstrous that he should not only be interfered with, but maltreated in such a way that serious results to his physical welfare are likely to accrue.

"The business of a professional football agent is a perfectly legitimate one and though we have not the slightest admiration either for the vocation or those who follow it, the law is with it and the law must be respected. The reflection cast on the Rangers Football Club by the assault is a most serious and damaging one."

Meanwhile, back in the FA Cup John Wallace Mackay's influence may have been diluted as Rangers approached the latter stages of the competition almost a year after his departure from the club, but they were still far from a team of choirboys – and certainly not, like the players from Old Westminsters, former public schoolboys.

The Londoners pitched up at Kinning Park for the quarter-final tie in February 1887 in an attempt to emulate at least their success of the previous year, when they had reached the semi-final of the FA Cup before being humbled 6– 0 by West Bromwich Albion.

Rangers were the sole Scottish representatives left standing in the last eight, as favourites Preston North End were also joined by West Brom, Darwen, Notts County, Aston Villa and Old Caruthians.

Old Westminsters may have been former pupils of Westminster College in the capital, but they were no slouches at football and went into the game against the Light Blues on the back of decent form, which had seen them lose only two of their 19 games played that season.

However, Rangers put in one of their best performances of the season and ran out 5–1 winners. The crowd was an impressive 6,000 ("the largest seen inside the ground for some considerable time" according to the Scottish Umpire), although only four goalscorers were recorded – Pat Lafferty, Matt Lawrie, Bob Fraser and Joe Lindsay.

As winter prepared to give way to spring, the progress of Rangers into the last four of the FA Cup was being recognised by observers beyond the potential for a Scottish side to lift the greatest prize in the British game for the first time.

A move from Kinning Park to their new ground at Ibrox in the coming August was agreed by Rangers at a special meeting of members on February 16. A seven-year lease, with a break available after three years, was signed for a site of "five or six acres" at the Copeland (sic) Road end of Paisley Road, with £750 being committed to building a pavilion, stand and enclosure, with further terracing taking the capacity of the new ground to around 15,000.

The respect Rangers were winning as they progressed to the latter stages of the FA Cup was also being viewed as a vital marketing aid to enhance the club's finances, as well as its reputation. Not only were they looking to attract glamour sides north for showpiece friendlies to boost gate receipts at their new home, but such matches would also attract a new generation of fans to support the now established Light Blues at their state-of-the-art ground.

As it reflected on Rangers' march to the semi-final, the Scottish Athletic Journal noted: "They will require several big attractions for the first two or three weeks of their tenancy of the new ground to allow the people to become acquainted with the new order of things.

"If they make a good appearance now, such English matches as they may desire will be all the more easily arranged. It will thus be seen that the club is looking to its financial standing as well as its reputation. It will be a proud moment for the Rangers if they succeed in getting so far as the final for the English Cup. Stranger things have happened."

Aston Villa, like Rangers, had reached the semi-final of the competition for the first time that season and were under the management of a Scot, Glaswegian George Ramsay (he is credited with helping establish the lion rampant on the Villa badge, where it still roars to this day, and he also dedicated a staggering 59 years of his life to the club, leading them to six championships and six FA Cup final successes).

Villa were given an immediate advantage by the FA's decision to play the game at Nantwich Road in Crewe, meaning Rangers had to travel 200 miles – four times the distance of their rivals – to fulfil the fixture. For their part, the FA believed playing the game at a ground no more than a stone's throw from a railway station that served Scotland and the Midlands was an appropriate compromise.

Ramsay took his players to Droitwich to prepare for the game, a ploy which was virtually unheard of in those days, and they went through a vigorous regime of training and salt baths to ensure they were in the pink for the biggest game in their history.

Their star man was skipper and forward Archie Hunter, another Scot who started his career with Third Lanark and Ayr Thistle before moving south. Tragically, he suffered a heart attack in a League game against Everton only three years later and died in 1894, aged just 35.

Rangers arrived in Crewe at 9.30pm the night before the game in the company of former player Hugh McIntyre, who had met them earlier at Preston. Rangers had previously doled out Villa's record defeat, 7–1 back in April 1882, but history was not to favour a repeat.

The clubs shared the same hotel across the street from the ground, the Royal, and a crowd of 10,000 turned out to watch the tie, the majority of them from the Midlands and bearing cards in the Birmingham club's colours of chocolate and light blue, reading 'Play up Villa!'

The sides, who changed at the hotel, took to the field and Hunter opened the scoring after only 13 minutes, maintaining a record he would continue throughout the competition of scoring in every round.

However, Lafferty equalised on 34 minutes and Rangers twice went close to adding to their tally, although Villa were always dangerous on the break against a Rangers defence that was, according to the Scottish Umpire, "not being of the best."

The Umpire's reporter, writing under the name 'Forward', had previously tipped Rangers to win through to the final, but his faith proved unfounded and his fearless punditry was reduced in the second half to barely concealed disgust over the performance of goalkeeper Willie Chalmers, who had lunched heartily with McIntyre before the match and was beginning to feel the effects.

'Forward' wrote: "The Rangers defence was much better than it had been in the first half, so far as the backs were concerned, but Chalmers was in very poor trim. A shot was sent across by Hodgetts and though Chalmers had plenty of time to get it away he just touched it along the ground, and Albert Brown dashed it through."

Hunter added his second near the end to secure his side's 3–1 victory and 'Forward' concluded: "They [Villa] played a much better game than the Rangers, who were not so good as I expected. Chalmers was the worst of the lot and seemed very nervous on the three occasions, besides the one that ended so fatally... The weak points of the Rangers were in deficient combination and dash of the forwards, rather weak defence and downright poor goalkeeping."

It was scant consolation that Rangers, on paper at least, were the only amateur representatives in the last four.

Villa's victory, added to a shock 3–1 semi-final win for their near neighbours West Brom over the mighty Preston North End, sent the Midlands into meltdown.

The Scottish Umpire revealed that: "when the results were made known, the Midlands went about delirious, and many got fou. Poetry cobblers were commissioned to write paeans in praise of the respective champions. The Villa almost went off their heads on Saturday night, especially when they heard of the Albion victory. They think they can now win, but did not favour their chances against North End."

Villa's confidence was not misplaced, as they defeated West Brom 2–0 in the final at the Kennington Oval on April 2 in front of more than 15,000 fans.

For Rangers, the recriminations continued for several weeks after the semi-final defeat and the Scottish Umpire noted: "From all accounts, Chalmers cracked his reputation by his Crewe performance. Was it that lunch that did it?"

It added: "The Rangers…can't get over their dismissal and the number of 'ifs' they have uttered would fill our columns from end to end. Let them forget the past and prepare for the future."

It was easier said than done for Chalmers, who was ditched by the club before March even came to an end, much to the disgust of the Scottish Athletic Journal, who finger-wagged: "The Rangers have lost the services of Chalmers, who has certainly not been very well treated by the club. It is most unfair to blame him for the loss of the Aston Villa tie… Chalmers has done good service during three years."

A fortnight earlier the Journal's English football writer, who penned his articles under the byline 'Rab', was less forgiving as he mischievously suggested a more sinister motive behind Chalmers' poor form.

He wrote: "I have it on the authority of a brother scribe, who was at Crewe seeing the semi-final, that the Rangers would have drawn with the Aston Villa but for the wretched goalkeeping of Chalmers. He says it was vicious such, in fact, as might have been expected from a novice. Chalmers got badly chaffed by the spectators, some even hinting that he had sold the match. Altogether his lot was not a happy one. The Villa were exceedingly lucky in their scores and, but for Chalmers, there was not much difference between them and the Rangers."

John Allan, in his jubilee history of the club, cut straight to it: "William was an excellent trencherman and Hugh McIntyre confessed, with some self-reproach, that it was he who, in a playful spirit, acted as agent to the goalkeeper's little debauch."

Rangers and Chalmers did kiss and make up – he had returned to the club by the start of the following season, though could have been forgiven for wishing he had stayed away as Preston North End rattled eight goals past him to mark the opening of the new Ibrox Park.

However, even that was not as bad as the 10–2 defeat Rangers suffered at snow-covered Kinning Park in February 1886 against Airdrie. That scoreline still stands as the Light Blues' heaviest defeat and Chalmers was also slated after that one for refusing to dive around his icy goalmouth.

Rangers' relationship with the FA Cup ended for good at the end of the 1886–87 season as the SFA finally forbade its clubs from competing in the cup south of the border. Their reasons were straightforward and justified: not only did their members' appearances in the FA Cup undermine their own Scottish Cup competition, they also ran the risk of losing control of football in their own backyard. It was inconceivable to the SFA that if two Scottish clubs met in the FA Cup and came to loggerheads, the association in London could argue for the right to resolve the dispute.

The Scottish Athletic Journal had argued as much in a stern editorial when it said: "It does rile us to see England thus claiming a jurisdiction over Scotland… How can the SFA prevent this assumption of a British jurisdiction by the English association? Easily enough. It only has to pass a rule at the coming annual meeting that no club under its control can take part in any cup competition, save that of the Scottish Association or one of its affiliated associations.

"At the same time, the Scottish clubs are to blame. What has the Queen's Park gained by competing for three consecutive seasons for the English Cup? Nothing, save disappointment and humiliation… the Rangers, with more than ordinary luck in the ballot, are now in the semi-final and were they even twice as good as they are they could not win the cup. If they do, they deserve a public banquet."

They never were so feted. However, Chalmers appears to have eaten on behalf of the whole team anyway.

FOOTBALL.—*Argill v. Clyde.*—A match was played between these two clubs on Tuesday evening, on Glasgow Green, and resulted in a draw. The game was very exciting, being played with great spirit by both sides. The Argill men pressed their opponents hard, and gave them hot work to keep the ball from being goaled. Players—Argill—M. M'Neill (captain), P. M'Neill, T. Vallance, W. M'Beth, J. Ryburn, A. Yuill, P. Campbell, W. Thomson, D. Smith (goal), J. Watson, D. Forrest. Clyde—J. Rankin (captain), D. Armstrong, A. Herriot, L. Herriot, W. Reid, R. Hunter (goal), H. Clunie, A. Gray, J. Clunie, J. Baird, D. Hill.

Allan key…the match report mentioned in John Allan's 'The Story of the Rangers' from the Herald of July 18 1873. The match was played three days earlier.

FOOTBALL.

Rangers (late Western) *v.* Clyde.—The return match between these two clubs was played on Saturday afternoon on the Glasgow Green. The ball was kicked off at 4.20, and on the elapse of 20 minutes the Rangers had made two goals, cleverly got by Mr. W. D. M'Beth. On time being called the Rangers had made seven goals, against one for the Clyde, made by A. Gray. The playing of the Rangers was greatly superior to that of their opponents, but Messrs. J. Rankin, A. Gray, and J. Baird played well to sustain the honour of the Clyde. The playing of Mr. W. D. M'Beth for the Rangers was most excellent and greatly admired, he having made five goals out of the total for the Rangers.

Glasgow News September 22 1873…we assert this match report is the first to ever mention the name of Rangers and provides strong evidence they had previously played under the name 'Western'.

Popular Football Players.—No. 20, Mr Wm. D. Macbeth.

The line drawing of William McBeath in 'The Chiel' from March 1885, discovered by Gordon Bell.

The line drawing was inspired by this photograph, discovered in August 2021.

Taken by the Collis studio in Torquay, it is the only photograph of William McBeath research has ever uncovered.

FOOTBALL.

WESTERN V. ROVERS.— A friendly football match was played between these two clubs on Saturday, on the South Side Park, the ground of the latter. When time was called, the match was proclaimed drawn—no goal being obtained by either side. The game was very keenly and evenly contested throughout, some good play being shown on both sides. The Rovers pressed their opponents rather hardly at the latter end of the game, although they failed in securing a goal.

We assert this match report of Western v Rovers, played at South Side Park (also known as Queen's Park) on September 13 1873 featured the team that would soon become Rangers.

G. GILLESPIE W.B. M⁵NEIL J.WATT S.RICKETTS
W. DUNLOP D.HILL T.VALLANCE P.CAMPBELL M.M⁵NEIL
J.WATSON A.MARSHALL

The Gallant Pioneers: The Rangers team that played in the Scottish Cup final in 1877. Back row (left to right): George Gillespie, William McNeil, James Watt, Sam Ricketts. Middle row (left to right): William Dunlop, David Hill, Tom Vallance, Peter Campbell, Moses McNeil. Front row (left to right): James Watson, Sandy Marshall.

Rangers played at Burnbank for a season between 1875-76. The pitches, of course, are long gone and now form a neighbourhood of tenements off Great Western Road. The Lansdowne UP Church still stands.

A view north from Park Quadrant circa 1867 shows Burnbank and, in the foreground, houses on what we know today as Woodlands Road.

The Marquis of Lorne, first honorary president of Rangers, before his wedding to Louise, daughter of Queen Victoria.

The late Heather Lang unveiled a plaque to her grandfather, Peter McNeil, and his friends at Glasgow Green in September 2009 watched by VIPs including Rangers legend Sandy Jardine.

Ibrox aristocracy: Heather Lang and her sister, Doreen Holland.

Iain McColl approached Glasgow City Council in 2006 with a plan to pay tribute to the Gallant Pioneers at Glasgow Green, leading to the unveiling three years later.

In the spring of 1872 four young boys, Moses McNeil, Peter McNeil, Peter Campbell and William McBeath left their rowing boat on the nearby River Clyde and upon these fields formed a football team.

This team was to be known as The Rangers Football Club It was their determination to succeed that led to The Rangers becoming one of the world's most famous clubs.

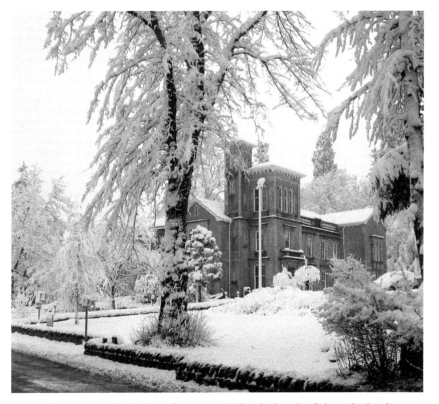

Belmore House, birthplace of Moses McNeil and where his father John lived with his family and worked as a master gardener under the Honeymans and McDonalds. It is now part of the Faslane Naval base.

ROSNEATH VILLAGE

The village of Rosneath, on the western shore of the Gare Loch, where Moses returned to live out his final years with sister, Isabella.

Rosneath old cemetery, burial place of Moses McNeil, who rests with sisters Isabella and Elizabeth and his brother-in-law, Captain Duncan Gray.

Waverley Hotel in Callander now and then.
It is where William McBeath was raised as a child.

'Honest' Tom…a man of fine sporting and business standing.

Taken too soon…Peter Campbell, Rangers founder and Scotland winger, was a pivotal player in the 1877 team.

POPULAR FOOTBALL PLAYERS.

NO. 2.—MR PETER CAMPBELL.

Only one photograph of Peter Campbell is believed to be in existence, from the 1877 team photoshoot. However, 'The Chiel' mourned his loss in a drowning tragedy with this portrait in October 1885.

RANGERS FOOTBALL CLUB.

Instituted 1872

GROUNDS—KINNING PARK.

THIS CLUB has been one of the most successful of our Scotch Football Clubs, having played on Glasgow Green as a Junior Club from 1872 to 1874. The rapid increase of Members necessitated the Committee to get Private Grounds, and being successsful in securing the Clydesdale's old Cricket Ground at Kinning Park, the Club at once placed itself in the first rank of Senior Clubs. The objects of the Club being the promotion of Football, all young gentlemen are eligible for election. The following is a list of the Office-Bearers :—

Hon. President.
J. S. STEWART, Esq., Ascog Hall.

President.	*Vice-President.*
R. B. KERR.	**A. HARKNESS.**
Hon.-Secretary.	*Hon.-Match Secretary.*
A. CAMPBELL, 85 Maxwell St.	**P. M'NEIL**, 21 and 23 Renfield St.
Hon.-Treasurer.	*Hon.-Assistant Treasurer.*
J. M. WATT, 4 Radnor Terrace.	**J. C. MARTIN**, 169 Berkeley St.

Captain.
THOMAS VALLANCE.

Directors.

GEO. GILLESPIE.	A. STEWART.	S. RICKETTS.	A. VALLANCE,
A. MARSHALL.	M. M'NEIL.	D. BROWN.	J. CAMPBELL.

SUBSCRIPTION FOR FIRST YEAR, 10s.; AFTERWARDS, 5s. ANNUALLY. HON.-MEMBER'S TICKETS 5s. Admits to Ground and Grand Stand.

Rangers were formed, beyond doubt, in 1872. Here is the evidence from one of the earliest SFA annuals.

George Goudie, saviour of Rangers, gifted the club £30 in 1883, shortly after becoming president, to prevent the fledgling club from going under.

H and P McNeil were prolific advertisers in the
Scottish press from the early 1870s until they closed
their doors for good in 1896.

The Evening Times captured the 'old contemptibles' in front of the Rowardennan
Hotel during their day out at Loch Lomond in September 1928, shortly before
Tom Vallance (seated front row, far right) jokingly revealed he was considering
a comeback.

IN MEMORY OF
PETER CAMPBELL
A FOUNDER OF RANGERS FOOTBALL CLUB

PETER CAMPBELL LEFT PENARTH PORT

ON THE 28TH JANUARY 1883

ABOARD THE ST. COLUMBA.

THE SHIP LADEN WITH A CARGO OF COAL

WENT DOWN IN A STORM IN THE BAY OF BISCAY.

ALL HANDS WERE LOST.

REMEMBERED ALWAYS

WASTAD YN BAROD

A memorial to Peter Campbell was unveiled at Penarth, South Wales, in July 2017. He left the port in January 1883 on board the St Columba with a cargo of coal, bound for India. The ship went down with all hands lost in the Bay of Biscay.

The inscription, in the Italian Gardens at Penarth, reads 'Always Ready' in Welsh, with the plaque fittingly made from local slate.

Author Gary Ralston and daughter, Jennifer, visited the memorial at Penarth during their summer holidays, July 2021.

Season   ~   1920 - 1921.

Directors.
Sir JOHN URE PRIMROSE, Bart., *Chairman.*
Ex-Bailie JOSEPH BUCHANAN, J.P.
Ex-Bailie DUNCAN GRAHAM, J.P.
WILLIAM CRAIG, J.P.   JOHN MACPHERSON.
W. R. DANSKIN.   GEO. SMALL.

Manager—WM. STRUTH.
Secretary—W. ROGERS SIMPSON, C.A.
Trainer—G. T. LIVINGSTONE.
Groundsman—ANDREW WOODROW.

The Rangers Club was founded in 1872, and was incorporated 27th May, 1899.

Kinning Park ground was closed on 26th February, 1887 ; Old Ibrox Park was opened on 20th August, 1887 ; Ibrox Park was opened on 30th December, 1899.

The total extent of the enclosure at Ibrox Park is 14·140 acres. The playing pitch measures 115 yards by 72 yards. The size of the running track is one quarter of a mile, measuring at one foot from edge of grass.

In 1898-99 the " Light Blues " made the record of winning every match in the course of the League competition, scoring 79 goals and losing only 18.

In League and Cup-tie matches last season, Rangers scored 144 goals and lost 34. This was the best record of any Scottish club.

Alex. Smith is Rangers record Internationalist —having been " capped " 33 times.

J. Gordon, J. Bowie, T. Cairns, A Cunningham, and R. Manderson were called upon last season to uphold the honour of the country of their birth.

Another Scottish League flag will be unfurled at Ibrox this season.

The Wee Blue Book of season 1920-21 acknowledged the year of the club's formation as 1872. No reference was made in the club publication in either of the following two years, but by 1923-24 the date had been changed to 1873, without explanation.

24

CLUB RECORDS, DATES, AND DATA.

The Rangers Club was founded in 1873 and incorporated 27th May, 1899.

Kinning Park ground was closed on 26th February, 1887 ; Old Ibrox Park was opened on 20th August, 1887 ; Ibrox Park was opened on 30th December, 1899.

The total extent of the enclosure at Ibrox Park is 14·140 acres. The playing pitch measures 115 yards by 72 yards. The size of the running track is one quarter of a mile, measuring at one foot from edge of grass.

Rangers have won the Scottish Cup four times, the Glasgow Cup fifteen times, the Glasgow Charity Cup eleven times, and the Scottish League Championship twelve times, and once joint with Dumbarton F.C.

In 1898-9 the " Light Blues " made the record of winning every match in the course of the League competition, scoring 79 goals and losing only 18.

The beginning of great things :—Total drawings at first Rangers v. Celtic Glasgow Cup Tie, £89 17s. 6d. Rangers' first League cheque from Celtic, ¼ share of gate, £34 3s. 10d. Compare this with the record attendance at Rangers v. Celtic Cup Tie Match, played at Ibrox on 6th March, 1920—80,493 spectators.

Last year Rangers finished first in League Table—five points ahead of the nearest challengers, Airdrieonians.

Since formation of Scottish League, 33 years ago, Rangers have never been lower than fourth on the League table, except in 1891-92, when they finished fifth.

On September 8th, 1888, Rangers played Canada on Old Ibrox Park ; result was a draw, 1 goal each.

Alex. Smith is Rangers' record Internationalist, having a total of 34 caps.

Rangers fans raised funds to place a commemorative headstone to honour William at his final resting place in Canwick Road Cemetery, Lincoln.

Then and now...Ibrox Terrace in the background gives an example of the scale of the first Ibrox Park compared to today.

Kinning Park closed for good on February 26, 1887 with a game between
the Ancients and the Moderns. The Ancients included players such as Tom and
Alex Vallance, George Gillespie, Sam Ricketts and William 'Daddy' Dunlop.
Moses McNeil (seated second row, far left, with cane) attended but did not play.
The Moderns won 3-2.

The stricken Daphne, which went down following its launch at Alexander
Stephen's Linthouse shipyard on the Clyde. In total, 124 lives were lost in the
tragedy, in July 1883.

Harry McNeil, pictured with his grand-daughters in his garden at Rutherglen, circa 1920. He was still a regular at Ibrox, with the children, at this time.

Moses, pictured in the 1930s, with nieces Mary Margaret Stewart (left), Isabel Scott and Mary Margaret's husband, Archie. Mary Margaret and Isabel were granddaughters of Harry McNeil.

Harry McNeil and his wife, Margaret Walker.

A S I watched the crowd assemble at Ibrox Park my memory turned back its pages, and I envisaged a Cup tie in which Rangers were engaged some years ago.

As a matter of fact, I believe it was their very first venture in the Scottish Cup competition. It was played on what we as youths termed the Cricket Park—Queen's Park recreation ground.

Their opponents were a team known as Oxford, and if memory hasn't tricked me Rangers won two-nil.

That match placed Tom Vallance in a niche in my temple of famous players. Picture it if you can, you who may not know what the surroundings were. The playing area was marked out by means of boundary flags. The goalposts had no crossbars, tapes did duty, and umpires and referee conducted the service.

Lined around the playing area were spectators. My view of the proceedings was obtained through the legs of one who, having brought me there to see, considerately enough ensured me vision.

It was a duel—a sort of man beat man. Concerted play came mostly from Rangers' left wing. I haven't a reference handy, but I do remember there were M'Neills as well as a Vallance, and to the Rangers' members they were giants.

It is a far cry, and when one, looking at the great spacious and splendidly-equipped enclosure that the Rangers now possess, trace their career from Glasgow Green to Ibrox, and dwell on their vicissitudes and triumphs, one is constrained, be he even churlish, to say of them that they have a just claim to be included amongst those "who have achieved greatness."

TOM MALEY.

Tom Maley, of that famous Celtic family, paid a warm tribute as he recalled watching Rangers in their earliest days.

'Genial' Peter McNeil, founding father, former player, honorary match secretary and vice president of Rangers and SFA treasurer.

The dressing rooms at Kinning Park were so small the players washed themselves outside, using buckets of water.

Scots Wha Hae: The Scotland team that defeated England 6-1 at The Oval in 1881. Tom Vallance is back row, centre. The match is also significant as it was the first time a black player, Andrew Watson of Queen's Park, played international football.

The Glasgow team from 1880 that defeated Sheffield 1-0, in Sheffield. Committee man Peter McNeil is seated on the floor, far right, next to brother Moses, on the chair. Rangers were also represented by William 'Daddy' Dunlop, third from right in the bottom row and goalkeeper George Gillespie, back row, far left.

The Light Blues lining up against Preston North End before the game to mark the opening of the first Ibrox Park in 1887.

The ground of 1851, and a great occasion. All-England batting against Twenty-Two of Glasgow at Kinning Park. From a painting by an unknown artist.

The Rangers ground at tranquil Kinning Park, captured on canvas in 1851 as a Glasgow select takes on England at cricket. The Grapes, The Red Lion and The District Bar would come later.

Garelochhead … a village the McNeil, Campbell and Vallance brothers knew intimately.

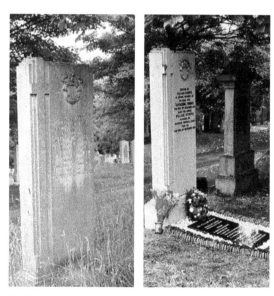

Bill Struth rests in his restored grave at Craigton Cemetery.

r their own benefit and the good of vould remind our readers that it is atter to criticise, and it is much oy than construct. Some critics tetic role, and like the augurer of ure events without regard to fulnise or fear of losing prestige. elieve that they have received a ct in the capacity of referee, and instance in which this important lestly told his auditors that he was)est referees in Scotland ! A man wledge of vessels, and yet be ingating the steam ferry across the like manner, a critic may know very club in the kingdom, and every week, and yet be altogether give a correct *resumé* of a game, cate the faults and merits of the therein. It is often amusing to es of an evening paper, published ternoon. The opinions expressed 1lated, and too often are the vapid ne embryo scribe who knows as tball as a Hottentot does about . In order that one may criticise atly, one must thoroughly undert : and we would counsel those ritics to become acquainted with bye-law, and at all times to act nd without partiality or prejudice.

Advertisements.

Match—Saturday, 19th March.

RANGERS
VERSUS
E OF LEVEN
3K (kindly lent by 3rd Lanark).)ff at 4 p.m. prompt. Ladies Free. Stand 6d. extra. *Tickets available to Ground.*

—Saturday First, 19th March.

CLYDE
● VERSUS
TTLEFIELD
ZD PARK, French Street (off eet). Kick-off at 3.30. hreepence. Ladies Free.

—Saturday First, 19th March.

RENTON
VERSUS
OWLAIRS
2K, Renton. Kick-off at 3.30. mission as usual.

VTRY CHAMPIONSHIP

Rangers undertook an ambitious fund raising drive to finance the first Ibrox Park.

Senior statesman: Tom Vallance,
pictured in the 1920s.

Garelochhead. The birthplace of Peter Campbell, whose family home lay around
the sweep of the bay to the left.

Moses McNeil in a family snapshot – the bowler hat was to remain a feature throughout his life.

Once upon a dream: Few would have thought a walk along these paths in West End Park would result in the birth of one of the world's greatest football clubs.

The Blues Brothers…Ian McColl (left) and Gordon Bell of the Founders' Trail and Rangers Graves Restoration Project.

11

TOM VALLANCE

The shabby goings on around the Rangers training ground in Milngavie as winter gave way to spring in 2012 and the Light Blues toppled into the financial abyss of administration were an affront to the memory of the man looking down on it all.

Day after day the media camped outside Auchenhowie, waiting from updates from management and officials, little knowing the final resting place of Honest Tom, at Hillfoot Cemetery, was framing the scene.

Former Rangers manager Graeme Souness surely never had Vallance in mind when he memorably opined that one of the biggest problems in Scottish football was the presence of too many hammer throwers.

Vallance, who rightfully earned the nickname 'Honest' throughout his glorious, one-club career with the Light Blues, could lob 16 pounds of solid steel with as much aplomb as he could run, jump, row or play football. Of all the gallant pioneers, he clearly boasted the richest and most varied talents.

This lad o' pairts from the Vale of Leven was a champion athlete and skilled oarsman, international footballer, successful entrepreneur and such an adept artist that his work was exhibited in the Royal Glasgow Institute and Scottish Academy. He would have needed a wide canvas indeed to reflect in oils on all he had achieved.

Tom Vallance was not present at the conception of Rangers in West End Park, nor its birth shortly afterwards against Callander, but he quickly developed a bond with the infant club that would remain virtually unbroken until his death from a stroke in February 1935, aged 78.

He nurtured its development to such an extent that he was club captain for nine seasons from 1873 and president for six years from 1883. He represented Scotland seven times, with four caps won against England in 1877, 1878, 1879 and 1881. Not once did he finish on the losing side against the 'Auld Enemy'.

Four men are correctly identified with the formation of Rangers but a fifth, Vallance, was also a towering influence – and not just because the powerful full-back stood 6ft 2in tall, a veritable giant of the age on and off the park.

Vallance was born at a small farmhouse known as Succoth, near Renton in the parish of Cardross, in 1856. His father, also Thomas, was an agricultural labourer from Lesmahagow and his mother, Janet, came from Loudon in Ayrshire.

They were married in Glasgow in December 1842 and by the time Tom was born there was already a large Vallance family, including Ann aged 12, James 9, Robert 8, and Margaret 2. The family unit would increase still further in later years with the birth of another two boys, Alexander (who also gave sterling service to Rangers) and Andrew (who went on to become the head gardener in Helensburgh for Neil Munro, the novelist best known for his 'Para Handy' tales).

When Tom was still young the family moved to the Old Toll House at Shandon, north of Rhu on the Gare Loch, and in all likelihood crossed paths with the McNeil brothers for the first time. After all, the new Vallance residence was only a short distance south of Belmore House, where John McNeil, the father of Moses and Peter, was employed as head gardener.

Tom Vallance senior is listed in the Helensburgh Directory of 1864 as a 'road man' – in effect, a toll collector for a stretch of highway that once hugged the shore of the Gare Loch between Shandon and Garelochhead, but which has long since been swallowed by the naval base at Faslane.

On the athletics field in his youth, Vallance was a regular prize-winner at the annual Garelochhead Sports, while his love of rowing was nurtured and developed initially on the local regatta circuit.

Newspaper reports from the 1870s and 1880s confirm his domination of the local sports scene. For example, on Ne'erday 1878 he competed in the annual Garelochhead Amateur Athletics sports meeting and promptly won the champion mile race for the parishes of Rhu and Rosneath, the 150 yards and 200 yards sprints, as well as the hurdle, 'hop step and leap', and the hammer throw.

Three years later, at the same Ne'erday meet, he won the 160 yards and 200 yards races, the steeplechase, the triple jump, another hammer event and the long jump. To rub salt into the wounds of the defeated and dispirited, his team even won the tug-o-war.

By that stage in 1881 Vallance, then aged 25, was at his athletic peak, underlined when he jumped an astonishing 21ft 11in (6.68 metres) at the Queen's Park FC sports. The leap pre-dated the formation of the Scottish Amateur Athletic Association (it would not be established for another two years) but was still passed as the initial Scottish record.

It was no fluke either, as Vallance also leapt 21ft 6in and 21ft exactly at two other sports meetings that year. Amazingly, Vallance's Scottish record stood until 1896 when Glaswegian Hugh Barr, another athletic all-rounder, beat it by two inches.

By 1871 the Vallance family had moved to Hillhouse in Rhu, where 14 year-old Tom was listed in the census as a 'civil engineer's apprentice'. If the work was not directly with his father at that time, it was almost certainly a position gained through his influence.

However, with a restricted economy based on farming, fishing and the infant industry of tourism, the Gare Loch proved inadequate to satisfy the career interests of Vallance and, like the McNeil and Campbell boys before him, he headed to Glasgow where he quickly found work as a mechanical engineer in the shipyards with the company P and W McLellan.

Schoolboy friendships formed would be cherished in the new, alien environment, so it was no surprise when Vallance teamed up with his Gare Loch chums soon after his arrival in Glasgow to boost their fledgling football enterprise. Nor would it have come as a shock to see the teenager seek out a rowing club at which to continue the pastime that had so captured his interest. According to the Scottish Athletic Journal, he chose Clyde Amateur Rowing Club – and therein lies a story.

For decades the Clydesdale Rowing Club, neighbours and friendly rivals of Clyde, believed Rangers were formed as an offshoot of their club, but there is no evidence to support their claims beyond anecdotes passed on by members through the generations.

Clydesdale generously opened up their minutes and membership lists dating from soon after their formation in 1857 for the research purposes of this book. Unfortunately, none of the names on the membership lists (which are extensive) from the period 1865–1900 match the gallant pioneers, other players or committee members from the earliest years of Rangers.

Of course, that is not to say Tom Vallance, the McNeils or the Campbells never splashed a ripple in the colours of Clydesdale but, more likely, it was Clyde, who were formed in 1865.

The reported evidence of the time in relation to Vallance apart, there is another strong clue – the star on the shirt of the 1877 Scottish Cup final team, the earliest known picture of a Rangers squad.

It has baffled the unknowing for years, but the puzzle is surely solved moments after stepping through the front door of the Clyde HQ at the boathouse on Glasgow Green when visitors are confronted by the club's motif on the wall – a light blue, six-pointed star, identical in style to the one on the shirts worn by the Rangers team over 130 years previously, which hints at a close relationship between the two clubs.

It is worth noting, in the 1877 picture, however, Tom Vallance is pictured with a lion rampant on his shirt, symbolising his status as a Scottish international that season.

Unfortunately, absolute verification of the Clyde link is impossible, not least because their earliest records, unlike those of Clydesdale, were lost long ago.

John Allan's first great history of Rangers paints a somewhat romantic picture of lusty, laughing lads. However, the truth of the rowing exploits of Vallance and Co. was likely to have been somewhat more down to earth.

Firstly, opportunities to row would not have been plentiful, not least because boats would have to be hired from specialist agents on the south of the river at Glasgow Green or loaned from the Clyde or Clydesdale clubs themselves. As recently as the 1960s, as many as six crews would share the use of one four-man boat.

Members of each 'four' would be under strict instruction to return to the boathouse within half an hour and only if there were no crews waiting on the bank for their slot could the time on the water be extended.

Furthermore, rowing on the Clyde for much of the latter half of the 19th century often involved a lengthy game of patience. Until 1887 there was a weir on the Clyde at Glasgow Green and, while it helped to hold a high tide longer that usual, it was impossible to take to the water at low tide as the river resembled little more than a narrow stream between two substantial mud flats.

For the most part, four-man teams on Glasgow Green raced a 1,000-yard course upstream between the Albert Bridge and St Andrew's Suspension Bridge, while single rowers favoured longer distances of up to four miles.

The demographic make-up of the Clyde and Clydesdale clubs at the time was white-collar – doctors and lawyers, but the gallant pioneers were aspiring middle class, serving professional apprenticeships.

Peter Campbell may have been a shipyard worker, but he was from entrepreneurial and privileged stock and he and his brothers, as well as the McNeils and Tom Vallance, would have felt at home on Glasgow Green, not least because rowing was such an integral part of their upbringing on the Gare Loch.

The clubs may have been perceived as elitist, but the sport was not. Employees of each shipyard on the Clyde, for example, designed, built and rowed their own boats under the auspices of the Trades Rowing Association.

In truth, it is more than likely that the founding fathers of Rangers were social rowers in Glasgow rather than competitive, not least because their new football team took up so much of their time and attention.

The highlight of the rowing season in the city was undoubtedly the Glasgow Regatta, and it is astonishing to think in the 21st century that as many as 30,000 spectators would cram the banks of the Clyde in the 1870s to watch the best rowers in the country.

There is no evidence to suggest that any of the club's founding fathers, even Vallance, took part in the main event on the Clyde, perhaps because it was generally held on the first or second weekend in September, when the football season was already up and running.

An examination of newspaper reports of the event throughout the 1870s failed to throw up the names of anyone connected with the Light Blues although, intriguingly, one ace rower was a Gilbert McNeil, while the regatta's energetic secretary was a certain John Banks McNeil.

The latter was the owner of the Clutha Boathouse and one of the principal hirers of small craft on the Clyde, not to mention the founder of the Glasgow Regatta itself. However, no connection between John and Gilbert and the McNeils of Rangers fame could be established.

As a footballer, Tom Vallance was without equal in the Scottish and English game in the latter part of the 1870s, with the skipper, like his team-mates, first rising to prominence in the memorable Scottish Cup final ties against Vale of Leven in 1877.

He played the final against the same opposition two years later and although the cup would leave the city in controversial circumstances on both occasions, the Charity Cup success of 1879 made some amends for the earlier disappointments.

Vallance was revered by commentators at the time, with respected football analysts such as D.D. Bone arguing that "for several seasons, but more particularly that of 1879–80, none in Scotland showed better form. His returns near goal were neat and clean, and without being in any way rough with an opponent Vallance's length of limb and good judgement often saved his club from losing goals."

The Scottish Athletic Journal reckoned: "He was worshipped by a very large section of the football community, and that worship at times had in it all the fire and enthusiasm which are commonly bestowed on a hero."

If he was playing today, Vallance would command a substantial eight-figure transfer fee, but in those innocent, amateur days football was only a past time for most.

Looking to the future, Vallance decided to leave his lodgings at No. 167 Govan Road in February 1882 and forge a career on the tea plantations of Assam in India. It was a bold move as it was a fledgling industry that had only become commercially exploited in the previous 50 years. However, conditions in the north east of India were far from idyllic.

Vallance moved to the foothills of the Himalayas to erect and superintend new machinery being introduced at the Corramore Plantation, which had been established in 1858 by Scot Robert Logan and named after the family farm in Lanarkshire. The Corramore Plantation stayed in the Logan family for 120 years before it was absorbed into Williamson Tea Holdings.

Assam historian Derek Perry has painted a picture of a remote, lonely region at the time of the emigration of Vallance. The conditions would have been daunting, even for a man such as Vallance at his physical peak, but he had little chance to settle as he was struck down by illness within a few months of his arrival.

On the basis of later accounts, particularly those which reveal that the illness compromised his football career on his return to Scotland, Perry suggests he was likely debilitated by the dreaded Kala-azar, or black water fever, a form of pernicious malaria.

Another attack could have been deadly and it was in light of concerns about his health that Vallance returned to Scotland after only a year away. A profile on Tom, published in the Victualling Trades Review in May 1891, admitted as much.

It read: "Unfortunately, even his strong constitution, hardened as it was by his great athletic career, fairly broke down and he was most reluctantly compelled to abandon his bright prospects of success in this sphere and return to Auld Scotia, where his native air, the bagpipes, the parritch and the mountain dew soon re-inspired him with his wonted vigour."

Tom played three times for Rangers in season 1883–84 but was a spent force. He kicked his last ball for the club in a 9–2 win over Abercorn at Kinning Park on March 8 1884.

The Scottish Athletic Journal sadly noted: "He still had a fancy for the game of football and donned the jersey several times but his eye was dimmed and his leg had lost its cunning and he was not even the shadow of his former self."

His illness had clearly forced Vallance into taking stock of his life and soon after his return from India he abandoned his earlier aspirations of pursuing a career as an engineer to become a travelling salesman in the wine and spirits trade, opening the door to a new and lucrative existence in the hospitality industry.

He was employed by James Aitken & Co. Ltd, brewers who

operated from Linlithgow and Falkirk, brewing their popular 'Aitken's Ale'. His working life quickly back on track, Vallance also set about re-establishing himself at Kinning Park. If he could not do it on the field any longer, he could certainly contribute off it and he was elected club president for the first of six seasons in May 1883.

During his 12-month absence John Wallace Mackay had come to the fore at Kinning Park. Vallance honourably resigned early in his presidency after that player coup moved to remove him as umpire for a match at Dumbarton and replace him with Mackay because he would not favour his own team in his decision making.

However, keeper George Gillespie issued a grovelling apology on behalf of the team and Vallance returned within a week, his grip on his portfolio tightened still further.

As a salesman he was undoubtedly familiar with flattery, but there also appeared to be a genuine streak of honesty and integrity running through Vallance to which people warmed. For example, he was an arch critic of Mackay and frequently stood up against the worst excesses of the honorary match secretary in his seemingly never-ending spats with the Scottish Athletic Journal.

On one occasion, following the half-yearly meeting in November 1884, Mackay attempted to coerce Vallance into lying on his behalf by denying claims in the Journal that the match secretary had said Queen's Park were on their financial uppers ahead of their move to the second Hampden Park.

In a fit of pique, Mackay had also recommended Rangers never play Third Lanark again after their Glasgow rivals reported them to the SFA for the 'Cooking the books' scandal. Vallance refused and, not surprisingly, was showered with praise the following week by the newspaper.

Increasingly, Vallance was dealing from a position of presidential strength as Rangers moved from a period of financial uncertainty to one of stability under his reign. Membership numbers increased and, with a far-sighted and energetic committee at the club, a move to the purpose-built first Ibrox Park was secured.

However, Vallance missed the grand opening of the new ground against Preston North End on August 18 1887 as he married Marion Dunlop, sister of former teammate, club president and friend William. Marion was from Glasgow and was six years Tom's junior.

The wedding ceremony was held in the Dunlop family home, with Tom's younger brother Alick acting as best man.

Within 18 months the couple's first child was born, Harold Leonard Vallance, on January 20 1889. By this time they lived at No. 89 Maxwell Drive in the south-west of Glasgow, before moving back into the city to No. 48 Sandyford Street a year later.

It was at this point that Tom's career was suddenly injected with an extra impetus, as he moved from his position with brewer James Aitken to become a successful restaurateur.

In 1890 he took on his first real business venture – a pub/restaurant located at No. 22 Paisley Road West at Paisley Road Toll. He called the restaurant The Club – generations of modern day fans know it as The Viceroy – and it quickly became a popular venue for the Rangers 'smoker evenings'.

He would also go on to own and operate at least two other restaurants in the city: The Metropolitan at No. 40 Hutchison Street and The Lansdowne at No. 183 Hope Street. His reputation among his business contemporaries was underlined in 1906 when he became president of the Restaurateurs and Hotelkeepers Association.

The happiness of Tom and Marion grew still further in 1891 when another son, James Douglas, was born. The Vallances seemed to lead a somewhat itinerant life at this stage as James was born in the new family home at No. 219 Paisley Road in Glasgow, before they moved to nearby Lendel Terrace then, soon after, back to Maxwell Drive and on to Kersland Street in the west end. Finally, in 1908 Tom and Marion settled at No. 189 Pitt Street in Glasgow city centre and the place they would call home for the rest of their lives.

In addition to his work with Rangers and his various business concerns, Vallance was also a member of the 'Old Glasgow Club,' a local history society.

He also found time for another passion: art. Self taught, he exhibited at the annual exhibition of the Royal Glasgow Institute at least twice, in 1897 and 1929, and his work was also displayed by the Scottish Academy. He never became as celebrated as contemporaries such as Glasgow Boys James Guthrie and James Paterson, or Scottish colourists Samuel Peploe or John Fergusson, but his work was popular and still occasionally appears at auction.

One of his final commissions was an impressive and dramatic canvas almost six feet in height entitled The Charge, which was presented to Cadder Golf Club in Bishopbriggs on its opening in May 1935.

The painting, which featured an army battalion on horseback, was so impressive it was even reproduced in the Daily Record in February 1934. Unfortunately, despite its size, the golf club lost track of the painting when it was removed during World War Two and its current whereabouts is unknown.

Sadly, the events of World War One were to have a lasting impression on the Vallance family. Harold Vallance joined the 7th Battalion (Blythswood) of the great Glasgow regiment, the Highland Light Infantry. Tragically, on September 28 1918, just six weeks before the end of the war, Second Lieutenant Harold Leonard Vallance, aged 29, was killed in one of the closing conflicts in the assault on the Hindenburg line in France.

He was buried with honour at Abbeville Communal Cemetery. He is commemorated on the memorial board at Glasgow's Western Baths, where he was a member, along with Peter McNeil's son, John Fraser.

Tom would know heartache in his life, not least the death of younger brother Alick at the age of only 38 in 1898, soon after the younger brother had taken over as proprietor of the Red Lion Vaults in Glasgow's West Nile Street.

The influence of Alick on the early years of Rangers should never be forgotten. Alick joined Rangers in 1873 as a 13-year-old, shortly after his big brother and, like Tom, was employed by the engineering firm P and W McLellan, initially as an office boy.

He was credited, supported by Tom, with securing Burnbank for the use of Rangers in 1875 and, the following year, he put forward the suggestion of Kinning Park, thus taking Rangers to the south side of the city for the first time. He would have known the area around Kinning Park intimately as P and W McLellan had opened the Clutha Ironworks in 1873 and it would stand as a neighbour of the Light Blues in the district for several years.

Alick also kept pace with his big brother in sport and it was estimated the Vallance boys won more than £300 worth of cups and medals across several sporting disciplines.

Indeed, Alick even put out a 12 sport challenge to any Scottish athlete in 1884 who fancied taking him on, but there was no-one willing and, as a result, he was lauded in the press as the finest all-round athlete in the country.

In addition to their membership of Rangers, the siblings were also long-standing members of the Clydesdale Harriers, which Alick helped establish in 1885. Alick also solely organised the first Rangers Sports.

Golf was another passion and he was one of the founder members and the first captain of Garelochhead Golf Club in 1895. He was also Scottish 120 yards hurdles champion in 1888 and he played over 100 times for the Light Blues in a career spanning 12 seasons from 1877–88.

Like Tom, he was a defender and, although he had a lighter physique than his older brother, he was every bit as gutsy. They played together in the Glasgow Charity Cup Final in 1879 when Rangers beat Vale of Leven 2–1 to win their first piece of silverware as a club.

Alick, who was a Rangers selector before being named captain in 1881, packed achievement after achievement into his life before his death.

He was secretary of the Shandon and Gareloch Rowing Club, the Shandon Mutual Improvement Society, a member of the of the Glasgow Wanderers Angling Club and even a member of the Queen's Own Yeomanry Cavalry. He was an award-winning poultry breeder and his love of dogs shone through as secretary of the Glasgow Canine club and membership of the Scottish Collie Club, as well as the Scottish Kennel Club.

Tom's life was also touched with scandal and sorrow of a different sort in January 1923 when his surviving son James was jailed for nine months and fined £250 for culpable homicide following a car accident on Gibson Street in the west end, a stone's throw from the former home of Peter McNeil.

On October 4 1922 James was driving up Gibson Street in a car purchased for him by his dad, by whom he was employed at the Lansdowne Restaurant in Hope Street. Painfully, no doubt, Tom admitted in court the distance between the accelerator and brake pedals in the vehicle was only an inch-and-a-half and the brakes were slack. He added that if the accelerator was touched at the same time as the brake, the car would shoot forward.

James, aged 30, then stepped forward to give evidence and told the court he had been travelling at 20 miles an hour, but had accelerated going up the hill at Gibson Street towards Bank Street.

Suddenly, two men stepped out in front of him and he swerved to the left to avoid them but could only conclude that as he tried to apply the brakes he hit the accelerator instead. The car crashed into a lamp post and although Vallance walked away uninjured one of the poor pedestrians, Alexander Doyle, was struck by the vehicle and died.

The jury returned a guilty verdict by a majority and Lord Alness passed sentence. He told Vallance: "I will not add to your distress by reading a homily with regard to the painful position you find yourself in because you have been convicted of a crime involving the loss of life." The devastation of the Doyle family, in part, would also have been shared by Tom and Marion Vallance.

Tom remained an ever present at Rangers throughout his life. He attended the dinner to mark the 50th anniversary of the club at Ferguson and Forrester's Restaurant on Buchanan Street in April 1923 and it must have been an occasion of mixed emotions following the death of Alexander Doyle and the imprisonment of his surviving son.

Tom was also present when the magnificent Main Stand was officially opened on January 1 1929. To think the pride he must have felt that day as he reflected on the club's humble origins at Glasgow Green and how far they had grown in little more than a half century.

Tom was given the Ibrox equivalent of a state funeral following his death at home on the evening of Saturday February 16 1935, with his burial three days later at Hillfoot.

Rangers chairman James Bowie took one of the cords as the gallant pioneer was laid to rest, while former teammate James 'Tuck' McIntyre, also in his late seventies and one of the oldest surviving former players at the time, took another. Bill Struth attended, along with other senior club officials, while a host of former opponents from clubs such as Dumbarton, Clyde and Third Lanark also turned out.

Fittingly, Rangers saw him off on the day of his passing with a 3-1 win over Airdrie at Ibrox.

12

HAPPILY WE WALK
ALONG THE COPLAND ROAD

It was a measure of the new-found confidence of Glasgow that the city hosted its first International Exhibition in 1888 on the stretch of parkland that had earlier provided a place of contemplation for four youngsters who were interested in forming the football club that quickly became known as Rangers.

Glaswegians grew giddy at the thought of the cosmopolitan delights of a showcase for their city that would eventually be nicknamed Baghdad on the Kelvin as a result of the eastern influence on the architectural structures that dominated Kelvingrove Park for seven months between May and November.

The Glasgow International Exhibition of Science, Art and Industry attracted almost six million visitors in total and was widely recognised as the first truly international exhibition since the great gathering at Crystal Palace in 1851.

In addition to showing off Glasgow's outstanding achievements as an industrial power and second city of the Empire, the exhibition was also aimed at turning a profit to fund a new gallery and museum at Kelvingrove.

Glasgow now boasted such a treasure trove of art and other valuable artefacts there was no longer room to display them at the McLellan Galleries, which was until then its main museum. The art gallery and museum at Kelvingrove opened in time for the next major exhibition in 1901 and still stands today as one of the country's top tourist attractions in all its refurbished splendour.

In total, there were 2,700 exhibits at the 1888 event, including an electrically illuminated fairy fountain of different colours and a Doulton Fountain, now restored to all its former glory and housed at Glasgow Green. The River Kelvin was even deepened and cleaned and the flow of sewage into its waters stemmed to such an extent there were regular swimming galas.

A gondola was brought to Glasgow from Venice especially for the exhibition and two gondoliers, nicknamed Signor Hokey and Signor Pokey, treated visitors to trips up and down the Kelvin.

H. and P. McNeil also took the chance to exhibit their wares – at court number two, stand 1241, according to their adverts at the time. Glasgow was letting its hair down, more confident of its place in Britain and the world in general. It was a bold display of self-assuredness that was being matched at the time by the leaders of Rangers.

The constant creep of industrialisation had long put pressure on land at Kinning Park, the ground Rangers had called their home, if not their own, since 1876.

At least twice the Light Blues had fought the threat of eviction from their landlord, but the writing was not so much on the wall as the gable ends of the tenements that began to dominate in the district. The factor, land agents Andersons and Pattison, duly arrived early in the New Year in 1887 and gave Rangers notice to quit their home by March 1.

It was a sad blow, not least because the £60 per annum Rangers paid in rent was considered extremely cheap for the time and the facility. Nevertheless, the move to evict came as no great surprise.

In the 1860s Kinning Park was a pretty patch of meadowland and even as late as 1872 the former ground of the Clydesdale Cricket Club sat in rural isolation.

However, by 1873 the Clutha Ironworks had been constructed nearby, followed a couple of years later by a depot for the Caledonian Railway Company. By the turn of the 20th century the green grass at Kinning Park would disappear forever and be replaced by a coating of dust from the sawmill of Anderson and Henderson. A move west to the undeveloped lands of Ibrox beckoned.

In the same weekend that Rangers booked their place in the semi-final of the FA Cup against Aston Villa in February 1887, the club's committee came together and settled on a seven year lease for a parcel of land of up to six acres at the Copeland (sic) Road end of Paisley Road.

They struck a deal with Braby and Company, a building firm from Springburn, to construct a new stadium at a cost of £750, which included a pavilion, a 1,200 capacity stand, an enclosure and a four-lane running track inside a terracing amphitheatre.

In addition to the ambitious plans, a playing surface would be laid out 115 yards long by 71 wide and space was even left behind each goal for tennis courts to be introduced at a later stage. The ground, it was claimed, would be little inferior to Hampden Park, then recognised as the best sporting arena in the country.

The Scottish Athletic Journal greeted the decision of the Kinning Park committee to forge ahead with plans for a new ground in February 1887 with glee. It reported: "The meeting was most enthusiastic, harmonious in tone and unmistakenly evidenced the deep desire of the Light Blues to take a higher stand in the football arena than they have hitherto done."

However, three years earlier it had foreseen only doom and gloom if Rangers ever moved from Kinning Park. In March 1884 it warned: "The Rangers have received notice to quit Kinning Park as the ground is to be immediately built upon. This is a serious blow to the Rangers – one from which they will scarcely recover.

"It almost certainly means extinction. Dissociate the Light Blues from Kinning Park and the club will soon collapse. One cannot think of the Rangers associated with any other park and grounds situated so near the city as Kinning Park is are not to be had."

However, a sub-committee under the guidance of convenor Dan Gillies was formed for the purpose of raising the necessary funds in the spring of 1887. The fears of the Journal would soon prove unfounded.

Rangers hoped the bulk of the finance would come from money already at hand and the following season's gate receipts, but fund-raising was also crucial.

To that end they organised a benefit concert at the Grand Hall of the Waterloo Rooms in Wellington Street in Glasgow city centre, with Tom Vallance acting as compere. The bill promised acts such as Cinderella, from the Gaiety Theatre pantomime, celebrated tenor Peter Kerr, eminent soprano Isa Grant and Irish comedian Dan Rogers.

There was something for everyone, including an American music band, The Dobsons, and even a French equilibrist, Monsieur Trewey, whose trick involved walking along tightropes.

Rangers also got the financial balancing act spot on – the night was a complete sell-out, a roaring success. The licence for the Grand Hall was extended to 2am to allow dancing into the night and, with ticket prices of sixpence and a shilling, the club coffers were swollen substantially and concerns eased that the move was a step too far for an organisation that was still just 15 years old.

These days, with its excellent transport links and relative proximity to Glasgow city centre, Ibrox is the perfect home for Rangers geographically, not to mention the strong spiritual links which have been forged with the district for over a century.

However, in the 1880s the move to the relative backwater was considered a risk, but it was championed by the club's honorary secretary Walter Crichton, who foresaw the spread of the booming city further westwards.

Glasgow had overtaken Edinburgh in terms of the size of its population as early as 1821 and by the time of the formation of Rangers in 1872 it was home to approximately 500,000 people, which rose to almost 660,000 by 1891.

For much of the second half of the 19th century Ibrox was still a rural district – in 1876, fields of corn grew to the very fringes of Clifford Street, which runs parallel between Paisley Road West and the M8 over a century later. An outward sign of the growth and prosperity of the district in the 1870s came with the construction of the original Bellahouston Academy, which still stands today on Paisley Road West near its junction with Edmiston Drive.

Districts such as Bellahouston, Dumbreck and parts of Ibrox were home to the well-to-do and they shuddered at the prospect of sending their children across the ever sprawling city for a premier education at Glasgow Academy, situated in the west end, and as a result Bellahouston Academy was formed.

Understandably, given its rural status, the history of Ibrox has tended to be overlooked, certainly in comparison to its near neighbour Govan, once the fifth-largest burgh in Scotland.

The oldest recorded mention of the place name now so closely associated with Rangers is Ibrokis, in 1580, and Ybrox in 1590. Indeed, in the 19th century there were still people who lived in and around the district that pronounced it as 'Eebrox'. The name is believed to come from the Gaelic 'broc', meaning badger, and 'I' or 'Y', an old Celtic word for island.

According to local lore, a water trough stood just off the head of what is now know as Broomloan Road, with its spring water origins at Bellahouston Hill. The water was so plentiful it occasionally spilled over to join the Powburn, a sluggish stretch of water that meandered through Drumoyne and into the Clyde at Linthouse.

A swampy island populated by badgers was formed at the Broomloan Road site where the two stretches of water met, hence Ybrox or Ibrox, the island of the badgers.

In more recent times, the land around Edmiston Drive now associated with the home of Rangers was field and meadowland. There were two large houses on the area now recognised as Bellahouston Park – Bellahouston House, sometimes called Dumbreck House, owned by a famous Govan family, the Rowans.

Another estate nearby was known as Ibrox or Ibroxhill and was owned by the Hill family, partners in Hill and Hoggan, the oldest legal firm in the city. Both estates were bought by Glasgow town council in 1895 for £50,000 and within 12 months had been absorbed into the city boundaries, opening their gates as Bellahouston Park.

An historical delve into the origins of the names of Edmiston Drive and Copland Road might also intrigue fans.

The former was named after Richard Edmiston, a senior partner in the auctioneer firm J and R Edmiston, who operated at West Nile Street for much of the first half of last century. Edmiston's family home, Ibrox House, was in the shadows of the second Ibrox Park and he was bestowed the honour when the street on which the stadium now stands was first opened.

He appeared to have had a philanthropic nature and in 1949 was even named a freeman of Girvan, where he owned a holiday home, after gifting the local museum several paintings by leading artists of the time.

Copland Road was named in the first half of the 19th century after a writer, William Copland, in tribute to the fact that his principal residence was at Dean Park Villa, at the west side of the thoroughfare near its junction with Govan Road.

The name of the street was correctly spelled out in maps and journals of the time, but was later changed to Copeland Road after a spelling blunder by builders who were constructing the local Copland Road School. The erroneous letter 'e' was allowed to stand unchallenged for much of the first half of the 20th century, but the street name has long since been restored to the original.

If the few residents who lived in the Ibrox district at the time of the Rangers' arrival had some reservations about their new neighbours, they were probably well founded.

A few months before the move, the Scottish Athletic Journal was forced to take Rangers fans to task, not for the first time, for their behaviour at a match, this time against Third Lanark.

It reported: "There were several of the Kinning Park rowdies at Cathkin on Saturday. Some of them seemed proud of their swearing abilities as they took advantage of every lull in the play to volley forth a few choice oaths which were heard all over the field. It is a pity an example cannot be made of some of these people."

Rangers toyed with the idea of taking over the lease of a ground in Strathbungo at a rent of £80 a year and the Journal warned that rents in the area would immediately go through the floor.

Perhaps Tom Vallance summed it up best of all at the cake and wine banquet for VIP guests the Wednesday before the official opening of the new Ibrox ground. He addressed the throng and admitted that Kinning Park was not always a place for the faint-hearted.

He said: "A certain stigma rested on the club owing to their field being in a locality not of the best, while the spectators of the game were not always of the best description, though they were simply such as the locality could afford. I have known very respectable people come to our matches and not renewing their visits but that has all gone and I am sanguine that in our new sphere we will be able to attract to our matches thousands of respectable spectators."

His claims proved prophetic. Almost a year after the opening of the first Ibrox, Provost Ferguson of Govan admitted there had been initial private misgivings among the burgh's leading citizens over the arrival of the Light Blues in their district.

However, he lavished praise on the Rangers fans, noting there had not been a single arrest in their first season. The Scottish Umpire gushed: "It is satisfactory to have such a testimony from the chief magistrate of such a football constituency as Govan as to the law abiding and peaceful character of the crowds which patronise the pastime."

Bad behaviour was not restricted to Kinning Park. Indeed, one of the most ugly and unsavoury incidents of the period involved Queen's Park, following a 3–0 defeat to Preston in the FA Cup in October 1886 at Hampden.

There were 14,000 at the game, including 500 from England, and the crowd invaded the field near the end to attack the visitors following a hefty challenge on star player William Harrower by Preston inside-forward Jimmy Ross, younger brother of former Hearts star Nick.

Queen's players were forced to leap to the defence of helpless Preston players as they were attacked by sticks and umbrellas as they made their way through the throng to the safety of the pavilion. Ross later ordered a cab to take him away from Hampden but the Liverpool Echo reported: "the vehicle was stormed and Ross was severely maltreated."

Nevertheless, despite its occasionally disreputable status, there was still a fondness for the old ground at Kinning Park that was exemplified by the turnout of former players to mark the end of its life as a sporting arena on Saturday February 26 1887, days before the landlord turned the key on the gates for good.

Rangers had tried – and failed – to lure Nottingham Forest and Blackburn Rovers north to play an exhibition match to mark the occasion, but it was perhaps more appropriate to field the moderns against the ancients, although the last-minute nature of the arrangements restricted the number of fans in attendance.

Old boys such as Tom and Alick Vallance, George Gillespie, Sam Ricketts and William 'Daddy' Dunlop all turned out and, although Moses McNeil did not feature on the park, the picture taken before the game shows him sitting proudly with his former colleagues, who were unlucky to lose 3–2 to the younger and fitter Light Blues.

Rangers were left to see out the last three months of the 1886–87 season as nomads, with 'home' games played at venues such as

Cathkin Park, Hampden and Inchview (Partick Thistle's ground at the time, in the Whiteinch district), while their soon-to-be near neighbours at the other end of Copland Road, Whitefield, offered their own Whitefield Park ground for training purposes, which was gratefully accepted.

Throughout the spring and summer, work continued at pace on the new ground, while the Rangers committee set about organising a grand opening that would later lead the Scottish News to comment: "The usually quiet district of Ibrox has never before witnessed such an assemblage."

The Rangers committee succeeded in persuading Preston North End to travel north to open their new ground. The visitors demanded a £50 appearance fee, a fair deal for Rangers on the back of eventual gate receipts of £340.

The Lancashire side, under manager Major William Sudell, became known as The Invincibles, with a team consisting predominantly of Scots who were among the first professionals in the sport. Players such as Nick and Jimmy Ross, David Russell, John Goodall and Geordie Drummond earned a fortune – comparatively speaking – as Preston won the first English league championship in 1888–89 without losing a game and clinched the double by going all the way in the FA Cup without conceding a goal. They also won the title in 1890, so Rangers fans were watching legends in the making as they turned up at Ibrox that August afternoon.

Rangers were keen to show off their new ground to a select audience ahead of the formal opening and 150 invites were sent out to dignitaries to attend the cake and wine preview the Wednesday before the Preston game (it was also a chance for Vallance to meet the VIPs ahead of his own big match with Marion Dunlop, which forced him to miss the game on the Saturday).

On the Tuesday night, a Rangers team playing under the guise of the Ibroxonians fought out a 2–2 draw with Whitefield at Whitefield Park as they prepared for Preston, although the Light Blues could only muster eight men to start the game.

Not surprisingly, the atmosphere at the cake and wine was jovial as the club was complimented for the quality of a facility few in British football could boast. Mr Luther, of builders Braby and Co., even noted that the sharp corrugated fencing around the ground would prevent fans from watching without paying for the privilege, as it made for an uncomfortable seat for supporters keen to sneak an illicit peek at their favourites.

Behind the scenes, preparations continued to accommodate fans from all over the city at the new ground. The Rangers committee asked for the 6pm train to Wemyss Bay to make a temporary stop at Ibrox, while the Glasgow Tramway Company agreed to run additional brakes from the city to Paisley Road at only twopence a head.

In terms of pre-match entertainment, the Scottish Umpire somewhat snootily noted: "The Fairfield Band offered to assist the Govan Police Band and Pipers at the opening ceremony. Declined regretfully. It is a football match, not a band contest."

The game and the opening of the new ground had clearly captured the public's imagination and, while the event was as popular as all associated with the club could have hoped, the capacity crowd of 20,000 revealed severe organisational problems.

Time was called on the action five minutes early amid scenes of chaos, even though many supporters had already given up and headed for home, setting a 19th-century precedent for the 21st century's so-called Subway Loyal, who turn for the exits as soon as the hand of the Ibrox game clock reaches out to touch 80 minutes.

Even the prophecy by Mr Luther of Braby and Co., who cheerfully predicted no climbing on the perimeter fencing, was wide of the mark.

The Scottish News lamented that the capacity, by kick-off time of 4pm, was "taxed to its utmost. There was scarcely standing room. Many spectators eager to obtain a good view mounted on the top of the corrugated iron fencing, on the sharp end of which they must have had a most uncomfortable seat. The stand was full to overflowing."

The pain of the posteriors of the Light Blues legions was nothing compared to the assault on their eyes as Preston opened the scoring after only two minutes through Goodall and raced to a 5–0 lead by half-time.

Goodall, born in London to Scottish parents and raised in Kilmarnock, notched up at least four goals (even the papers of the time stopped naming the North End scorers after a while). The Lancashire cracks had just scored their eighth goal, right near the end, with only a solitary response from Andy Peacock, when the game was ended prematurely.

Seven minutes from time, as Rangers mounted a rare attack, fans who had been forced by weight of numbers onto the track around the field crowded to the touchlines for a closer look.

Inevitably, spectators spilled on to the field itself, crowding the players in the process. The players eventually made their way through the throng to the safety of the dressing rooms. Rangers were victims of their own success, and claims by the builders for a capacity of 20,000 were clearly straining credulity as thin as the patience of the Preston party, who were understandably upset by the conduct of the crowd.

The News explained: "The accommodation outside the railings was found to be too limited and the officials were obliged to allow the spectators to go inside on the track, which made room for thousands demanding admission.

"The spectators, evidently weary of a very slow game, began to troop out of the game some 15 minutes before the allotted time had run. The policy of allowing the people in on the track proved a fatal one, as the crowd who stood there gradually edged their way in on the field of play and finally all control was lost over them.

"Before the game was concluded the police tried in vain to clear the spectators off the field. The Rangers coming close on the visitors' goal was the last straw as the people fairly swarmed round the players and the field was a black mass of living beings. It was no use now to attempt further play and the game came to an abrupt close five minutes from time. The players were followed into the pavilion and some were cheered. Others, especially Goodall, being hooted."

Rangers hosted Preston at the official banquet that evening in the favoured restaurant of the Light Blues, Ancell's in Glassford Street. In the absence of Vallance, it was left to vice-president Peter McNeil to address the players and officials and he enthused about the strides the club had made in the previous 15 years and the hopes for a new era symbolised by the new ground. Not surprisingly, the on-field events of a few hours earlier merited only a passing remark.

McNeil said: "I have been a member of the Rangers since it was ushered into the world and I cannot recollect an event which will bear comparison with the event we have been celebrating today and which has ended so gloriously for the club.

"We, as a club, have reason to congratulate ourselves on the splendid success that has attended the opening ceremony. There was, it is true, a curiosity shared by all to see the new ground but what attracted so large a crowd was the reputation of the North End more than the novelty that surrounded our enterprise.

"I am expressing the sentiments of every member of the committee when I say that we are deeply grateful to the North End for coming at this time and should it ever turn out that building extensions force them from Deepdale to some other ground the Rangers, if they are asked, will willingly go to Preston and perform the part that has been so well performed by the North End today.

"There is no need to say much about the game. It was played in a spirit of honest rivalry and with a true appreciation of the finer points of the game. I again express the wish that this day, which is undoubtedly the most memorable in the history of the club, will be followed by results, financial and physical, that will place the Rangers in a position that will be the envy of many and the possession of few."

Preston manager Major Sudell replied briefly, complimenting Rangers on the construction of such a spectacular new ground, but calling on the press in Glasgow to educate local fans in the matter of manners after the events of earlier in the day.

The get-together broke up shortly afterwards and Preston players and officials boarded the last train south from Central Station. They did not look back as they headed for the border.

Pretty soon, neither did Rangers. Even the brand new home that drew so many admiring glances from rival outfits would soon prove too restrictive for the ambitions of a club that would go on to earn a cherished status as the most successful in Scottish football history.

13

A NEW ERA

Alexander Graham Bell had already invented the telephone by the time Rangers and Celtic first crossed swords on 28 May 1888, but thankfully Guglielmo Marconi still had another eight years to go before his work on wireless transmission would reach its defining stages.

In truth, even if radio phone-ins had been an integral feature of the media and sporting landscape at the time, it is doubtful whether many among the Light Blues' legions would have rushed to spin the dial and pour out their hearts in dismay at the 5–2 defeat that had just been suffered by their favourites.

Rangers made the short journey to the east end in the spirit of sporting friendship, to help the newly formed Celtic play the opening match at their recently constructed ground at Parkhead, built in their spare time by volunteer supporters of the club.

Celtic were following in the footsteps of the country's other great outfits of Irish influence, Hibernian of Edinburgh and Harp of Dundee. The Old Firm has gone on to forge one of the most appealing yet controversial rivalries in world football, but these were more innocent times.

Celtic's 5–2 victory in front of a crowd of 2,000 against opposition featuring more second-string players than usual came courtesy of an opening goal from a former Ranger, Neil McCallum.

After the match, played in an atmosphere of genuine bonhomie, both sides retired to the local St Mary's Hall, where a supper was laid on for 70 guests and a concert enjoyed as toasts were raised to the ongoing success of both clubs.

The friendship between the teams was strong. The Scottish Sport, reflecting on a forthcoming Scottish Cup tie in 1892, reported: "Financially, Dumbarton or Queen's Park might have pleased treasurer Maley better, but for a genuine good match the Light Blues are favourites with the Parkhead crowd."

Perhaps it was coincidence that brought the two clubs together that early summer evening, a quirk of fate that the two teams who would become so associated with the Scottish game, and indeed each other, would meet at the very first opportunity.

It also certainly made sense for Celtic to approach Rangers to play their first match, not least because of the relationship between Celtic secretary John McLaughlin and the Ibrox side, but also because the Light Blues were a draw, a prized first opponent for any club kicking off an infant venture.

However, there is a hitherto unacknowledged relationship between two of the greatest figures in Celtic's history, Tom and Willie Maley, and Rangers players, committee members and other senior club figure.

Together in May 1885 they helped establish the first open athletic club in Scotland, the Clydesdale Harriers, bringing the sport to a wider audience than previous, gatecrashing the elite of the university and public school system. This was Glasgow united against the likes of the Fettesian-Lorettonian Club, Edinburgh Collegiate AC and St Andrews University.

The influence of Rangers on the fledgling athletic venture was there for all to see, not only in the membership list but also on the choice of venue for the club's first event on June 3 1885. It was a 300-yard handicap which attracted 54 entrants to Kinning Park, with athletes such as a certain William Wilton cheered on by approximately 500 spectators.

Wilton failed to emerge from his heat, finishing sixth of seventh runners – scant consolation, surely, that he just held off R Shiels, 'a plucky little youngster of 12 years,' according to the Scottish Umpire.

The judges that summer evening included the notorious honorary match secretary JW Mackay, the handicapper was committee member WW Tait and clerks of the course included former 1877

Scottish Cup final forward James Watson, who would go on to become vice-president and president of Rangers, further underlining the commitment of the Light Blues to the new cause.

By 1887 the Harriers boasted 120 members, rising to 650 and then more than 1,000 before World War One.

The Rangers influence was striking, from the appearance in the early years as life member of John Stewart of Belmore (one of the brothers credited with gifting Willie McNeil that first ball with which the young Light Blues played on Glasgow Green) to John Mellish, who rose to become vice-president of Clydesdale Harriers and president of the football club.

The membership lists of Clydesdale in its first decade are packed with great names from the history of Rangers. Peter McNeil was a member and H and P McNeil were official outfitters to the Harriers. Brother Willie was also a Harrier, although there is no record of Moses, a gifted runner in his youth, ever becoming part of the club.

Tom and Alick Vallance were Clydesdale Harriers, as were other players including, but not exclusively, Scottish internationals James 'Tuck' McIntyre, John Cameron, Donald Gow and his brother, John Robertson Gow.

The organisation that had helped bring Rangers to the fore in the decade or so preceding the establishment of the Harriers was also evident in the development of the athletics club.

In some cases, future Rangers office holders cut their teeth in the athletics division – for example James Henderson, president of the football club in 1898–99 when they went through the season without dropping a point in the League, was a Clydesdale Harriers committee man in 1887, as was John C Lawson, Rangers' honorary secretary between 1891 and 1892. In 1887–88 the Harriers' membership list also included TCB Miller and JF Ness, who had each held honorary treasurer positions at Kinning Park.

The Clydesdale Harriers even had a short-lived football division in the late 1880s as Celt Maley joined forces with Rangers men John C Lawson and AB McKenzie (a director at Ibrox between 1899 and 1911) to oversee a new enterprise.

The Harriers attracted players from most senior clubs, although Rangers were in the majority. Athletic members also played for clubs including Queen's Park, Third Lanark, Cowlairs, St Mirren, Morton, Hamilton Accies and Celtic.

When arranged, football matches were mostly of the challenge variety and clubs such as Third Lanark and even the mighty Preston North End were put to the sword. Clydesdale Harriers also entered a team in the 1889 Scottish Cup and knocked out Celtic from the competition, but football was soon dropped to allow members to focus more fully on the track and countryside runs.

Certainly, Tom and Willie Maley were likely to have had more pressing sporting concerns on their minds in 1887, when Celtic were officially formed following a meeting at St Mary's Hall on November 6.

Within a month the founders of the new club, including Brother Walfrid, made the capture of Tom a priority, banking on his sympathies with the charitable Catholic principles of Celtic, initially at least, and relying on his talents as a player with clubs such as Hibs, Partick Thistle and Third Lanark.

On a visit to the family home in Cathcart, Brother Walfrid was also impressed by the maturity and physical strength of younger brother Willie, whose stature had grown, in part, as a result of his endeavours on the track as a sprinter with Clydesdale Harriers.

A trainee accountant, he also worked at the time for Andrew Dick, then secretary of the Harriers. Willie was thus invited to join his brother at the new club and he accepted the invitation with alacrity. He kept his membership at Clydesdale long after he joined Celtic and also became a promoter of athletics at Parkhead. His career in the sport culminated with him being elected president of the SAAA in 1921.

The links between Rangers and the Clydesdale Harriers remained strong until the 1920s, but complacency was to cost the athletic venture dear as they failed to move to secure their own sporting acre.

For sure, the club handbook in 1889 discussed sourcing their own ground with a cinder track "but so long as the present friendly relations are maintained with the Rangers FC, the committee consider there are no grounds for moving in this matter."

For the most part, Clydesdale Harriers trained at the first and second Ibrox Parks and their annual meetings were held on the Rangers' grounds bar a couple of years at the turn of the 20th century when they switched to Parkhead and also Meadowside, then home to Partick Thistle.

The last reference to Rangers hosting the Clydesdale Harriers came in 1921 and the sports day ended on a financial high, but the balance in the bank could not be maintained by the athletics club and they cancelled the meeting the following year as a result of the industrial depression and uncertainty surrounding the response from the paying public.

Attempts were made by Clydesdale to resurrect the annual sports in 1923 and 1924, but they were in vain and nothing came of the efforts. Rangers had only recently celebrated its jubilee season, but the Harriers were already on their way to being relegated to a foot-note in the history of the football club.

The relationship with Celtic, of course, was to become enduring. The new club had quickly established itself as a major player in the Scottish game and brought new enthusiasm to the scene at an exciting and turbulent time for the development of the sport.

Celtic were formed to provide assistance where needed among the Catholic population of the east end of Glasgow, most of whom were first or second generation Irish and many of whom, like local Protestants, suffered appalling living conditions.

The main objective of the club was to provide the St Vincent de Paul Society with funds to maintain dinner tables for needy children in the local St Mary's, Sacred Heart and St Michael's diocese, and the Catholic community in the city quickly rallied around their club.

Brother Walfrid was also motivated by the fear that his congregation would be moved to abandon their faith, particularly with a number of Protestant soup kitchens already established in that part of the city.

As latecomers to the scene and with strong political and business acumen to guide them, Celtic decided to go for revolutionary growth rather than organic progress and players were quickly lured from the country's most prominent Catholic club, Hibs.

Undoubtedly, financial inducements were offered and the Edinburgh side lost six players to an act of footballing larceny those at Easter Road with long memories and a keen knowledge of their club's history still recall bitterly today.

Celtic were admitted to the SFA in August 1888, alongside long-forgotten sides such as Temperance Athletic from Glasgow,

Britannia from Auchinleck, Whifflett Shamrock from Lanarkshire and Balaclava Rangers from Oban, and their on-field strength was highlighted in the first season when they reached the Scottish Cup final, only to lose out to Third Lanark.

Inevitably, perhaps, the cash cow potential of the Parkhead outfit became a source of friction between those labelled by Celtic historians as idealists or opportunists.

Celtic had quickly become one of the best-supported clubs in Britain, and in only its second season was attracting attendances of up to 25,000, such as witnessed a Scottish Cup tie against Queen's Park. By December 1897 the club had managed to buy Celtic Park outright from their landlord, even though the lease still had four years to run.

Brother Walfrid, the strongest supporter of the club's charitable ethos at its foundation, had been transferred to London by 1892 and the idealists lost their strongest ally.

Celtic became a public limited company in March 1897 and within a year they boasted a British record turnover of £16,267 (approximately £3,000 more than Rangers in the same season) and paid a dividend of 20 per cent, but no donations were made to charitable causes.

If Rangers had been blessed with such a privileged existence, their move to the first Ibrox Park in the summer of 1887 would have heralded the beginning of a happy ending to the 19th century for the Light Blues visionaries. However, this was a club for whom nothing had ever come easy.

In a short period of time the rise of Celtic undoubtedly focused the minds of the Ibrox hierarchy – between 1889 and 1894 the income of Rangers quadrupled from £1,240 to £5,227, for example.

Initially at least, things would have to get worse for the Light Blues before they got better, and their silverware collection would extend to some of the game's other major prizes. As it was, the memory of their sole success in the Charity Cup Final of 1879 was fading fast in the minds of many club members as the 1890s approached.

That 8–1 trouncing against Preston North End in August 1887 apart, the season immediately following the move to Ibrox was not without its merits, financially at least. The club reported an annual income of £2,232 – an impressive sum – almost half of which was allocated to offset the cost of building the new ground.

The turnover was boosted by gate receipts of £400 from a demanding five games played at various venues across the city from November 1887 to January 1888 against Springburn side Cowlairs in the inaugural Glasgow Cup. Rangers eventually prevailed, winning the fifth match 3–1, but the tie was not without the element of protest pantomime that was so widespread in the Scottish game in the period.

This time, Rangers were chided by Cowlairs after the fourth game, which they won 2–1, for playing a professional striker, Bob Brand. Cowlairs brought evidence to the SFA claiming Brand had received £1 from his former club Queen of the South Wanderers to buy a suit in 1885.

Their allegation was as threadbare as the cloth would have been after almost three years of wear and tear and was dismissed, but Brand was suspended for two months anyway after the officials discovered he had been paid £1 to play for Hearts earlier in the season.

Almost inevitably, a replay was ordered. Rangers lost the very first final played in January 1888 to Cambuslang, going down 3–1. They finally ran out of steam in a season that was also memorable for the first floodlit match staged at Ibrox, with the Scottish Corinthians (in effect, the Scottish national team) turning up for an exhibition under electric light in March.

The gate receipts went to Govan charities as the Scots triumphed in the 'sunlight fixture', but the darkest season in the history of the Light Blues lay just around the corner.

The statistics for season 1888–89 were, quite frankly, woeful: 39 games played, 19 lost and seven drawn, with 108 goals conceded as annual turnover dropped by £1,000.

Rangers were knocked out of the Scottish Cup in a second round replay after a 3–0 defeat against Clyde and in the third round of the Glasgow Cup Celtic came to Ibrox and won 6–1. At the start of the season Rangers had taken the innovative step of appointing the club's first trainer, John Taylor, but he was struggling to make an impact.

The club were toiling as much off the field as on it, as the committee structure was in chaos and even the omnipresent Tom Vallance was struggling to make his influence felt as one embarrassment followed another.

On New Year's Day 1889 Rangers were losing at Blackburn at the same time as Aston Villa arrived in Glasgow expecting to play their old FA Cup foes in a match they believed had been previously arranged.

Nine men turned up for a game against Morton, the team lost 8–0 to Vale of Leven and even the much-heralded Ibrox Park was being criticised for a pitch that resembled a potato patch.

Meanwhile, the concept of a capacity crowd similar to that which had witnessed the opening of the ground against Preston was a dim and distant memory – only 500 fans could be bothered turning up for a match against Partick Thistle. One newspaper noted: "Such apathy and the name and fame of grand old Rangers will soon be but a distant memory."

These were desperate times and temperatures were running so high that the club's half-yearly meeting in November 1888 was adjourned for a week.

Seven days later resentment was still simmering and after nine hours of debate it was finally agreed to extend the numbers on the committee from five to seven in a bid to widen the circle of experience and expertise.

It also marked the end for the direct, decision-making involvement in Rangers of the gallant pioneers, as Vallance stepped down at the end of the season after six years as president to be replaced by John Mellish. Rangers were moving on.

Indeed, stagnation was not an option and William Wilton was the man to take them into the 20th century. More than anyone it was his vision, passion and commitment at a crucial watershed in the development of Scottish football that relegated to the annals of history the internecine squabbles that had so characterised much of the 1880s for the Light Blues.

Wilton was born in Largs on June 9 1865, a son to James and Janet Wilton. William's father, a stonemason, died aged 52 in Millport in March 1873 and soon after the family moved to Govan, where Janet set up home in Crookston Street with William and his brother Daniel, seven years his senior (they had at least one other brother, Charles).

By the age of 15, William was working as an office boy at a sugar broker and he would later earn promotion to the position of mercantile clerk, thus setting out on a career path that suggested organisation, diligence and discipline, the very traits for which he would soon become so respected and cherished at Rangers.

In his spare time, William was a member of the Glasgow Select Choir, a fine tenor by all accounts, and it is to the eternal benefit of Rangers fans that he could hold a tune better than he could his position on the football field.

He became a member of Rangers on September 24 1883, aged 18, but his skills as a player with the second team 'Swifts' were open to question. What could not be doubted, however, even at such a tender age, were his leadership abilities off the field and he was quickly promoted to match secretary for the second string.

His responsibility stopped short of picking the Swifts' team, but he organised fixtures and travel details and soon became an integral and influential figure behind the scenes at Kinning Park and Ibrox.

In 1887 he argued successfully at a members' meeting for an increase in the numbers making up the selection committee after that poor run of results at first team level. In May 1889, at the age of 23, he was put forward for the key position of match secretary of Rangers and saw off the challenge of James Gossland, an experienced committee man who had been honorary secretary of the club as early as 1883.

The promotion of Wilton was vital for several reasons, not least the drive and energy he brought to the club at a time in which the landscape of Scottish football was changing forever.

The Football League had been established in England in the summer of 1888, the brainchild of a Scot, Aston Villa patriarch William McGregor, and a natural consequence of the move to professionalism south of the border in 1885.

In total, 12 clubs started the first season in the Football League, all of them from north of Birmingham – Accrington, Aston Villa, Blackburn Rovers, Bolton Wanderers, Burnley, Derby County, Everton, Notts County, Preston North End, Stoke City, West Bromwich Albion and Wolverhampton Wanderers.

A structured set-up of regular fixtures was crucial, not least for the club moneymen, who were charged with turning over sizeable sums to pay the weekly wage bill. The new division was a roaring success and in its first season the English clubs attracted 602,000 fans to their games, an average of 4,600 per match. By the outbreak of World War One the Football League, by then 20 clubs strong, was attracting almost nine million fans a year, an average of 23,100 at every game.

Inevitably, in 1890, Scotland followed suit, although professionalism would not be officially recognised in the game until 1893, in part to stem the tide of players travelling south to earn their riches legitimately, rather than under the table in their homeland.

Peter Fairly, the secretary of Renton, set the ball rolling on a Scottish League on March 13 1890 when he sent a letter to 14 clubs across the Clyde–Forth Valley, inviting them to send two representatives to Holton's Commercial Hotel in Glassford Street, Glasgow, on Thursday March 20 to consider the question of organising a league for Scottish clubs.

In effect, there was a central belt bias and the Dundee clubs, for example, would soon express fears over their inability to attract clubs to play them on Tayside. Mellish, as president, and Wilton, as match secretary, attended for Rangers.

All but two of the clubs invited sent representatives: Queen's Park and Clyde. Clyde would later be welcomed into the fold, but Queen's Park were opposed to the new set-up as the avowed amateurs correctly foretold the arrival of a professionalism they considered elitist and selfish in what they had always considered a gentleman's game.

In addition to Rangers, the clubs who turned out for the meeting were Abercorn, Cambuslang, Celtic, Cowlairs, Dumbarton, Heart of Midlothian, Renton, St Bernard's, St Mirren, Third Lanark and Vale of Leven.

The proposal to form a league was given the backing by the majority of those present, but with conditions. Clubs were still keen to operate under the umbrella of the SFA and there were clearly further discussion to be held on the distribution of gate monies.

The Scottish Sport newspaper admitted it was disappointed with the contribution of Mellish to the debate, chiding him for adding little that had not already been said previously.

Journalist Number One went on: "Mr Mellish's words…were few, but were those of a diplomatist. In conjunction with Mr Wilton, he had come there to listen and report. Provided the league was got up in a proper way and for the benefit and furtherance of Scottish football he could see no harm in the departure, but it must be strictly amateur and recognise the SFA as the governing body. He had no instructions to act definitely."

A seven-man sub-committee, including Wilton, was formed to draft rules and a constitution for the fledging Scottish League and it was formally inaugurated on April 30 1890, with 11 clubs competing (St Bernard's were not elected by their fellow clubs in a dispute over professionalism, in addition to the no-shows from Queen's Park and Clyde).

As part of the new set-up it had also been agreed that league games should take precedence over all others, Scottish Cup ties excluded, and teams were forbidden from playing friendlies in a town or city where a Scottish League fixture had been arranged that day.

The boot was now on the other foot and, almost two decades after Queen's Park wrote to Rangers refusing their request for a game because they had no private pitch to call their own, it was now the turn of the Light Blues to send a rejection letter to the amateurs.

Along with every other club in the new Scottish League, Rangers politely declined a request from Queen's Park in the summer of 1890 for challenge matches in the forthcoming months as they were already committed to the new structure. Wilton was to remain a key player in the new set-up, firstly as Scottish League treasurer and then, in 1895, as secretary.

History records Rangers as the first champions of the Scottish League or, more accurately, co-champions as they shared the trophy with Dumbarton. In truth, the new competition at that stage was still considered a poor relation to the Scottish Cup and Glasgow Charity Cup, although that would soon change.

Off the field, Wilton's firm guidance was proving invaluable and on it the leadership of new signing John McPherson was to prove invaluable in the decade that lay ahead as a lynchpin of the first of the Rangers super teams.

McPherson, a forward, was signed from Cowlairs in June 1890 and he went on to make a sterling contribution in almost every position for the Light Blues, particularly inside-forward.

He scored the first ever hat-trick in the Scottish League, against Cambuslang in the first month of the new competition, and in total he won five championship medals, three Scottish Cup badges and 13 Scotland caps, in addition to seven Glasgow Cups and two Charity Cups.

He retired in 1902 and became a director of Rangers in 1907, serving the club diligently until his death in 1926.

Until the closing weeks of that debut league campaign Rangers had lost only once, against Dumbarton, and with three games still to play were just four points behind their rivals.

Dumbarton had the chance to clinch the title when they travelled to Ibrox for their last game of the season, although the Light Blues still had two further games to play. However, Rangers triumphed 4–2 in front of a crowd of 10,000, with such healthy numbers underlining the importance fans had already begun to attach to the new competition.

McPherson scored once in the hard-fought victory and Rangers knew three points from their last two games would clinch the Championship outright.

They were not secured, thanks to the efforts of Celtic, who won 2–1 at Parkhead on the second last day of the season courtesy of a late winner from Johnnie Madden.

Rangers were still two points behind Dumbarton as the final regular game of the League season approached and a 4–1 win over Third Lanark at Ibrox took the title to a play-off at Cathkin Park.

Again, a crowd of 10,000 emphasised the importance of the occasion in the eyes of the fans and, although Rangers raced to a two-goal lead at the interval, with strikes from David Hislop and Hugh McCreadie, the Sons hit back in the second half with two goals as the game ended in an admirable draw and a title shared.

Rangers had lost out in the Glasgow Cup that season in the quarter-final stages after three replays against Third Lanark (the free and easy way Third Lanark full-back Smith had used his hands to control the ball during these games was a major factor in the introduction of the penalty kick rule the following season).

Rangers did not compete in the Glasgow Charity Cup as a result of pressure of fixtures on the back of the new league season. Their Scottish Cup campaign ended in the first round with a 1–0 defeat at Celtic and, although the season was considered a success, Rangers – and other clubs in the Scottish game – were becoming more and more mindful of the strength of the new team from the east end of Glasgow.

The old order of the Scottish game was changing for good as the influence of Queen's Park waned on the back of their stubborn yet noble support for amateurism. Fittingly, perhaps, they won the last of their 10 Scottish Cups in 1893 with a 2-1 win over Celtic, just weeks before professionalism was publicly embraced in the Scottish game.

However, Queen's Park survived into the 20th century and continue to thrive in the present day, finally embracing professionalism in recent years despite being shifted to Lesser Hampden following the sale of the national stadium next door to the SFA.

Within a decade of the establishment of the new Scottish League six standard-bearers had gone to the wall: Abercorn, Cambuslang, Cowlairs, Renton, Vale of Leven and Dumbarton, although the latter would emerge again.

To think, as recently as 1888 Renton had been acclaimed champions of the world after the Scottish Cup holders thrashed the FA Cup winners West Brom 4-1 in front of 10,000 fans at Hampden and followed it with another victory against The Invincibles of Preston North End.

Financially crippled, they tendered their resignation from the Scottish League five games into the 1897–98 season, with Hamilton Accies stepping in as replacements.

A none-too-subtle shift was taking place as the early clubs from small towns and villages such as Renton and Alexandria gave way to sides from bigger industrial centres. Rangers were at the forefront of the changes, with Wilton the dominant figure as the endeavours of the previous two decades finally helped to deliver a sustained period of success on the field and startling progress off it.

Before the decade was over they had won the Scottish Cup three times, their first success a 3-1 win over Celtic at Hampden in 1894. Old Firm fixtures had quickly become vital for bragging rights as the the new rivalry was shaped and formed. Rangers won the Glasgow Cup four times in the 1890s, including a win over Celtic at Cathkin Park in February 1893.

The Scottish Sport of February 21 told the delightful tale of the urchin who ran all the way from the Third Lanark ground to Paisley Road Toll to deliver the score to the customers of publican Tom Vallance, gathered outside his popular bar, 'The Club.'

In those innocent times of limited media and no mobile phones or internet access, it reported: "A crowd was patiently waiting the verdict…the first news merchant to arrive was an urchin, who had done the distance in record time.

"He had little more than sufficient wind left to exclaim: 'Rangers 3, Celtic 1.' At first this was considered too good to be true, so the lad was pounced upon, and not until he had solemnly declared: 'Strike me deid if it's no true,' did the crowd break forth into…we will leave the rest to the varied imagination of our readers."

Rangers also won the Glasgow Charity Cup twice that decade, to add to their earlier success in 1879. Rangers may have had to wait another eight years for their next championship success after 1891, but it was worth it as they romped through the 18-game card without conceding a single point, a world record that still stands to this day. Business was booming, with the club's annual turnover that year an impressive £15,800.

Wilton, as Scottish League secretary, sounded almost abashed as he praised his Rangers for their achievement. He said: "Modesty, born of my close connection with the champions, hampers my eulogising them to the extent their great performance warrants. A world's record, however, especially when it is an unbeatable record, is an achievement that will speak for itself as the years go by."

It was a watershed year in more ways than one as Rangers Football Club ceased to exist, replaced on May 10 1899 by Rangers Football Club Limited. In total, £12,000 of shareholder capital was raised to fund the new Ibrox Park and secure still further the club's long-term future, with Wilton appointed manager and secretary.

The move to a second Ibrox Park had been on the cards for several seasons as the popularity of the team and the booming population of the south side helped push crowds ever upwards.

As early as 1892 the club had been forced to extend the first Ibrox Park, including a new grandstand, but even a 36,000 capacity proved inadequate in the end.

The arrival of the subway at Copland Road in 1896 added to the already existing railway station that served Ibrox on the Glasgow to Paisley line and made accessing the stadium even easier for fans from other parts of the city.

Crowds of upwards of 30,000 for major matches were commonplace and there was another solid economic argument for a new ground as Rangers sought to keep pace with Parkhead and Hampden and attract major cup finals and international games to the area.

A new era had been entered in the 1890s and the door to further prosperity had opened by the turn of the 20th century with the move to the new ground.

Rangers have known hardships and heartaches since 1872, none more poignant than the memory of almost 100 fans tragically killed in two disasters in 1902 and 1971.

All the while the team has carried the hopes and aspiration of millions of supporters at home and abroad onto the field of play wherever and whenever they have performed. There have been rich harvests of success and occasionally the barren crop of failure; however, Rangers have never stood as anything but their club to the proud people who have supported it since those earliest days on Glasgow Green.

The gallant pioneers have long gone, their voluble chatter no longer echoing around West End Park as they discuss the formation of their infant enterprise. However, the passion remains, recorded in every hoarse shout and cry from supporters on a matchday at Ibrox.

Moses and Peter McNeil, William McBeath, Peter Campbell and Tom Vallance were the standard-bearers. In their shadows, generation after generation have been happy to follow follow.

14

FOREVER IN OUR THOUGHTS

For Gordon Bell, it was sparked by a trip to Ibrox as a kid with his local supporters club from East Kilbride. For Iain McColl, it was a burning desire as a teenager to know more about the club he was always destined to follow follow.

Iain said: "During my childhood I had been handed that wonderful old book 'Rangers – The New Era' but there was scant mention of the lads who formed Rangers and I developed a deep curiosity about the founders of our club."

By coincidence, the 1966 tome from William Allison also significantly influenced Gordon, even if he didn't know it at the time.

He recalled: "I was just a young boy and my local supporters' bus, the Westwood RSC, organised a tour of Ibrox. At the end, everyone was given a copy of 'Rangers – The New Era'. I took my copy home, flicked through the pages and the pictures, then stuck it away at the back of a cupboard.

"Fast forward more than 30 years and the internet kicked off big time. Message boards sprung up and there was a tsunami of Rangers related information. Among the chat about the form of the team or the memory of favourite players, the historical anecdotes always had me engrossed.

"The names of Vallance, McNeil, Campbell and McBeath were often mentioned, but I knew nothing about the founders of the club. Where was that old book?

"Reading 'The New Era' again was just the start of my journey as visits to the Mitchell Library became commonplace and the information I discovered around the early years was stacked up and posted online.

"I didn't know Iain at that time, but he was a kindred soul. He was also posting his findings on the message boards and it wasn't long before he contacted me to arrange a meeting.

"I knew from the reaction of the posts Iain and I were putting online that there was a real thirst for the history and formation of the club."

Both men bleed blue and the wider Ibrox support – and the club itself – have reason to express thanks and gratitude for their passion for the history of Rangers, particularly its early years.

Since they first launched the Founders' Trail in 2009, almost 10,000 supporters have come from far and wide to be educated and entertained on a bus tour around Glasgow.

They visit key venues and Iain and Gordon tell the stories of the characters who helped shape the spirit and identity of the club in the 19th century.

Such is their commitment they have even gone to the fans in recent years too, with Founders' Trail roadshows taking the incredible story of the formation of Rangers to supporters groups and organisations from Aberdeen to Plymouth and Fort William to Belfast.

Gordon added: "In the autumn of 2009 we did our first Founders' Trail – on foot! – and then later that month by bus. Now we have taken thousands of supporters on the Founders' Trail and introduced the story to fans on the back of numerous presentations at supporters clubs across the UK.

"We also established our Restoration of Rangers Graves Project and take pride in restoring the final resting places of the men who worked so hard for the club, as well as those of the victims of the Ibrox Disaster.

"Our research continues to this day – in truth, I don't believe we'll ever stop learning. To say we have come a long way is an understatement."

Iain was introduced to Rangers by his late father. Archie even met his wife, Emma, on a supporters' bus that ran from Anderston in Glasgow in 1947. It's no surprise, when their son was born, that he was named after that fabled Iron Curtain defender.

Iain was soon bitten by the Light Blues' bug. His earliest memories were the European Cup Winners Cup semi-final at Ibrox against Bayern Munich and the Centenary Scottish Cup final victory over Celtic 12 months later in 1973.

He was a member of the Edmiston Drive RSC with his brother, Stuart. His son is also called Stuart, but he's named after a certain Mr McCall and grandsons George and Lewis are, unsurprisingly, already following in the family's footballing footsteps.

Gordon was born in Australia but his dad, William, and mum, Nan, returned to Scotland in the late sixties when he was only two-years-old, having left as '£10 tourists' a few years previously.

His earliest hero was Derek Johnstone and Gordon regularly stood in the Broomloan Road end because the East Kilbride bus parked in nearby Helen Street. He was used as a decoy every other Saturday – his scarf always hid the adults' half bottle of Whyte and Mackay, while he carried a flask of piping hot Bovril "and didn't get my tongue back until the Tuesday."

Iain said: "I first seriously accessed the internet in 2005 and my research into the young boys who formed the club began. I contacted Gordon two years later, we compared notes and then set off on our research journey together. Rangers Football Club is a huge part of our lives."

The Founders' Trail is so well established even the current Ibrox board have taken part, reminding themselves of the stories and legends of those who have gone before and the Restoration of Rangers Graves Project has also come to prominence in recent years.

Subscriptions and donations raised by the Rangers fan base worldwide has now allowed for 63 graves and memorials to be restored since 2013, as well as new stones laid. Iain and Gordon are proud the work has allowed them to honour all levels of the Light Blues' constituency, from past presidents to fans.

Iain said: "We first met Gary Ralston when he was researching The Gallant Pioneers. He had discovered the final resting place of Peter McNeil and other McNeil family members, including Willie, at Craigton Cemetery.

"After decades, the grave had fallen into a state of disrepair. However, thanks to the fundraising efforts of the Rangers support, we restored the original monument and placed new stones honouring the contribution Peter and his family made to the club.

"We knew Bill Struth was buried at Craigton and soon our research revealed it was also the final resting place of a number of former players, including several from the 1877 team, trainers and club administrators.

"Most of the graves were unmarked or in need of repair and the generosity of the Rangers support allowed us to go to work. However, I must stress we always seek permission of family members, if they can be traced.

"We also liaise closely with council and cemetery officials to ensure everything we do is safe, lawful and appropriate and over the years dozens of Rangers fans have offered their services to help us clear plots that have remained hidden for a long, long time.

"Their efforts are truly appreciated."

Several members of the fabled 1877 Scottish Cup final team are buried at Craigton, including Willie McNeil, Sandy Marshall, Sam Ricketts and James Watt.

A memorial stone to Moses McNeil was placed at St Modan's Parish Church in Rosneath in 2014, while at Cathcart Cemetery graves restored include those belonging to William Wilton, RS McColl, ex-chairman William Craig and another two 1877 boys, William 'Daddy' Dunlop and James Watson, who also went on to become club president.

One of the most touching stories, back at Craigton, involved the final resting place of James 'Tuck' McIntyre, an early favourite of the Rangers crowd at Kinning Park and the first Ibrox.

Born in 1858, he died in March 1943 and was so revered for the decades he dedicated to the club, including 12 years as a player and captain from 1880, that he was granted life membership – the ultimate 'thank you'.

Gordon said: "We noticed back in 2015 that flowers were being left regularly on 'Tuck's' plot. We hoped it was a family member and in an attempt to make contact we left a note in a waterproof bag with our contact details and a brief explanation of the restoration project.

"It was a wonderful moment, the following week, when we received a phone call from his grand-daughter, Vivien. We met and asked permission to restore her grandfather's plot and thankfully she agreed.

"She also gave us some wonderful little gems about James including the fact that, yes, he was nicknamed 'Tuck' because he had a portly figure.

"In his later years, James lived at 13 Walmer Terrace which today is 407 Paisley Road West, a stone's throw from Ibrox Stadium. Vivien told us a supporter once offered to buy him a house in Largs as a gift for his contribution to the club over many years. However, James turned him down as it would take him too far from his beloved Rangers.

"Apparently, 'Tuck' would often sit at the window of the flat on Walmer Terrace and the supporters would shout and wave to him on their way to the game, which brought him great comfort in his later years.

"Stories like that, which give a real insight into the men who played such an important role in the development of our club, make it all worthwhile."

By strange coincidence, Tuck's grave offered a signpost to the other, sadder side of the history of Rangers – those who have lost their lives in support of the club, particularly on Stairway 13.

Gordon and Iain were working on Tuck's restoration when their eyes were drawn to another stone across the pathway at Craigton.

Iain said: "It was the final resting place of George Nelson, who died on Stairway 13 after an Old Firm match on September 16, 1961, with another supporter, Tommy Thomson. Tommy was 29 and George was 22. Such tragedy.

"We will forever remember our brothers. We made contact with George's family, who live in Govan, and they kindly allowed us to have the stone cleaned and re-lettered. Shortly afterwards, 15 of the family joined us on the Founders' Trail and that was a very poignant occasion."

Sadly, too few lessons were learned from the passing of George and Tommy, on a night when 50 fans were also injured as they tried to leave the ground after the 2-2 draw. Less than a decade later, 66 fans lost their lives on Stairway 13 in what was the worst tragedy in British football history.

The Restoration of Rangers Graves Project has now helped 23 families associated with the Ibrox Disaster of 1971, although many of the relatives of the 66 who died that January afternoon, understandably, have requested their grief be borne in privacy.

Iain said: "People move home and after 50 years many people, including mothers and fathers of the 66, as well as brothers and sisters, have passed away. We have always held dear the memory of those who died that day in 1971 and respected the privacy of those who have requested it.

"A large number of the victims of the Ibrox disaster were cremated but, with the support of families, we have erected plaques in the memorial gardens of cemeteries such as Daldowie and Lambhill. The families now have somewhere to go and lay flowers.

"One of the most touching stories came from an approach by the families of Alex McIntyre and Hugh Addie. Alex and Hugh were two pals who were raised together, went to school together, watched Rangers together – and died together.

"They were proud Barrhead boys but, such were the council and district boundaries of the time, they were cremated in Paisley. The families asked if there was any way we could place a memorial stone in the town in which they were born and raised.

"We liaised with the local council and a place was found at Barrhead Cemetery where we could erect a stone in their memory. We attended a very touching ceremony and the families hosted a lunch afterwards. I think they found some contentment in knowing those boys have never been forgotten."

Of all the towns and villages affected by the Ibrox Disaster, none was left more devastated than Markinch, Fife. The close knit community suffered its darkest of days when 13-year-old Peter Easton, 14-year-olds Bryan Todd, Ronald Paton and Mason Philip and 15-year-old Douglas Morrison were among the 66 victims. Four of the boys lived in the same street.

There were few more heartbreaking scenes than that in the BBC documentary to mark the 50th anniversary of the Ibrox Disaster when Celtic fan Shane Fenton, a close friend of the boys, recalled a trip to the local railway station.

It was there he gathered, with the rest of the community that fateful night in 1971, waiting for the last train to arrive, desperately hoping those five kids would be on board. The train pulled away towards Dundee. No children had alighted.

Shane said: "Eight of us went to Glenrothes that day to catch the supporters buses to the game and being a Celtic supporter I was in a different part of the ground. I waited late into the night in the hope that they would return on the last train or bus, but they never did."

Iain added: "A Rangers supporter, Chris Beglin, made a pilgrimage to Markinch every year to tie a scarf to the memorial bench placed there several years ago in honour of the boys.

"Unsurprisingly, after many years, the bench had become weather beaten and it just so happens Chris restores benches for a living. He offered to restore it as a labour of love, if permission was received from the families and the local church. It was duly given. He did a magnificent job."

The only female victim of the Ibrox Disaster was Margaret Ferguson, from Maddiston near Falkirk. She was just 18 when she died, one of 31 teenagers who lost their lives on Stairway 13.

Iain said: "We met Margaret's sister, Mary Gibb, at Muiravonside Cemetery. Margaret is buried there and she also has a memorial bench nearby, which Chris again took away with permission and restored beautifully.

"We are proud to have helped remember those who died watching the club they loved, but it is only possible because of the generosity of our fellow fans."

The pandemic may have put the lives of everyone in the UK and beyond on hold for at least 18 months and had a terrible impact on society. However, as 2021 gives way to 2022, there have been signs of normalcy returning, not least the arrival of capacity crowds once again inside Ibrox.

The Founders' Trail is also up and running after its enforced hiatus, with new projects also springing up on a monthly basis for Iain and Gordon and the graves' restoration programme.

Iain said: "I could never have imagined, when I first started studying the early years of the club, we would come so far so quickly. Bringing the story of the lads who formed Rangers to a wider audience has given me and Gordon a real sense of personal pride.

"It has also been an honour to remember and pay tribute to the memories of those who have helped make this such a great club, whether they pulled on our famous shirt, worked in the boardroom, or supported from the terraces. They all made a commitment we will never, can never and should never forget."

Gordon added: "Even now, when I take my seat in the stadium and watch players such as Allan McGregor and Steven Davis, who have contributed so much, I still can't help but think of the past.

"My mind wanders back to Moses and the two Peters, William and Tom and those early games on Glasgow Green, Queen's Park, Burnbank, Hampden, Hamilton Crescent and Kinning Park.

"They could never have known the club they formed, really just to give them a sporting outlet on a Saturday afternoon, would grow to be so strong, successful and influential.

"I still think the formation of Rangers is one of the greatest stories in sporting history. I'm delighted Iain and I get to tell it to so many, so often. It's an absolute privilege."

DEDICATIONS

We would like to thank members of the Rangers family for supporting 'The Gallant Pioneers – 150th Anniversary Edition' and are delighted to include their dedications to loved ones below:

To a special brother, always in our hearts, always remembered. A true blue and a great football player. In memory of Scott Burns from Bishopton, gone but never, ever forgotten. From your brother Drew.

**

For my wonderfully staunch Bluenose parents Jim and Robina Clark. Thank you for a lifetime of love and support. To Jack, always love your team. In memorium Mattie Jordan. Love, Tom.

**

For my son Jordan Elder, a Bear since birth, as we celebrate 150 years of the Rangers. Follow we will.

**

Dedicated to my dad, William Govan. Thank you for introducing me to The Rangers. Love, Billy.

**

Simply the best Granda, love Becca and Jess.

To my dad, Brian Mitchell and our good friend Stevie. Two real True Blues. Lots of love, Elaine.

In loving memory of William and Lewis Broadley and to many more years of following the Rangers with Megan and Alan Broadley.

To our lifelong Rangers supporter Scot Lauder, celebrating the greatest club in the world and a tribute to our founding fathers, The Gallant Pioneers. We were, we are and always will be, the people!

For Greg Saini, proud to have a son who Follow Follows like his dad.

Tam Henderson 10 October 1949 – 1 August 2019. He loved the Rangers.

Simply the Best team to Simply the Best brother, Albert. Merry Christmas LVV The Bairds.

To my ever-beloved dad, Donald McNiven, who has followed Rangers near and far, and who has taught me to likewise follow on. Love, always, from his son, Robbie.

Dedicated to my personal Gallant Four – my mum and dad, Iain and Linda Sutherland, Uncle John and Aunty Phyllis Mercer, equally responsible for my love and obsession of THE Rangers.

**

William & Zara Graham – Dedicated to my Dad, David Crooks. A loyal fan who watched us win 55 from above.

**

To our dad, Davie Richardson – who bought us our first Rangers strips, who took us to our first match at Ibrox, and who brought us up the right way – to be Rangers Fans. Love from Callum and Lewis. Happy 50th Birthday, dad.

**

Dedicated to my brother Paul Govan. Thank you for the memories of watching The Rangers with you. Love, Billy.

**

Calum, Lindsey & Aila Graham. Here's to the next 150 years! WATP.

**

David Minnes, Happy 30th WATP.

**

To William Henery Dad, Grandad and True Blue Lots of Love, Charles, Dawn & Elizabeth.

**

For my nephew Jamie Skelton. In memory of your father, Jim – a good Bluenose who sadly passed away before we completed our journey back to the top.

**

Dedicated to my brother Jim Skelton, a lifelong Bluenose who passed away before we completed our journey. Rest easy big guy – we are, and always will be, the people.

**

We Are The People – James Reid.

**

Happy Birthday Campbell Farquharson, a real True Blue.

**

For David Aitken, a real True Blue and Rangers through and through. All my love, Joanne.

**

I dedicate this book to my dad and my two brothers, Alan and Craig, my son Ryan and nephew Luca. Last of all, 55 was for you Big G – GBNF WATP.

**

Derek and Ethan Ritchie. Losing you just seems so wrong, it's with loved ones you belong. Tenderly we treasure the past, with memories that will always last.

**

To all members past and present of the Stevenston Crosskeys Rangers Supporters Club, from Raymond and Chloe Bennett.

**

Daniel Dingwall, who took me to my first game. From his son, Mark.

**

To William Henery – Dad, Grandad and True Blue. Lots of Love from Charles, Dawn and Elizabeth.

**

To Dad, lots of love from Donald and Kade.

**

Remembering Lachlan and Dora McIntosh, love from Cameron.

**

In loving memory of my dad, Les Wilson, and his beloved brother, Uncle Bertie – resting in peace, but never forgotten. Remaining forever in our hearts. Simply the Best.

**

Five generations of our Hutton family have now followed on and we pray there will be many more to follow hereafter. Forever Blue.

**

To our son James Watson, Rangers through and through. Your Papa would be so proud of the young man following in his footsteps. Love Mum, Dad and Caitlin.

**

Remembering all those who stayed loyal through adversity but sadly never completed 'The Journey'. Wilf Marshall.

**

To Ellie Mitchell. We Are The People. Love from Aunty Vonny and Aunty Liz xx

**

To Grahame, told you we'd get to 55 some day. You're on the bell when I get there. Jamie.

**

For Allan, a very special son and friend. Thank you for everything you do for me. Lots of love, mum xx

**

For my dad, Billy Poynton, and his much missed mate Charlie Letham.

A book to be shared by father and son, handed down like the support of our club, for Paul Snr and Jnr.

**

Every day I think of my dad, Hamish Campbell, particularly when I am at Ibrox. He did not see 55, but I hope he is looking down on Rangers' success.

**

In memory of Kenny Craig – 'And with the angels I'll be singing, Up in heaven there up above, I'll be singing Follow Follow, to the Rangers that I love'.

**

The Louden Tavern is delighted to celebrate the 150th anniversary of Rangers Football Club with The Gallant Pioneers.

**

To Stevie – Rangers forever. We Are The People.

**

Thomas Boyce 1914, Thomas Boyce 1936, Thomas Boyce 1961, Thomas Boyce 1983, Thomas Boyce 2007.

**

For my dad, James Hunter Lindsay, who taught me how to be a true Rangers fan – Brian Lindsay.

**

To my big mate in Sandy Row from your wee mate in Paisley QS, FGAU.

**

Joe and Liz Crawford, Follow Following for 70 years. Simply The Best.

**

Fraser and Yvonne McLean WATP.

**

In memory of my dad, Jimmy Ferguson, who took me to Ibrox for the first time in 1972. Also dedicated to Linda, Jamie and Calum.

**

Dedicated to my daughter Aimee Coyne as we celebrate the 150th year of Rangers. Don't ever change. Love, mum.

**

What a fantastic 150 years. Congratulations to the Founders Trail for keeping the story alive and doing our generation's job in handing down tales of our founding fathers to the next generation. Sons of Struth Football Academy.

**

To Diane, a Jambos aristocrat, from her Bluenose boyfriend. January 5, 2021.

**

To Danny, from one loyal Rangers supporter to another – Jim Cleland.

**

To Calum, from one loyal Rangers supporter to another – Jim Cleland.

**

For my son, Greig Taylor, with love from your dad – and also to my brother-in-law, Jamie Richards. From a proud Bluenose, Kenny.

**

To Alan and Elsie and all the Fitzys. Milton's finest – thanks for helping introduce me to the Rangers.

**

For a True Blue, Paul Jamieson, on his wedding day. All my love, Uncle Kevin.

**

For Alec Brownridge, an exceptional family man, socialist and True Blue. Love you big man, Kevin.

**

To Robert, happy 60th birthday. Love from your brothers Cameron, Ross and Scott. Enjoy this book from a great writer and friend – and from one Bluenose to another.

**

In loving memory of big Scotty, who never lost that Govan feelin. Those European nights in The Linden will always be cherished.

**

For Frank and our mutual friend. Forever proud that you fought them on the beaches – and won.

**

For Dad, Mum, Amy-Louise and Brady. From Davy.

**

To Sandy, Happy Christmas 2021 – love from Liz, Robert, Victoria and Jessica.

**

To my husband and son, Colin and Billy Irvine, may your trips to Ibrox to see The Famous last a lifetime. Simply The Best! Xx